ON LUXURY

A CAUTIONARY TALE

Also by William Howard Adams

The Paris Years of Thomas Jefferson (1997)

Grounds for Change: Major Garden Designs of the Twentieth Century (1993)

Gouverneur Morris: An Independent Life (2003) (nominated for the Pulitzer Prize)
Awarded the Sons of the American Revolution Award

Roberto Burle Marx: The Unnatural Art of the Garden (1991)

Denatured Visions: Landscape and Culture in the Twentieth Century (editor, 1991)

L'Art des Jardins: ou La Nature Enbellie (1991)

A Proust Souvenir (1984)

En Souvenir de Proust (1984)

Les Jardins en France (1980)

Atget's Garden: A Selection of Eugène Atget's Garden Photographs (1979)

Thomas Jefferson and the Arts: An Extended View (editor, 1976)

Related Titles from Potomac Books

The Revolutionary Years, 1775-1789;
The Art of American Power during the Early Republic
—William Nester

The Hamiltonian Vision, 1789-1800;
The Art of American Power during the Early Republic
—William Nester

ON LUXURY

A CAUTIONARY TALE

*A Short History
of the Perils of Excess
from Ancient Times to
the Beginning of
the Modern Era*

For Chip

William Howard Adams

WILLIAM HOWARD ADAMS

Potomac Books
Washington, D.C.

Library of Congress Cataloging-in-Publication Data
Adams, William Howard.
  On luxury : a cautionary tale, a short history of the perils of excess from ancient times to the beginning of the modern era / William Howard Adams.—1st ed.
    p. cm.
Includes bibliographical references and index.
ISBN 978-1-61234-417-1 (hardcover : alk. paper)
ISBN 978-1-61234-418-8 (electronic)
1. Luxury—Moral and ethical aspects—History. I. Title.
BJ1535.L9A33 2012
179'.9—dc23

                                          2012029360

Printed in the United States of America on acid-free paper that meets the American National Standards Institute Z39-48 Standard.

Potomac Books
22841 Quicksilver Drive
Dulles, Virginia 20166

First Edition

10 9 8 7 6 5 4 3 2

Seek not proud riches,
but such as thou mayest get justly,
use soberly,
distribute cheerfully,
and leave contentedly.

—SIR FRANCIS BACON

Contents

1

A WORD OF WARNING

―――――⚬᙭᙭⚬―――――

On the soft bed of luxury most kingdoms have expired.
—EDWARD YOUNG

The saddest thing I can imagine is to get used to luxury.
—CHARLIE CHAPLIN

It may be the most bankrupt word in the English language—and irredeemable in others as well. Yet in the West for more than twenty-five hundred years, the specter of "luxury" and its baggage of moral hazards has represented one of the most enduring restraints to manage human excesses, thus insuring social harmony. Luxury's reputation as a metaphor for vice or sin grew out of the belief that it was both a cause and a symptom of social disarray, the opposite of virtue or what some might call "clean living." Its presence signaled the subversion of simple necessity and ordinary human pleasure, and it stirred up real trouble: succumbing to the destructive forces of "corruption and greed" (an all-purpose label for appetites beyond prudence or common sense) brought its own retribution. Such weakness not only threatened the moral welfare of the individual, but it could also infect the body politic and lead to society's collapse. Indulging in luxury was a disease that had to be purged.

Through the centuries, this moral concept of luxury grew increasingly powerful, complex, and controversial as opposing sides in matters of politics, religion, and economics used it to identify those faults of human nature to beware of. It was a conspicuous element in understanding class, race, gender, and the besetting price of celebrity.

Excess in any form—not merely "goods" and "stuff" in our contemporary sense—was denounced as a sign of unmanageable passions. By the eighteenth century as material consumption increased with unsettling repercussions, the Anglo-American and Continental perception of luxury began to change in the shifting debate that took center stage in what we now see as the beginning of modernity. The full-blown "consumer revolution" would emerge in the nineteenth century, that rambunctious era of materialism, urban crowds, and the dogma of progress. In a universe awash in the mass-produced, everyday "things" become the object of fetish and addictive desire. And at this tense moment, luxury—the notion, the metaphor, and the word—underwent a radical transformation from generic vice into useful marketing tool of the new capitalism. Luxury's association with what was once thought to be base gratification of the body and destructive human ambitions—a central focus of religion and the afterlife—became archaic and neurotic, a lapsed sentiment without historical or metaphysical resonance. It ceased to function as a moral barometer foretelling the "decline and fall" of empires and sinners alike.

Unable to constrain the energies of "democratization" as a feared vice, luxury now became a palpable virtue available to everyone everywhere, serving the transient pleasures of "fashion," "style," "amusement," and the cult of "good taste," as the ad-speak of the market economy would spin it. And as the concept of universal political equality became popular, supposedly undermining hierarchy, society insisted on the leveling ministrations of the marketplace and its products. Spending became the way people established their fluid social position in an affluent society. The conversion of this ur-vice into a potent social and economic asset altered the structure of Western human consciousness, and in the process it has obliterated any alternative direction for our self-indulgent existence. Of all the visions of extravagance that have filled the popular imagination in which excess has played an overwhelmingly creative and disturbing role, nothing can remotely compete with the fantasies of the American dream factories of Hollywood in the twentieth century. Film was the perfect medium for the celebration of consumption in all of its overblown forms; its technology could produce spellbinding illusions of luxurious life-styles on the stage sets of Hollywood studios, reaching far beyond entertainment and instantly settling into the psyche of its audience.

The "de-moralization" of luxury was a boon for the chaotic new laissez-faire culture; extravagant behavior was divorced from moral judgment. With so many worlds to conquer in the name of luxury, the impact of limitless (and now global) consumption on the environment had not yet been recognized; it remained out of sight and out of mind as a moral issue through most of the nineteenth and twentieth centuries. For the consumer, the only drawback was the anxiety over keeping up with one's neighbors and the apprehension that one's failure to contribute to the GDP could bring on economic collapse.

"Luxury" in the modern sense has remained remarkably stable in its everyday banality—a car dealer's or real estate agent's sales pitch, merely a piece of market jargon. The latest high-rise apartment developments can be described as "sky-piercing luxury and can't-miss quality." Like most things subject to the unfathomable quirks of human behavior, luxury possesses an irresistible allure, and the unforeseen, unintended consequences of overindulgence have kept it entangled with the unpredictable dynamics of politics, religion, and, above all, personal ambitions and desires.

When plague and famine struck Florence in the spring of 1496, turning the city's annual pagan carnival into a dance of death, the zealot friar Savonarola saw it as divine direction to organize an assault on the luxurious vanities that had dragged the city into wickedness. He and his followers lost no time in building their famous bonfires that would enter our moral language.

When a disastrous earthquake struck New England, the Reverend Cotton Mather told his congregation in Boston that it was a direct signal from God that he was upset with the widespread "excesses and vanities" of the people. "Let all exorbitances and extravagances be rebuked and retrenched," Mather warned his flock.[1] Down the street at Old South Church, the Reverend Thomas Prince added his apocalyptic voice, claiming that the earth's shaking was because of God's irritation with the colonists' lust for "extravagant apparel, building, furniture, [and] expensive, and pompous ways of living."[2] Of course, pomp and grandiosity disguised as necessities of state—those extravagant pretensions employing the best artists and craftsmen who are using the most expensive and rare materials—have historically been an accepted part of the tableau of high civilization. They were the acknowledged machinery of official power and authority, both earthly and celestial. To announce their supremacy and proclaim their virtue, kings, emperors, and prelates have asserted their uncontested might, not only with armies but also with gloriously costumed courts, splendid buildings, sculpture, paintings, gardens, and rich furnishings.

All agreed that "this politics of splendor" in the words of the diarist Count Harry Kessler, was a natural part of the life of God's designated voices of authority. Sovereigns large and small adopted dazzling ceremony and profusion as key elements of their unquestioned supremacy. The oriental extravagance of Queen Elizabeth I's wardrobe left no doubt of her divinity, her right to rule. The queen's dizened image came before policy. Importantly, its visual intensity in person and in portraits helped to subdue her public and convey her political power. "She wore ruffs and lace of almost inconceivable complexity," in the vivid words of J. H. Plumb, and "her hair elaborately adorned with pearls and jewels, her vast and ornate dresses alive with rubies, sapphires and diamonds" were so heavy that she had to be carried in a litter. Plumb continues,

> Naturally this divine monarch was surrounded by her high priests and priestesses, whose clothing too marked them off from the common herd; aristocrats with velvet breeches studded with elaborate emblems in gold thread, sporting codpieces that proclaimed their more than mortal manliness, and ladies-in-waiting whose beflowered skirts and intricate ruffs were the result of years of patient embroidery that no mere mortal could afford.[3]

Once these lavish artifacts and their grand architectural settings were no longer connected with the power they represented and for which they were made, their symbolic and practical functions of state, they would survive as flotsam and jetsam to furnish our historical imagination—both spectacular works of art and commonplace leftovers utterly denatured of their original utility. In Elizabeth's case, the magnificent wardrobe recorded on paintings has assured her of a cinematic immortality far surpassing the glamour of her stiffly official portraiture.

Since the nineteenth century, the celebration of the might and splendor of monarch and church has faded as TV entertainment, to be replaced by the conspicuous consumption of the new centers of power created by the industrial and political revolutions. Except for its military purpose of impressing supposed enemies, elaborate ritual display is no longer an emblematic necessity of governing. Putting aside the expressions of corporate ego in gleaming high-rise headquarters, the vulgar celebrity lives of the elite industry and finance tycoons—including the most recently created mass-market affluent of the twenty-first century—merely update, repackage, and repeat a predictably hackneyed formula of material display of often unremarkable, everyday extravagance. For the most part, the contemporary record of material excess, measured by quantity, scale, and degree of megalomania, reveals a depressing lack of imagination and is often coupled with blind hubris, what Joseph Epstein calls "that ample pride that goes before that total fall."[4]

Bill Gates's 66,000-square-foot "dream" house (called Xanadu 2.0—Xanadu was the film estate of Citizen Kane) outside Seattle that cost $147 million is just an up-to-the-moment West Coast interpretation of Cornelius Vanderbilt II's ornate Manhattan mansion of 130 rooms, built in 1883. Gates was inspired to place on the wall of his library, apparently without irony, the brooding line that occurs near the end of *The Great Gatsby*. F. Scott Fitzgerald's words heralded the decline of the American Dream and its moral values, signaled by overarching greed in the pursuit of lucre and aimless pleasure: "He had come a long way to this blue lawn, and his dream must have seemed so close that he could hardly fail to grasp it." The next line was not included on the library's wall: "He did not know that it was already behind him, somewhere back in that vast obscurity beyond the city, where the dark fields of the republic rolled on under the night."[5]

As for luxury yachts, that hoary cliché of immeasurable wealth made famous by J. P. Morgan, the only thing that now separates the richest at the top from the rest is not greater tonnage or speed, but whose behemoth is the longest.[6] In 2005, a wealth management service asked its richest private banking clients what would make them feel more secure and content. Their pedestrian answer was simplicity itself—more cash. Clearly they had not yet sated their avarice with all that money can buy and the expectations of luxury's illusion of more to come.[7] After all, most of us would agree with John Kenneth Galbraith that "wealth is not without its advantages and the case to the contrary, although it has often been made, has never proved widely persuasive."

The so-called free market of advanced trickle-down capitalism pumping up enormous phantom paper riches is itself morally sacrosanct, beyond economic or ethical reproach, and most importantly beyond environmental censure. There is the usual amount of hypocrisy in the "good" work that foundations of the corporations and the rich perform and publicize with tax-free dollars as a tradeoff for their entitlements of material possessions and social status. Alexis de Tocqueville got it right when he observed that hypocrisy of virtue is in every age but "hypocrisy in matters of luxury belongs more particularly to democratic ages."[8]

The spin of expensive hypocrisy is often a cover for calculated scams. Think of Chrysler's state-of-the-art $1.1 billion corporate headquarters in the Detroit suburbs, where the executive staff later presided over the company's bankruptcy. Or, take Enron's dazzling skyscraper in Houston, successfully concealing one of the largest financial swindles in Wall Street history. People with too much money, parading their wealth and power, arrive at a moment when they simply "can't stop themselves from tempting the fates," as one *New York Times* Op-Ed columnist put it, "The next thing you know their world, and sometimes ours, has crashed."[9]

Whatever we call the demon of unchecked greed—lust, wantonness, cupidity, or any other alias it has used throughout the centuries of human struggle against it—the worship of luxury has been singled out and condemned by every religious system from Hinduism to Christianity. None of these ancient synonyms, all linked to basic human examples of misconduct, goes very far in revealing the extent of luxury's deeper roots. The consistent tone of righteous indictment resonates even in the ancient Sanskrit epic *The Mahabharata*, written more than two thousand years ago:

Yudhisthira said; I desire, O bull of Bharata's race, to hear in detail the source from which sin proceeds and the foundation on which it rests.

Bhishma said: Hear, O King, what the foundation is of sin. Covetousness alone is a great destroyer of merit and goodness. From covetousness proceeds sin. It is from this source that sin and irreligiousness flow together with great misery. This covetousness is the spring also of all

cunning and hypocrisy in the world. It is covetousness that makes men
commit sin . . . it is from covetousness that loss of judgment, deception,
pride, arrogance, and malice, as also vindictiveness, loss of prosperity,
loss of virtue, anxiety, and infamy spring. Miserliness, cupidity, desire
for every kind of improper act, pride of birth, pride of learning, pride
of beauty, pride of wealth, pitilessness for all creatures, malevolence towards all, mistrust in respect of all, insincerity towards all, appropriation
of other people's wealth.[10]

After he had made his sizable fortune, Sallust, Roman-politician-turned-
historian and friend of Julius Caesar, declared that "setting your heart on
money . . . was a kind of deadly poison, which ruins a man's health and weak-
ens his moral fibre." The angst he describes is familiar to brash Wall Street
executives suddenly worried about their next multimillion-dollar bonus in a
volatile financial market. Sallust sounds as though he is speaking from experience—he had raked in a pile as the provincial governor in Africa—when
he claims that luxury's addiction requires unlimited and accelerating wherewithal to maintain a steady supply. Like any drug, it "knows no bounds and
can never be satisfied."[11]

The consumer revolution is so advanced and we are so accustomed to fab-
ricated marketing psychology inflating our desires, it is now impossible for
us to fully grasp why luxury was once considered so risky and a prime target
of moral condemnation. The concept has totally lost its original registry of
meanings that served as some of the most important "Thou Shalt Not" principles ensuring a stable, orderly society. The Greeks, who famously opened the
debate in the West on the immorality of excess versus a détente based on rational moderation and restraint, did not, however, cast their ethics in the "Thou
Shalt Nots" of the Old Testament nor along the lines of the church's mortal
sins to be regularly forgiven. In contrast to the Ten Commandments, their
reasonable pagan ethics might be condensed to one short, if overly simplistic
phrase, *meden agan*, "nothing in excess," conveniently found on the chaste
Doric Temple of Apollo at Delphi.

The classical meaning of the Latin word "luxus" referred to effeminate
sensuality, a passion for splendor and pomp. "Luxuria" implied riot, excess,

moral weakness, and extravagance, and it was understood as a serious ethical failing. "Incontinentia," "licentia," and "libido" were included in luxury's all-purpose moral opprobrium. In his novel *Cousin Bette*, Honoré de Balzac's portrayal of the stunning venality of bourgeois Paris society in the 1830s focuses on the bankruptcy of a society defined solely by money and the dynamics of the marketplace, making us sharply aware of the connection between luxury (*luxe*) and lust (*luxure*).

Even after the emergence of the consumer society, defined by the later half of the eighteenth century, luxury's tainted past continued to fade as more material possessions, once considered luxuries, became necessities of comfort and convenience.[12] Many defenders of the consumer society and its Sisyphean goals to make everyone happy have concentrated on the positive qualities of luxury and its gratification, which serve divergent, democratic, and personal purposes as constructive forces in an ever-expanding free market. Somehow, these passions of pleasure, possessions, and power in a bourgeois world (built on a classically self-regulating economy) would check one another and avert the usual dangers. The pursuit of one's private economic interests with minimum government interference was supposed to tame and domesticate the wasteful pursuit of excess that had once bred wars, tyranny, and political instability. Mankind was presumably no longer destined to live and die by the dynamics of long-outmoded martial values.

And at another level of cliché, the hedonist argued that the pursuit and consummation of human desires had produced society's greatest creations, allowing aesthetics to trump any question of morality. "Why rant against the passions?" Rodolphe whispers to Madame Bovary as he plans her seduction. "Aren't they the only beautiful thing on earth, the source of heroism, enthusiasm, poetry, music, the arts—everything, in fact?"[13]

The Norwegian American economist Thorstein Veblen, in his critique of the "leisure class," which some have called a satire, labeled his subjects "higher barbarians." This links the significance of limitless consumption beyond necessities to the human urge to distinguish oneself and maintain status. "Throughout the entire evolution of conspicuous expenditure, whether of goods or of services or human life," Veblen wrote in *The Theory of the Leisure Class*, published in 1899, "runs the obvious implication that in order to effectually mend the consumer's good fame it must be an expenditure of super-fluities." In order to hold on to public esteem, "it is not sufficient merely to possess wealth or power. The wealth must be put in evidence for esteem is awarded only on evidence." Throughout the book, Veblen's use of language was exact and often ironic. He made clear, for example, that the word "waste" meant the matter-of-fact spending on nonessentials, adding perversely that he used it without any "undertone of deprecation." In order for such consumption to be reputable, Veblen sardonically declared, "it must be wasteful. No merit would accrue from the consumption of the bare necessaries of life . . . the most prosaic and unattractive level of decency."[14] Extending Veblen's analysis into the contemporary realities of a global economy, it is easy to see the unintended consequences of third world countries emulating the West. Their predatory pursuit of "status"—Veblen's "evidence for esteem"—would require ever-greater levels of wasteful, nonessential consumption on a global scale, based on the catastrophic assumption that natural resources would sustain an ever-expanding population.[15]

Considering the environmental issues raised since Veblen's day, I should note that the primary and original meaning of the word "consumption," according to the Oxford English Dictionary, is an act of destructive and wasteful expenditure. It turns up in the sixteenth century, used to describe the Second Coming of the Lord when the world is "consumed" in flames. More ominously, earlier in the fourteenth century "consumption" became the name for the deadly scourge tuberculosis. It is also worth noting that Thomas Mann, in his great novel *Buddenbrooks: The Decline of a Family*, published at the turn of the twentieth century, traces a commercial dynasty that is finished off by bankruptcy because of the family's lack of restraint expressed in the overstuffed furnishings of their estate and the death of the last prodigal son who dies of "consumption."[16]

Before it lost its ancient moral clout, luxury conveyed portentous warnings, buzzwords with the ring of judgment. Ostentation, extravagance, excess, sensuality, immorality, dissolution, decadence, carnal appetites—all were used to underline luxury's more exotic (and erotic) qualities, which seemed to exceed the admittedly fluid definition of what was recognized as either a necessity or a luxury. This bristling clump of now unfashionable synonyms makes it a thematic challenge to focus on the main concept of luxury's history as a powerful taboo. Like most abstract judgmental words and notions, such as "decadence" until it was transformed beyond recognition, "luxury" was also caught up in the thicket of linguistic and historical background. Soft living and sumptuous feasting, voluptuousness and effeminacy were all implied in the ancient world's nuanced understanding of luxury's perils, which remained a part of its historic legacy. It is no surprise that when Plato writes on the importance of educating the warrior class, he expounds for pages on dissolute citizens who succumb to the attractions of soft beds, bad diets, and little exercise, rendering them unfit to defend the city.

To any sensible Greek, a certain amount of wealth was necessary to support "the good life" according to his social station, signified by a dignified accumulation of worldly goods. Aside from a few spoilsport philosophers living hand to mouth and making a virtue of their rags, no one was prepared to condemn wealth without good reason. It was only a problem if it got out of hand, became an end in itself, and was not used for ordinary social purposes like entertaining one's friends, or if it was not at least hedged around with virtuous sanctions and pious disclaimers.

Looking at the success of the early Roman Republic before it also succumbed to internal civil friction brought on by imperial ambitions and the cultivation of what appeared to be wholesale debauchery, Polybius, another Greek writing on Roman history and a favorite of early American politicians, linked the virtues of the citizen with the quality of austere republican manners, traditions, and laws: "When we see a community in which private life is characterized by greed and avarice and public conduct by injustice," he writes, "then clearly we have good reason to pronounce their laws, their particular customs and their constitution in general to be bad."[17]

Luxury's contribution to the decline and fall of societies as well as individuals—the transit from a mythic Golden Age of natural, frugal virtue to an age of random, irrational excesses and collapse—was once tightly woven into arguments concerning morals as well as economics. The specter of luxury (and all of its destructive possibilities) still remains an unacknowledged spur to humankind's resistance to dissolute misconduct. We tell ourselves that we expect empires to fall as well as rise; otherwise, we might coast on forever just as we are, a condition even more terrifying than falling into the abyss.

This notion of society's inevitable slippage and erosion reaches back to Homer's *Iliad* and Hesiod's *Works and Days* at the dawn of Greek awareness. The familiar metaphor reflected nature's organic, inexorable rhythm and cycle— the approach of darkness at the end of the day, the coming of autumn's decay and the dead of winter, the phases of aging and death of all plant and animal life—was the commonplace lesson of the cosmos. No one could imagine a golden future on earth until the advent of Christianity, and then such a future existed only in God's kingdom.

Dio Chrysostom, the Hellenic historian writing in the first Christian century, lays out the classic case against what he believed to be luxury's corrupting role in Rome's imperial history:

> It would be a vast undertaking to attempt to catalogue all who through luxury have suffered ruin: the Lydians long ago, the Medes, the Assyrians who preceded them, and lastly the Macedonians. For the Macedonians, although they had but lately shed their rags and were known as shepherds, men who would fight the Thracians for possession of the millet fields, vanquished the Greeks, crossed over into Asia, and gained an empire reaching to the Indians; yet when the good things of the Persians came into their possession, the bad things followed in their train. Accordingly both scepter, royal purple and Median cookery and the very race itself came to an end, so that to-day if you should pass through Pella, you would see no sign of a city at all, apart from the presence of a mass of shattered pottery on the site. And yet the districts belonging to the cities and peoples I have named still remain just as they used to be, and no one has diverted the rivers into other channels, nor was anything else of that sort different from what it is today; but in spite of that, whatever is touched by extravagance and luxury cannot long endure.[18]

The seven cardinal Christian sins were not put forth as such in the Bible. They were normal human instincts first sorted out by the early church fathers, who were forced to recognize them if the sinner were to be redeemed and reunited with God. These deadly sins (some have called the virtues just as deadly) named six of luxury's delinquent progeny: lust, greed, pride, gluttony, sloth, and green-eyed envy. This power to generate other sins gave luxury its primary position linking the rest one way or another to the curse of bodily pleasures, especially sex and vice in hedonistic congress. For centuries the mortal sins remained the test for humankind's incorrigible passions.

Greed, the lust for wealth and its ill-gotten gains, approximates an important aspect of luxury's ancient negative quality as in Saint Paul's bald dictum: "The love of money is the root of all evil." His ideology of poverty would remain the Christian ideal. Like greed, the lineage of gluttony, the boundless lust for food and drink, also set off a chain reaction of sins the apostle traced back to Adam and Eve's delinquency in the Garden of Eden. If only Adam had practiced moderation or abstinence, we might all still be there, enjoying its cornucopia of eternal (and organic) produce. As many have preached, when Adam and Eve ate the apple, they discovered sex and gluttony, followed by lust—excesses that have been part of luxury's makeup ever since. And as Lord Byron remarked on Eve's unseemly lust for apples: "Since Eve ate apples, much depends on dinner."

In his provocative study of the role and dynamics of luxury in the genesis of capitalism, Werner Sombart's gloss of Saint Paul's warning takes a Freudian step further, linking money with sex, the progenitor of luxury throughout history:

> All personal luxury springs from purely sensuous pleasures. Anything that charms the eye, the ear, the nose, the palate or the touch, tends to find an ever more perfect expression in objects of daily use. And it is precisely the outlay for such objects that constitutes luxury. In the last analysis, it is our sexual life that lies at the root of the desire to refine and multiply the means of stimulating our senses, for sensuous pleasure and erotic pleasure are essentially the same. Indubitably, the primary cause of the development of any kind of luxury is most often sought in consciously or unconsciously operative sex impulses.[19]

Throughout the Renaissance and the era of a permissive Church of Rome, the Reformation, and on into the early portents of the modern era, luxury's offspring still promote the obvious items of sinful transgressions, particularly pride, greed, lust, and gluttony. Significantly, in the list of sins Pope Gregory laid out in the sixth century (appropriated from the Romans), *luxuria* replaced *fornicatio*. In his expansion of Gregory's list of sins, the pedantic Thomas Aquinas's luxuria included the compulsive behaviors of lechery and concupiscence as well as the moral blindness of narcissism. Luxury's threat was so insidious that it could undermine all the virtues and become the inescapable defining character of humanity. The inevitable cycle from "naïve sensuality followed by refinement, debauchery, and finally perversion," according to Sombart, "encompass the deepest tragedy of human destiny: that all culture being an estrangement from nature, carries in itself the germs of dissolution, destruction and death."[20]

With all of their irreconcilable theological disputes and their reaction to Rome's extravagance and pomp (not to mention its libidinous underground bureaucracy), the new Protestant Church revived the moral lessons that luxury's abuse had to teach. A major source of trouble was that the Catholic Church had sold salvation in the form of indulgences to cover the cost of its expensive habits. Useless spending for the sake of effect became the defining gesture of the age in the churches of Martin Luther, John Calvin, and the English Puritans, the classic notion of luxury received a renewed place in the moral vocabulary of the pre-modern Western mind. This meant that for the majority of mostly Protestant Europeans transplanted to the American wilderness, there was also a resurgent distrust of riches, a demon that could short-circuit direct communication with God, the central belief of the Lutheran and Calvinist Reformation.

The first generation of American colonists, whose background was for the most part an "economy of scarcity," were deeply troubled by the paradox that the potential abundance of their new Paradise might be their ultimate undoing. There was a nagging unease that they could become victims of their own good fortune: honest work leading to wealth, followed by excess and inevitable Fall from grace. Instead of receding after the colonists' victory over the British in 1783, American anxiety about corruption, fueled by success and sudden prosperity, continued to spread in the pulpits, press, and political debates of the major cities of the former colonies.[21] In his *Essay on the History of Civil Society*, published in 1767, a conflicted Adam Ferguson had tried to pin down a definition of the luxury that might breed this corruption. Most people agreed that it meant "buildings, furniture, equipage, cloathing, train of domestics, refinement of the table, and, in general, all that assemblage which is rather intended to please the fancy, rather than obviate real wants, which is rather ornamental than useful." But now men were "far from agreed on the application of the term *luxury*, or on that degree of its meaning which is consistent with national prosperity or with the moral rectitude of our nature." While it signified civilization, the arts, commerce and national greatness, it also portended "degenerate manners, the source of corruption, and the presage of national declension and ruin . . . proscribed as a vice."[22]

Americans enjoying post-Revolutionary prosperity believed that the disturbing signs of the public's growing indifference to religion and the destabilizing political perils hidden in luxury's temptations would undermine the very foundation on which their daring experiment in government was founded. Addiction to luxury and godly ingratitude went hand in hand. Old Revolutionaries like John Adams and John Jay worried over the decline of both public and private virtue they detected wherever they went.

The embryonic "consumer revolution" and consumer society had stirred up questions regarding luxury's growing ambiguity and a moral unease about where it fit into the equation of human desires and pleasures. If it fed the appetites of the masses and promoted laziness, shorter working hours and more holidays would follow, and it would undermine traditional economic efficiency. And if men became resistant to the value of physical work, they would become soft and injure their health. The wilderness would never be subdued. Or, take the dicey question of the inequality of the distribution of luxury's bounty. In the burgeoning market economy of the twentieth century, there was the age-old question, now recast by technology, of just what separated luxury from necessities and comfort. If knockoff kitsch for the many was a solution, wasn't the enjoyment of luxury itself somehow cheapened by the loss of its former costliness, the exclusive privilege of the few?[23]

But for many new Americans, the traditional Christian condemnation of avarice flew in the face of all the temptations pouring into the ports of Boston, New York, and Philadelphia. It was evidence of God's providence sealed by His gift of a successful Revolution. For those who had the energy and ambition, they were now free to pursue their goals of commercial conquest wherever they might lead.

The implications of the transformed meaning of luxury—from the perils of excess to an acceptable, natural element of a prosperous and supposedly self-regulating marketplace—would set off a long, contentious debate. Faced with the wealth-and-virtue conundrum and the guilt it produced, many thought that the future direction of American society built on republican restraint was at stake, implicating private morality, the form of its laws and constitutions, even the quotidian aesthetics of the New Republic and its public and domestic architecture. Recalling Apollo's temple at Delphi, a flawless expression of moderation and balance in its pure, understated Doric order devoid of useless decoration, post-Revolutionary Americans, notably Thomas Jefferson, adapted Greek Revival porticoes to houses, churches, banks, courthouses, and college buildings throughout the new country, a visible ideal of chaste perfection so reassuring to the newly minted, insecure citizens of the first modern republic.

When the new president, George Washington, asked his friend Gou-. verneur Morris to order in Paris some presidential porcelain for his table in New York (this had not yet become the duty of First Ladies), Morris reported that he had found a perfect dinner service of "noble simplicity, made by the Angoulême factory." It is "of great Importance to fix the Taste of the Country," he reminded the president, "that every Thing about you should be substantially good and majestically plain: made to endure."[24] Both men understood the unspoken need to firmly uphold a due sense of proportion and conservative restraint in all things public and private. Simplicity in taste not only reflected classic republican virtues; it was also a statement of authenticity, a troubling issue in times of change at the beginning of an untested form of government. Some fifty years later, the retired president Andrew Jackson joined the national dialogue on excess, dismissing it in all forms when he rejected a Roman sarcophagus of the imperial era as his final resting place. It had been offered by an admiring naval officer who had brought the marble souvenir from the Middle East in 1845, believing it had once held the remains of Alexander Severus. In death as in life, leaders of the republic should "fix the Taste" for "plainness," "economy," and "simplicity," Old Hickory declared. "True virtue cannot exist where pomp and parade are governing passions. It can only dwell with the people, the great labouring and producing classes that form the bone and sinew of our confederacy."[25]

ℰℭ

My argument so far has been that there are two ways of looking at luxury. First, there is the only one we now know: using it instinctively to punctuate the tired language of commerce to stimulate our desire to spend and consume. A word reduced to a worn adjective, it is now only a label on a product to guarantee a "lifestyle" that needs no further explanation or apology. The other notion of luxury, once of powerful moral potency with an impressive pedigree, is now badly endangered to near extinction. Madison Avenue has recently been told by marketing specialists to drop it from its lexicon.

In the chapters that follow, my narrative will focus on the original, complex, anachronistic word of warning and danger as it was used by the ancients and translated into Western history to sort out and identify irrational self-interest, a taboo maintaining luxury's long, critical influence to the end of the eighteenth century. This traditional morality expressed a preference for self-control in consumption that avoided the risk of corruption, which would subvert our ability to aspire to higher things. It would help to shape the American character and how Americans regarded themselves during the critical debates of the formative years leading up to the Revolution, and the individualism of liberal democracy, focused exclusively on unfettered economic freedom.

Bearing out the cautionary tale, with its inevitable sting of morality, is staggering evidence in the twenty-first century that the vice of predatory excess is still causing massive trouble. But as the historian Brad Gregory has pointed out, "technology does not drive history; rather since the Middle Ages human desires have driven technological innovations, which in turn influence human desires."[26] The voracious system we have built thrives on unending waste and assumes the existence of bottomless pits for its disposal, so the once provocative, salutary history of luxury's susceptible turpitude is still relevant to our contemporary debates about the commonsense limits of consumption, and particularly its relentless environmental impact, alienation of nature, social divisiveness, and misplaced priorities, including the alarming neglect of the public sphere.

Exploitation, competitiveness, and mindless waste have made innocent, gullible consumers into victims of the prevailing economic system. Trained to chase the mirage of the "good life" that "makes up the banality of the social order," we have been blinded to any other possibility.[27] There is no time or energy left to cultivate other realms of pleasure and satisfaction and public service that require little in the way of material goods. This was the heart of President Jimmy Carter's controversial "malaise" speech to the nation in July 1979, although the word itself did not appear in his text. In his prescient but premature "sermon," he spoke of the country's spiritual depression: "In a nation that was proud of hard work, strong families, close-knit communities and our faith in God, too many of us now worship self-indulgence and consumption. Human identity is no longer defined by what one does but what one owns." However ill-timed and impolitic Carter's warning was considered on the eve of the Reagan era, it was as eloquent as anything a Puritan leader might have said within the first decade after arriving in Boston, or William Penn later in Quaker Philadelphia, or Presidents Thomas Jefferson and Franklin Roosevelt, who all preached a message of moderation as a matter of public policy.[28]

After 9/11 and our continuing failure to secure a humane source of alternative energy to satisfy our addiction to consumption—with its devastating global ramifications—we have moved unmistakably "into a new way of being." In the new Age of Limits, as many economists and social observers have pointed out, luxury as we have known it is already passé and unsupportable.[29]

The sky's-the-limit spending spree has succumbed to a lethal overdose, disrupting the financial system, and exhausting our dwindling natural environmental resources along with our moral faculties of outrage. Maybe it is time to add up the true cost of how we have been living beyond our means, and measure things differently. Yet it remains to be seen if any word of moral caution will help us articulate and understand this new time of transition, when the notion of the luxury of excess in all its forms may be forced to return to its ancient role, acting once again as a fraught moral omen and warning.

2

THE GREEKS
Less is More

———✿———

In the end they were Greeks. Nothing in excess, Augustus.
—C. P. CAVAFY, *JULIAN SEEING INDIFFERENCE*

There was one thing philosophers of ancient Greece could agree on: consuming passions, if left unchecked, would lead to selfishness, rampant animal appetites, hubris, or worse. Over a long stretch of evolution, the best minds concluded that moderation and resistance to excess in all of its incarnations were the heart of the matter. The gods' messages also regularly urged mankind to recall that necessity and mortality placed limits on the individual. The acceptance of limits in all forms helped to define the balanced life that was the key to human happiness. But as everyone knew, moderation was a hard sell.

The Greek word for "happiness" (*eudaimonia*) had a much broader meaning than its English translation; it suggested a substantive well-being, something universally desirable. But when pleasure was pursued for pleasure's sake, reaching beyond reason and into indulgence that upset natural order and stability, its ravages would inevitably bring on self-destruction. It was important to recognize pleasure and happiness as distinct conditions, and the latter—the ultimate goal in life—was in no way dependent on the former.[1]

The Greeks, with their celebrated rationality (morality had not yet been hijacked by religion, and sin was not a Greek notion), wisely accepted that the temptations of luxury leading to excess were a part of man's natural, psychological makeup and instincts, and that those all-too-human impulses could not be completely eliminated. After all, as Gibbon observed, Greek philosophers drew their morals from the nature of man rather than from that of God, and in their long and deep inquiry they expressed both "the strength and weakness of the human understanding."[2] For the Greeks and later the Romans, human pleasures were sorted out in a hierarchy from the "refined" down to the "vulgar" and base. One gets the sense that the omens and warnings of limitless pleasures gave the moralists a vocabulary that actually increased the subversive appeal of the forbidden while yet proscribing it. For the good of mankind, these desires could only be corralled, discouraged, and managed, particularly among the more disorderly, susceptible run of mankind. In his *Nicomachean Ethics*, Aristotle declares that "bad is of the unlimited, as the Pythagoreans surmised, and good is of the limited." Would-be tyrants boasting a despotic hauteur and a limitless appetite for high-priced dinner parties, chariot racing, and love affairs they couldn't afford required particularly close watching. Their obsessive appetites encouraged predatory isolation that destroyed social relationships in the family and the community.

Temptations of excess could also impose unexpected surprises and suffering on the human community as a part of their tragic condition. In his epics *Works and Days* and *Theocracy*, Hesiod introduces the goddess Pandora, made in the image of a beautiful woman speaking "wheedling words" and bearing her seductive gifts—greed, vanity, and "wearing sicknesses."[3] Unpredictable fate was always just around the corner or in Pandora's jar ("box" is another translation) of "sad troubles" waiting to tempt hapless mortals. "Gold and the good life drag men out of their right minds—the lure of power!" the chorus of Euripides exclaims, warning Heracles of what is merited and what is loaded with hazard. "None dares to think how time may flip him over—racing past the law he smashes the black car of his luck."[4]

One important but overlooked element contributing to the Greek preoccupation with the ethical problem of license versus limits and prudence is the introduction of money in the form of a universally acceptable coinage, and its inherently unpredictable, unstable power. As the British classicist Richard Seaford described in his study of money and the early Greek ethics, the Greeks, toward the end of the seventh century BC, were the first people in history to use money as an impersonal currency of exchange in the modern sense. The very dynamics of money and the unlimited ability to accumulate it gave a whole new dimension to the concept of luxury and its inherent perils. The collective confidence in money to mediate social relations belied the authority of the gods—a human construct establishing monetary value on all aspects of life. Tragedy first appeared on the stage not long after. By the fifth century, tragic playwrights such as Sophocles recognized its limitless, unregulated power to create dangerous, insatiable appetites in men and drive them from their families and communities, encouraging tyranny and destroying cities. "No current custom among men as bad as silver currency," Creon cries in *Antigone*. "It shows men how to practice infamy and knows the deeds of all unholiness."[5]

The unprecedented phenomenon of money was its unlimited power—the power to acquire things in limitless quantity. This power, in turn, created a boundless desire for it without any natural restraint to its accumulation, expressed in contemporary Wall Street terms as an "isolating passion for individual gain" regardless of the consequences. Its fungible abstractness and impersonality concealed (and continues to conceal) its potential for unforeseen dangers and tragic consequences. The myth of Midas dramatizes the risk of focusing solely on money when Midas asks Dionysus for the power to change anything he touches into gold. The first shock is when he picks up his food on the banquet table and tries to drink the wine. All becomes hard, cold metal.

The unlimited power of money concentrated in the hands of a single individual established the tyrant. But beyond power, the dynamics of money also allowed pitiless impoverishment or base unconscionable enrichment. "Of wealth," Solon the statesman and poet writes, "there is no limit that appears to men. For those of us who have the most wealth are eager to double it." The results would be the inevitable enslavement of the poor by the rich. In order to prevent such instability, in both the polis and the soul of the individual exposed to insatiable desires, reasonable limits must be central to morality.[6]

In their forensic efforts to apply some sensible rein on the pursuit of pleasure (or even contentment) for its own sake, it was clear, at least to the more philosophical of Greeks, that frugal self-sufficiency based on the needs of everyday existence must not be overwhelmed by "insolence and anarchy and prodigality" of luxury's incipient, irrational excesses—possessions, fame, the satisfaction of every Dionysian whim—things they could rationally live without. The message of Apollonian restraint would later be transformed into a matter of Christian faith and become a part of the spiritual discipline to master "the art of quenching all desire," in the words of the early church father Tertullian, which the Puritan immigrants in their own vernacular would bring with them to New England in the early seventeenth century.[7]

The very survival of Greece and its meager natural resources depended on carefully managing human appetites. But the Greeks no doubt would have agreed with Patrick Leigh Fermor, that enthusiast for living well, and his equally sensible rejection of the notion that sin existed only in matters of excess. After all (and ignoring the price), "how can one eat caviar in moderation?"[8]

Reading the ancient Greek philosophical debates over what constituted the good life of virtue and how to find it without falling into the throes of luxury brings to mind Nat King Cole's classic riffs in "Body and Soul." But unlike the yearning harmony of the words and melody of the song, where body and soul are united in an emotional bond of love, the Greeks' conception of the "body" and the "soul" as separate polarities stirred up a long, divisive polemic marked by confusion and anxiety over which one exactly was in charge. They were impenetrable abstractions that would fuel intense debates for several millennia. In the Platonic view, the three aspects of the soul were located in the human brain, heart, and liver. The "rational soul" was seated in the brain, where reason controlled the other two parts. The "irrational soul," governing passion and anger, was found in the heart, while baser appetites of desire and lust, both useful and wicked, were found in the liver. It was this tripartite soul, popular in later Christian circles, that linked moral virtues and vices to the soul's health.[9]

The Oxford classicist E. R. Dodds took the side of Dionysus, that appealing Greek god of unpredictable enthusiasms, arguing that the irrational is a central creative force in human experience, contrary to the conventional view that Greek culture represented the triumph of the rational. According to Dodds, before Plato, the soul or *psyche* was thought of "as the seat of courage, of passion, of pity, of anxiety, of animal appetite . . . but not the seat of reason." It had not yet developed any puritanical or metaphysical qualities. The psyche was the life and spirit of the body without any fundamental antagonism—quite content, not the body's prisoner. But over time, philosophers and men of God spread the concept of a soul or "self" separate from the body and older, destined to survive it. "It was here that the new religious pattern made its fateful contribution: by creating man with an occult self of divine origin, and thus setting soul and body at odds," where the irrational always threatened the soul's piety. Dodds concludes that at some point these beliefs alien to the Greeks encouraged a revulsion of the bodily experience and the life of the senses, new, unchartered psychological territory that provided rich soil for the growth of what we call puritanism and the cult of self-punishment.[10]

But even if they did not fully accept the metaphysical divisiveness of the belief that the body was the soul's prison or tomb, those upholding the priority of Apollonian moderation argued that it was far healthier for the social order to exercise some restraint. Licensing the body to do whatever it wanted, following the old Club Med slogan of "Everything in Excess" and ignoring the consequences, was a prescription for civic and personal disaster. For all the creative potential of wild, unbridled energy, the familiar and destructive debauchery of Bacchanalian revels in the woods demonstrated the civilizing importance of good manners. The widespread collapse of social standards was thought to be as sure a sign of more catastrophe to come just as the sudden ominous failing of springs and water fountains could foretell an impending volcanic eruption.

In "A Dialogue between the Resolved Soul and Created Pleasures," the Elizabethan poet Andrew Marvell casts the mortal combat between the higher virtue of the soul and pleasure's irresistible distractions in terms that would have been understood by Solon's generation. Marvell might have been inspired by the First Epistle of Peter, when the disciple exhorts the faithful to do battle: "Dearly beloved, I beseech you as strangers and pilgrims, abstain from fleshly lusts, which war against the soul." It was a message at the center of Puritan ethics.[11] While Plato conceived of the soul as incorporeal and the source of moral qualities guided by reason, the Stoics and Epicureans held bodily or materialistic views of the soul as a "body" in itself. But outside the thinking classes, most people would have agreed that the "soul" remained "a vague kind of stuff."[12]

Since the basic human needs—food, clothes, shelter, procreation—that could be seamlessly transformed into excessive indulgence are connected to the body, this metaphysical distinction becomes an important element in luxury's dark, controversial history. Plato complains in the *Phaedo*, his dialogue on the immortality of the soul, that the body "fills us up with lusts and desires, with fears and fantasies of every kind and any amount of trash, so that really and truly we are never able to think at all because of it."[13] The philosopher compared the soul to a winged chariot with Reason as charioteer driving a team, one white horse representing Honor, and the other, a black one, unmanageable Pride and Insolence. The metaphor demonstrates how the bodily senses were linked to the soul, whose spiritual and rational parts were affected by the body's rogue desires. If they were not controlled by the soul's high-minded reasoning, and a heavy hand on the reins, all would end up in the abyss, a vision with a long, troubling history. In Plato's *Republic*, a life ruled by passions and appetites is totally rejected in favor of the philosopher's chaste model, detached from all troublesome human conflicts.

The voracious body—with its mysterious, sensual antennae searching to satisfy the desires of the stomach, eyes, ears, glands, and, above all, greedy imagination—never understood the limits of the soul's capacity and appetite for good or evil. Or was it the other way around? In the event, the Greek legacy of this separation of the soul (or higher "self" of divine origin) and the body's irrational instinct to let down its guard and overdo whatever it was doing would be a troubling gift to humanity, haunting the spiritual life of the West to the present day as it continues to search for the root of mankind's wickedness.[14]

When luxury appeared, dressed to the nines in all its seductive guises, it was a sign that this war was going the wrong way. Body and soul would blame each other for the outcome, and both sides went out of their way to torment and best the other.[15] As a student of the conflict, Democritus, a younger and mostly forgotten contemporary of Socrates, blamed the soul for greater responsibility as the governor of life, emotion, and conscience, according to a quotation from a surviving fragment by Plutarch, the Greek historian. Democritus mused that if he were to judge a case in which the body took the soul to court, accusing it of causing all of life's pain and torment,

> he would gladly find the soul guilty for having ruined the body with neglect
> and dissolved it with drunkenness, for having debauched and distracted it
> with indulgence, just as the user of a tool or equipment in bad condition
> is held responsible for its reckless misuse.[16]

Whatever the soul's "contributory culpability," maintaining an untroubled enjoyment of life remained the primary goal. Guided by an enlightened hedonism of moderation and reason, along with the steady discipline of human desires, contentment should not be impossible to achieve, even when threatened with the most alluring temptations. After all, things could only go wrong in one direction: toward excess, pulling everything over the cliff with it.

In Book II of Plato's *Republic*, the philosopher lays out his celebrated case against luxury as evil, a morality tale and an indictment that would continue to reverberate throughout much of Western history. In the course of his examination of the fundamental nature of justice and injustice—of the city as well as its citizens—Plato decides that the origin of the city was to be found in the communal effort to supply the common, functional necessities: food, dwellings, and clothing that are required by the body. But he realizes that many people will not be satisfied with the Zen-like minimalist existence of such a primitive community, a boring heaven. Over time, his true, healthy city will evolve into a fevered urban center, fired up over the tempting possibilities of luxury's bounty created by artists, poets, and dancers. It then becomes "inflamed" by the growing intemperance of its citizens as they begin to indulge in "fancy" foods, clothes, and houses decorated with gold and ivory. Predictably, "they will be adding sofas and tables, and other furniture; also dainties, and perfumes, and incense, and courtesans, and cakes, all these not of one sort only, but in every variety."[17] With the appearance of courtesans, "fancy" women whose role is something more than normal procreation, luxury is linked to lust and lechery, Christian sins that, born of biological impulses, would require much stern discipline. As we will see later, the German economist and sociologist Werner Sombart will link the role of "fancy" ladies in the seventeenth and eighteenth centuries to the invention of capitalism.

We can see what's coming in Plato's parable of the rise and fall of civilizations. All this urban energy will generate many specialized craftsmen, artists, and workers (Plato does not mention the ubiquitous slave) to make and maintain the increasingly complex production of luxuries for an increasingly insatiable public. The predictable and most significant consequence of Plato's original city falling into a luxurious condition is that it will need more and more physical territory to accommodate its growing population and fulfill its imperial ambitions. Since the only way to appropriate more land is to take from one's neighbor, force will be the obvious resort. So the life of luxury has intro-

duced warfare; this, in turn, will carry the city to ruin in pursuit of the ultimate evil of unlimited wealth, which becomes necessary to pay for its voracious
military-industrial complex that protects and defends its increasingly compulsive, irascible obsession.

To avoid Plato's "luxurious" city, Aristotle places temperance (or self-
control) at the head of his lists of virtues, just after courage. Both belonged to
the most temperamental parts of the soul. "It is the pleasures of the body, then,"
at the center of licentiousness and corruption, "that are the concerns of temperance."[18] If a majority of the populace followed the example of good men of
judgment and controlled their passions and appetites, then they were less likely
to fall into corruption and debilitating temptations.

Aristotle does not say much explicitly about luxury, but his negative assumptions of luxury's influence, countered by the virtues of moderation and
self-restraint, underpin much of the future discussions about luxury's detrimental effect on morality. He rooted his morality not in rules but in the virtue
of good habits and dispositions and common-sense conduct that make us content. By Aristotle's measure, the true gentleman—that most virtuous model
of good conduct—knows by habit that he must learn to control his appetites,
"holding a mean position with regards to pleasure," separating useful, or at
least innocent, pleasures from the harmful. This also implied a firm control
over venal, aimless ambition to produce a lifetime of virtuous behavior reflected in good manners. In Aristotle's words, "the temperate man desires the right
things in the right way and at the right time," by developing a nature that will
support a properly functioning healthy soul. To eat or drink too much or do
anything else in excess beyond what nature or the situation required was rude,
unhealthy, and unsettling to a well-ordered society.[19]

> Drink or food that is above or below a certain amount destroys the health,
> while that which is proportionate both produces and increases and pre-
> serves it. So too is it in the case of temperance and courage and the other
> virtues.[20]

Conversely, the man who falls into intemperance and vulgarity spends
more time and money than he can afford. Aristotle notes,

He uses trivial occasions to spend large sums of money and make a jar-ring display: that is by entertaining the members of his club as if they were wedding guests, and (if he is financing a comedy) by bringing on the chorus in purple robes at their first entrance. . . . And all this he will do not from a fine motive but to show off his wealth, expecting to be admired for this sort of conduct; spending little where he ought to spend much, and much where he ought to spend little.[21]

While these vulgar vices may not be particularly harmful to disapproving neighbors or may not cause a public disturbance, it reveals a poverty of the soul (not to mention style) on the part of the individual, a lack of what became all those dignified, upper-crust aristocratic virtues of "magnanimity, proper pride and self-respect . . . greatness of soul" so much a part of Aristotle's ideal.[22]

From Plato's Academy and Aristotle's Lyceum to Zeno's Porch and Epicu-rus's Garden, the ability to resist luxury's viral allures became the true measure of one's philosophical temperament, physical well-being, and morality. It was a vital test of the individual's—and society's—ethical immune system, a standard of virtuous conduct that would persist into the beginning of the modern era.

The importance of cultivated austerity and self-control versus excess and luxury, according to Plato's philosopher-king, was to conserve the commu-nity's natural, physical resources for any emergency: war or famine or plague. Any material surplus was to support the "music" of philosophy. By judiciously feeding the body, the body in turn would serve the soul. But the body's desires were always threatening to get out of hand, upsetting the ideal spiritual equi-librium and disrupting the "music." For Socrates, the outcome of this internal civil war was imperative; the soul must triumph and rule the body, laying down the basic virtue to work intelligently, use any prosperity wisely, and set common-sense limits to bodily needs. Wealth, or a desire for it, was not a bad thing in itself if it were not abused. But without careful management, riches could become "the root of all evil," the cause of hubris—Aristotle called it "the vice of the rich," overweening success calling forth the envy of the gods. "Excess breeds hubris, whenever wealth attends upon an evil man and upon anyone without an upright mind."[23]

All agreed that the individual's abuse of luxury through overindulgence—too much food and drink, sexual pleasure, lack of exercise—could damage one's health and well-being, producing pain in the body as well as confusion and despondency in the mind. For example, drinking could be the source of all manner of obvious problems, not to mention a drain on the pocketbook, according to Critias, a character in Plato's dialogues. As for too much sex, it posed a special problem for the Greeks since both genders tempted men and increased the odds of seduction. In his *Memoirs of Socrates*, Xenophon recalls the philosopher lecturing him in particular about the potential dangers of seductive boys: "Poor thing. Do you have no idea what will happen to you once you have kissed a handsome boy? Without a doubt you'll become an instant slave instead of a free man, you'll spend large sums on harmful pleasures, you'll have no time for the business of a decent gentleman and be forced into pursuits even a madman would eschew."[24]

The ongoing anxiety over "excessive" behavior, signaled by an obsessive embrace of soft, sybaritic living, and the many devious paths it opened, had deep social and political implications. Greek words used to discuss the issue—implying wantonness, lewdness, riot, arrogance, prodigality, laziness, incontinence—give an idea of the lexicographic as well as the ethical perils. Whatever afflicted or weakened the individual citizen—his body, his moral compass, and his character or "soul"—threatened the delicate balance between him and the city-state, the complex, dynamic relationship that produced classical Greek democracy in the fifth century BC.

The care and exercise of the body as well as the cultivation of the inner man became an obsession for the Greeks, and if these efforts could be synchronized, living well might just be the best revenge in a universe filled with the inexplicable surprises regularly cooked up and delivered by the gods. As a part of the discipline required to reduce the tension between body and soul, young men in Athens were to spend the day rigorously training their bodies at the *gymnasia*, eating lightly, and avoiding too many baths, then lift some heavy discourse in Plato's nearby Academy, or later at Aristotle's Lyceum. Both schools of philosophy took their names from the neighborhood health clubs. Noticing that his companion Epigenes looked as though he had not been near the gym recently, Socrates told him quite frankly that he needed to get in shape. When Epigenes wanly replied that he was not an athlete, the philosopher told him that that was no excuse and proceeded to give him a lecture on bad health and its connection to the safety of Athens should its citizens suffer from "bodily weakness." The obvious "results of physical fitness are the direct opposite of those that follow" from indolence and sloth, conditions related to self-indulgence.[25]

For the majority of people in the poor, hardscrabble, democratic society of early Greece, there had to be something more than pursuing the elusive mirage of material goods and overenthusiastic pleasures available only to the elite. Probably 90 percent of the population lived regularly in the non-urban countryside, a place where luxury in its classic sense has rarely found congenial or stimulating. As late as the fifth century, most Athenians actually lived outside the polis (imperfectly translated as "city-state"), that characteristic mode of Hellenic social existence.[26] For the overwhelming majority, even the thought of "urban" luxury was impious, undemocratic, and probably subversive. Only a small, privileged, wealthy few in Athens and in prosperous port cities could buy Carthaginian carpets, fancy pillows, Indian peacocks, a basket full of eels, and hire expensive chefs to prepare sumptuous symposia banquets. Aristotle dismissed as empty vanity the excesses of the few, such as the peacock owner who ostentatiously refused to show his prize bird to the public. Greek funerals were notorious for their pretentious displays of extravagance, parading the gold trinkets and jewelry of the deceased through the streets of Athens. They were shows that did not impress Socrates who famously declared that he was only interested in "the wealth of wisdom."[27]

If life's objective was to secure some degree of contentment, how could the body's passions and the soul's higher dreams manage to produce in the best of all worlds this elusive state of well-being? Recalling the repeated advice of the choruses of the tragedies of *Oedipus*, *Agamemnon*, and *Heracles*, that no man could be called happy until he was dead, the Greeks knew the jealous, pitiless gods would have the last word. Their eyes were wide open to the true condition of man's mortal fate and they did not pander to hare-brained optimism.

Trying to follow the difficult and rocky road leading to a happy (or, by Greek definition, a contented) life in a democratic society however imperfect by later "enlightened" standards, it was recognized that unlimited wealth, ambition, and the luxuries they brought might be besetting distractions; worse, indulging in them might become compulsive, dehumanizing, and possibly criminal. The issue was not so much a material fact as it was a question of ethics and politics. If life was only a matter of satisfying bodily desires, then, in Socrates's dismissive observation, a human being was nothing more than a leaky barrel that needed to be continually refilled. Dissipation and debauchery, produced by the demands of luxury's insatiable appetite, would only disrupt nature's harmony, weaken the body, and play havoc with the soul's loftier ambition of struggling to achieve a virtuous existence.

Anticipating by centuries the iconic Christian sins, the Greeks were well aware that luxury could also be divisive in a democratic community, loosening its social bonds by stirring up avarice, envy, and pride, and encouraging gluttony and sloth. If hard times and famine loomed, squabbles would quickly erupt over squandering scarce resources on excessive eating, drinking, and whoring. It was also understood that widespread, unchecked opulence could threaten the state by weakening the collective will of the community to take up arms to defend itself.

While open-range grazing of goats and sheep has added several millennia of environmental devastation to the modern Greek mainland and its islands, it was always a poor place: rocky, thin soil, denuded mountains with feckless rainfall. The playwright Menander speaks of "a typical Attic farmer, who struggles with rock that yields nothing but thyme and sage, and gets nothing out of it but aches and pains."[28] Such as it was for the average peasant—hard work at farm labor, resistance to invidious human desires, and saving were the only ways to nurture a meager nest egg that passed for wealth, well hidden from envious neighbors.

One did not have to embrace the voluntary poverty of the self-denying Cynics or the more stoical Stoics to see the need to live with the greatest restraint. It embodied the great rule "Know thyself," propounded by Socrates and followed in his own uninhibited style by the unworldly Diogenes, who expressed himself by wearing a barrel, one of the ancient world's most enduring fashion statements. The rule had nothing to do with modern Freudian self-analysis; rather it was a way to rationally penetrate man's inner nature and soul to bring about self-control over his passions and animal qualities. Frugality was also an economic necessity enshrined in popular myth and philosophical imperative that defined human survival in the ancient world. The "Hymn to Thrift," by fifth-century Athenian poet Crates, could have been sung by Andrew Carnegie when he arrived penniless in America in 1848 to make his fortune and become one of the foremost industrialists of the nineteenth century:

> Hail! Goddess and mistress, delight of the wise,
> Frugality, the child of famed Temperance.
> All those who practice justice honor your virtue.[29]

The myth of Greek superhuman courage in battle was an expression of the reality of scraping out a living in the country's rugged, mountainous, impoverished landscape. It became a critical virtue enabling Greece to defeat its richer and more powerful enemies. The image of the lean, muscular citizen-soldier also made a nice, straightforward contrast of moral superiority over their vastly stronger enemies, the Persians. The latter's reputation for decadence was a metaphor for foreign corruption, as they were usually obese Eastern rulers who lacked virtuous self-restraint and saw gluttonous feasting, for example, as a normal way to express their power. One of the continuing legacies of Persian potentates is the power banquet as a metaphor (a required ritual and protocol for heads of state in all modern societies); hegemony had to be communicated in the opulent spread even if it strained the public coffers. Following suit, Greek tyrants didn't hesitate to tax, confiscate, and steal to pay for their despotic appetites and entertainments. Corrupting excess would become a part of the myth of the decline and fall of nations.[30]

One way to avoid wandering into luxury's minefield was to achieve self-sufficiency, the only kind of true wealth that mattered. It was a time-honored and widespread Greek ideal not limited to the philosopher class. In a country with limited natural resources, it was common sense. For Plato, temperate frugality as public policy was the definition of the Ideal Good. Aristotle concluded that the ideal life was not dependent on worldly possessions. Xenophon's Socrates saw divine wisdom in "needing nothing, second best to lack as little as possible." The philosopher's tyrant who had to steal and bribe in order to hold onto his power saw no need to "pity people as poor when they can *honestly* come by everything they need."[31]

Endlessly chasing after too many good things of life merely to satisfy the body's appetites at the soul's expense was the high road to slavery. "It is the profligate and the incontinent who really engage in menial tasks [slaves] as they are for ever running back and forth trying to fill their leaky jars of desire," a dismissive judgment surviving from the fourth century BC that may still resonate with the modern consumer in the local mall who has just "dropped" from exhaustion trying to fill a bottomless shopping bag like filling Socrates's leaky barrel.

The Greek maxim "Nothing in excess" was a big step forward from the primitive Bronze Age societies of the seventh-century AD: blood guilt and rites of purification gave way to personal responsibility and recognition of one's limitations. Even if Plutarch, who ended his life as a priest at Delphi, provides the only historical reference to the quotation, it is a useful reminder of "the harmony of due proportion of the higher and lower elements of human nature," the familiar and strikingly Greek notion. It is significant that Themis, the ancient goddess of limits and measure, was also an Oracle at Delphi, adding her support of civilized existence established fair weight, custom, right manners, and social order in contrast to Dionysian anarchy.

In the sixth century, the legendary Solon, a poet and statesman who had a reputation for prudence, gave the Athenians a constitution of sorts when he was called in to resolve a political crisis brought on by the widespread greed and poverty that threatened the state. Following his controversial resolution laying a foundation for Greek democracy, he volunteered, according to Plutarch, to go abroad for ten years to prove that his solution had nothing to do with his presence or personal interests. During his travels he is said to have met Croesus, king of Lydia, the richest man in the world. After inspecting the king's sumptuous luxuries and furniture, the Greek was famously asked if there could be anyone happier than he. Studiously indifferent to all of Croesus's loot, Solon baited him by suggesting a few unlikely candidates. In exasperation the king shouted, "But what about me?" Solon politely replied with a classic lesson on Greek temperance and self-control:

> God enjoined us Greeks that we behave with moderation in all things, and the moderation gives us an idea of virtue which seems timid and common-place: nothing regal or flashy about it. When we look at the ups and downs which never fail to upset human lives, it stops us being proud

of our possessions or admiring the happiness of anyone subject to the caprices of time. Everyone's future is mutable, and based on uncertainties. We regard as fortunate the man whose luck holds till the end. But to flatter the happiness of someone still alive, open to all the dangers of human life, that's like calling someone a winner and giving him the championship, when the fight is still going on.[32]

Although he was writing nearly three quarters of a millennium after Solon and other legendary Greek worthies had disappeared, Plutarch's intimate knowledge of earlier Greek texts allowed him to capture something of the essence of their virtues, as well as their flaws and weaknesses—human virtues and failings that seem to have changed little in the intervening centuries. Take for example his portrait of the politician and military leader Alcibiades, whose sensational reputation dating from the great imperial days of the fifth century BC has fascinated historians and moralists for centuries. Bold, brash, beautiful, the Athenian's dangerous celebrity became a parable on the fundamental Greek virtue of the moderation required in public life as opposed to the limitless excess and hubris leading to tyranny.[33] Alcibiades's mutable and unprincipled character was documented in Thucydides's famous account of the Athenian's showoff insolence at the Olympic games, the premier political and religious celebration held every four years. His accusers did not suspect him of an attempt to overthrow the state but they "found evidence in the unruly and undemocratic nature of the way he lived his life." Plato reports that he turned up drunk at Agathon's well-ordered symposium, leaning on a flute-girl with a huge wreath falling over his eyes. By outspending the ordinary citizen to win the famous chariot races, the incipient demagogue might be tempted to overthrow the state simply to get himself out of debt. Or he might become a traitor, as he, in fact, did.

Several qualities of character linking lust for luxury and power typical of tyrants are exemplified in the personality and career of Alcibiades, who believed that he was unique in his superiority, claiming to be a favorite of the gods. An aristocrat who with cool cynicism knew how to manipulate his audience, he could be all things to all people. In his *Essays*, Montaigne notes how easily Alcibiades was able to change according to the occasion, "now outdoing the Persians in luxury and pomp, now the Lacedaemonians in austerity and frugality." His is an all-too-familiar type of unprincipled tyrant-in-the-making, even in the twentieth and twenty-first centuries with many parallels of similarly imposed political tyrannies.[34]

The democratic city-state of Athens had extensive experience dealing with outsized personalities whose lust for power, along with their colossal vanity and charisma, stirred up both admiration and fear. But the layers of tradition and recorded histories of the fifth-century political and private life of Alcibiades are richer than those of any other figure in the Golden Age of Greece. With his uncommon good looks, natural gifts, and seductive charm, Alcibiades had the larger-than-life stereotype qualities of a Greek hero of greatness, as well as a demagogue inclined to psychopathy. The very force of his individuality and excessive pride placed him outside the rules of the community, allowing him to violate the protocols of civic and political affairs demanded of the ordinary citizen, whom he held in contempt. Like the heroes of myth and cult, there were also extremes in his temperament and passions, an unpredictability that led some to detect "the habits of the tyrant" in his exhibitionism and insatiable appetites of the body, particularly for drink and sex but also for praise and flattery. The signs of narcissism suggested a man who would be unable to control himself in the political realm, thereby threatening the body politic, someone who was "incapable of being ruled" or trusted in a democracy. To many, Alcibiades's shameless bragging, his "drunkenness, debauchery and insolence," his flaunting of "effeminate dress," trailing "long purple robes" through the marketplace all hinted at possibly fatal weaknesses in his brilliant but erratic character. Athenian suspicions were borne out when he went over to the Persian side in the middle of the Persian Wars.

Alcibiades let the cat out of the bag when he used the sacred festival at Olympus to advertise his "barbaric" behavior violating the civic values and traditional pieties by pursuing personal pleasure, fame, and honor for himself rather than for the greater glory of the country, the purpose of the games. He was seen as an extravagant opportunist planning to make himself a tyrant as the only way he could support his compulsive private spending on luxuries. In the words of British classicist James Davidson, it was more a tyranny of desperation than of aspiration.[35]

The conduct of Alcibiades at the Olympics of 416 BC is the turning point, when he had the cheek to enter seven chariot teams in the races and walk off with the top four prizes. Thucydides reports that Alcibiades understood the connection between the unprecedented extravagance involved in the Olympic competition and his unquenchable thirst for power and status. His king-size spending was so lavish that it overshadowed the public displays of Athens and the other cities at the races, upsetting the relationship between the citizen and the community. He made sure that his exotic "Persian" tent was larger than the official tent of Athens and even appropriated the city's sacred processional vessels for his victory parade. "I ordered everything in style worthy of my victory. The general sentiment honours such magnificence; and the energy which is shown by it creates an impression of power."[36]

The conventional wisdom was that to achieve ideal happiness and moral goodness, one must resist or even renounce material satisfactions and temptations, beginning with the pleasures of the table and creature comforts. Among his telltale lapses, duly noted by one of his disapproving biographers who accompanied him on his ill-fated Sicilian campaign, Alcibiades slept on a comfortable rope bed in an alcove of his trireme's afterdeck instead of on the hard deck planks like the common sailor. This small but telling mark against his character was picked up and later passed on by Plutarch, who considered him both "unscrupulous" and "entirely careless." The historian also noted that the Greek general had Eros emblazoned on his shield announcing his dedication to frivolous pleasures and sex while in the middle of battle.

Before the loot poured in to Greece from imperial adventures beginning with the defeat of Xerxes's Persians, the early Greek fixation on hints of ostentation seems obsessive in an economically challenged society where the ability to show off was limited by lack of resources and few opportunities to be conspicuously reckless. The words of Herodotus's Demaratus, king of Sparta, who told the Persians that "Greece has always had poverty as its companion," sum up the country's hard-bitten economic condition. The need to be frugal and sparing was a fact of life for both citizens and peasants, for the gods from the heavens delight in frugality or are at least indifferent to worldly luxuries. It was the source of Greek bravery against crushing odds on the battlefield. Or as the moral critic Isocrates observed in the fourth century, the richest cities and states usually adopt the worst public policies: "Riches and power are attended and followed by folly, and folly in turn by license: whereas poverty and lowliness are attended by sobriety and great moderation."[37]

The innate Greek distrust of luxury also reflected the universal military training of citizens of the privileged class. Luxury carried with it an unmistakable suggestion of a feminine, Oriental softness—the opposite of athletic, martial manliness. All adult male citizens were strictly equal as warriors, and from the age of eighteen to sixty, military service was mandatory, including exercise and sports each summer. The citizen warrior in turn was expected to privately discipline members of his household. It was also his duty to see that the male members of warrior age were physically fit and resistant to self-indulgence, ready to face all physical dangers in the ranks of a phalanx meeting the external enemy head-on in honorable combat.

The defeat of the Persians by the Spartans became a legendary cautionary tale in Herodotus's description of Xerxes's abandoned camp of gorgeous tents, filled with mounds of uneaten food and jugs of wine all hung with gold and silver decorations pitched on the barren Greek plain after his defeat. Athens suddenly became a rich city, no longer forced to make a virtue of its poverty. The spoils of imperialism in silver, gold, piles of oriental silk robes sewn with jewels, and, of course, prisoners turned into slaves brought an irreversible transformation. After he sacked the Persian stronghold of Byzantium, Cimon used the spoils to replant the trees in the agora and transform the dusty patch called the Academy "into a well-watered shady grove." The great south wall of the Acropolis was also built with his patronage, later to be crowned with Athena's great temple, the Parthenon. But as Voltaire pointed out, luxury has always been both loved and feared; "Vanity will always invent more ways of distinguishing inself than the laws are able to forbid."[38] While the dazzling new public buildings and temples Pericles placed at the top of the Acropolis "created amazement among the rest of mankind," his enemies saw it as "an act of bare-faced tyranny," paid for out of misappropriated public funds earmarked for the war against the Persians. The imperial glitter, the result of Pericles's personal ambitions to beautify the city "as if it were some vain woman decking herself out with costly stones and statues and temples worth millions" would in the end leave Athens, in Plutarch's words, "polluted by a rank growth of corruption and wrongdoing after Pericles' death."[39]

This fear that foreign conquests would lead to the pitfalls of empire was real, and it has a long history in the thinking and experience of the ancient world and later. Looking back from the perspective of a hundred years, Isocrates believed that imperial aggression "in the name of democracy" had in fact caused the collapse of Greek democracy "under which our ancestors lived and were the happiest of Hellenes." He made his attack on the imperialist hawks represented by a dangerous class of rich oligarchs who lacked all self-control, applying the rules of private morality to the state, a significant strategy in the "war" on luxury:

> Set not your heart on the excessive acquisition of goods, but on a moderate enjoyment of what you have. Despise those who strain after riches, but are not able to use what they have. . . . Try to make money a thing to use as well as to possess; it is a thing of use to those who understand how to enjoy it and a mere possession to those who are able only to acquire it.

As private citizens, the powerful oligarchs could not be trusted to serve any interest other than their own, at the expense of the public welfare. The ancient suspicion of empire was later expressed on several occasions by the senate members of the Roman Republic when they refused to accept and exploit more foreign territories, believing they would cause serious damage to themselves and the state. Wealth produced by the empire inevitably spawned a plutocracy that would use and abuse the state, promoting vice rather than the nobility of the soul and encouraging "indolent living and luring the young to pleasure."[40]

While they attacked the war backed by the imperial hawks, and associated luxuria with foreign conquests, the critics mostly ignored the fact that the discovery of silver at Laurion in 482 BC paid for the victorious fleets of triremes that brought about the eventual defeat of the Persian forces following the naval Battle of Salamis in 480 BC. More important, it was the "luxury" of ten- to twenty-thousand slaves to work the Greek silver mines and help power the Greek navy (some two hundred ships requiring thirty-four thousand oarsmen) that provided the wherewithal to lay the economic foundation of Athenian liberty.

Critics of Periclean extravagance regularly pointed to the example of Sparta after its defeat of Athens in the Peloponnesian War: the sudden surge of wealth, followed by the inevitable temptations of soft, enervating living, undermined Sparta's military power and its fragile democracy. According to Plutarch, only the famous constitution of the legendary Lycurgus was able to restore Spartan austerity, with his hardly credible decision to remove all "odious distinction" among the Spartans by closing down the luxury trade. In Plutarch's imaginative version of the life of Lycurgus, all gold and silver coinage was peremptorily replaced with money made of iron with little value. This revolutionary move not only brought a halt to robbery and political bribes, but imported luxuries including "rhetoric-masters," "fortune-tellers," and "harlot-mongers" also disappeared from the markets, making a sumptuary ordinance to outlaw "all needless and superfluous art" redundant: no "gold or silversmith, engraver, or jeweler set foot in a country which had no money; . . . so that luxury, deprived little by little of that which fed and fomented it, wasted to nothing and died away of itself."[41]

The effort to reform Sparta's eating habits, always an index of self indulgence, was as radical as replacing gold and silver coins with worthless iron, and it fits in with the mythology of the military asceticism of Spartan communal equality. With all the lavish imported food and wine served by the rich after the Peloponnesian War, Lycurgus (now dismissed by scholars as probably fictitious) knew that conspicuous consumption thrived in the dining room. Striking at the target dead-on, his extraordinary law ordered the rich to sup with the poor at the same table, declaring that all citizens should eat together "in common, of the same bread and same meat, and of kinds that were specified, and should not spend their lives at home, laid on costly couches at splendid tables, delivering themselves up into the hands of their tradesmen and cooks, to fatten them in corners, like greedy brutes, and to ruin not their minds only, but their very bodies."[42] Anyone who refused "to eat and drink like the rest" was dismissed as "dainty and effeminate," the ultimate insult to a Spartan in 500 BC.

Without any austere idealism or religious beliefs dictating the daily menu, meals of most ancient Greeks probably consisted of lettuce, peas, lentil soup, figs, and beans. The only variation was that the most ascetically orthodox Cynics philosophically ate their food raw, washed down with water instead of wine. They blamed Prometheus for undermining mankind's natural hardiness and goodness with his gift of fire for cooking. Except for the elite, clothing was minimal for most people. There was, of course, a small, closed patrician class of mostly large landowners whose wealth came from agriculture, aside from the plunder and profits of war and politics. Their tables, set with silver cups and ewers and surrounded by soft reclining couches, were loaded with exotic imported fare:

> From the Hellespont mackerel and salted fish of all kinds.
> From Thessaly puddings and ribs of beef,
> From the Syracusans pigs and cheese,
> From Euroia pears and well-fleeced apples,
> From Phoenicia the fruit of the palm and finest flour.[43]

For the most part, the Athenians, who ate their Syracusan cheese with "well-fleeced apples" from Euroia, were rich absentee landlords whose estates were run by slaves and indentured tenants. This prodigal aristocracy became the regular target of the moralists who wanted to prevent the *gratin* from wasting the community's resources in showoff living and idle leisure, making the state vulnerable in the case of war or a natural catastrophe. Since most luxuries—food, spices, perfumes, silks, furs—were imported, widespread dependence on foreign supplies could also undermine public policy on trade that might in fact be against the long-range safety and welfare of the state, much as the addictive consumption of imported oil currently does in the West.

Demosthenes, one of the richest men in Greece, thought he had detected disturbing symptoms of compulsive excess in the expensive new houses being thrown up by Athenian politicians.[44] To his jaundiced eye, they seemed the result of some unchecked character flaw supported by political shenanigans, sharp dealing, bribery, and corruption. His example of Meidias, one of Athens' big spenders near the end of the classical period, would not have received a footnote in Thorstein Veblen's examples of the "conspicuous consumption" of the Robber Barons. Nor can it compare to the grotesque displays flaunted by celebrity elites on the pages of *Architectural Digest*, who have lifted Veblen's label to stratospheric heights of staggering exhibitionism. "He has built at Eleusis a mansion huge enough to overshadow his neighbors," Demosthenes grumbled; "he drives his wife to the Mysteries or anywhere else that he wishes, with a pair of grays from Sicyon; he swaggers about the market-place with three or four henchmen in attendance," loudly bragging about his collection of fancy drinking cups and horns. Demosthenes caps his dismissive scruples by saying that a man should not be admired for his pompous, run-of-the-mill ambitions in his McMansion and his three-chariot garage but by his private generosity and public service. It is worth noting that in the history of the West's attempts to curb shameless extravagance, though architectural excesses have often been fair game for attack on aesthetic grounds, they have seldom been a target of moral critics. To impress their followers, successful TV evangelists conspicuously vie with one another and with entertainment stars to see who can build the most grotesque architectural monstrosity, proof of God's blessings.[45]

The very tone of Demosthenes's criticism of the jumped-up politician's vulgarity may expose his class prejudice. In democratic Athens, statesmen, no matter how profitable their public offices, were supposed to live discreetly like everyone else. "In the good old days" (a common preface to a blast at excess), "the houses of men such as Aristides or Meidias or any famous citizen of those times was in no way more distinguished than [those of] their neighbors." Meidias's boorish insolence—flaunting his wealth, raising the hackles of the better sort—adds another dimension to luxury's complex social register of taste and lifestyle that still survives in the "fashion system" of mega houses.[46]

After the death of Plato in 347 BC, and Aristotle twenty-five years later in 322, the study of ethics and the pursuit of the art of living through a philosophically secure understanding of the nature of things moved from the Academy and Lyceum to the Epicureans in their Garden, and the Stoics sitting in the shade of their colonnaded Porch. To our modern ear, "epicurean" suggests the sensual life of the sybarite, a languorous hedonist who lives only for the pleasure of the senses. In his dictionary, Dr. Johnson dismissed the epicure "as a man given wholly to luxury." The word could easily be confused with the dubious qualities of the "epicene." But Diderot's encyclopedia entry on Epicureanism challenged this popular definition: "Never has a philosophy been less understood and more calumniated than that of Epicurus."[47] As for "stoic," it continues to sound severe, grim, or at least weak and passive, yet in the expression "stoic calm," it still manages to capture something of its ancient essence. But the popular notion of a vulgar Epicurean hedonist challenging the puritanical

Stoic on the question of luxury is a caricature of the two schools of philosophy. They both would have agreed on the virtue of moderation and the rewards of simple living and high thinking.

Both the Epicureans and the Stoics endorsed the dichotomy between the necessary and natural on the one hand, and material excess on the other. It is easy to see how Epicurus was dismissed in his own lifetime as a subversive promoter of overindulgence, a libertine, or worse. His letter to his friend Anaxarchu was provocative:

> You need only possess perception and be made of flesh, and you will see that pleasure is good. I summon you to continuous pleasures—and not to virtues which are empty and vain and which hold out troubling expectations of rewards. We say that pleasure is the beginning and end of a happy life; for we recognize it as a primary and innate good, and from it we begin all choice and avoidance, and to it we return, judging every good thing by the standard of that feeling.[48]

While Epicurus professed that "the beginning and root of every good thing is the pleasure of the belly," the study of nature convinced him that the perils of hedonism meant that Epicurean pleasure, the things that give pleasure, must be rationally selected on the clear empirical evidence of sight, sound, taste, smell, touch, and validated by one's rational judgment and experience. "The pleasant life" is not the sensual life of profligates, nor is it produced by "continuous drinking and revels, nor the enjoyment of women and young boys, nor fish and other viands that a luxurious table holds, which make for a pleasant life, but sober reasoning, which examines the motives for every choice."[49] If the rule were ignored, the next day's headache, regrets, or guilt would inflict their predictable misery and pain on both body and soul.

To restore a sense of moral integrity to hedonism, a true Epicurean must be virtuous as well as sober, for it "is not possible to live pleasurably without living sensibly, justly and temperately." Epicurus's Garden in Athens, where his followers gathered, was not a formal school but more of a relaxed community retreat where sympathetic friends could demonstrate (and afford) a certain style of ascetic life by taking directions from nature. These lines from a letter to a friend promoting "the simple and inexpensive diet" turn the popular notion of hedonism upside down sounding like a promotion for an expensive health spa:

> We regard self-sufficiency as a great good, not that we may always have the enjoyment of but a few things, but that if we do not have many, we may have but few enjoyments in the genuine conviction that they take the sweetest on luxury who have the least need of it, and everything easy to procure is natural while everything difficult to obtain is superfluous. Plain dishes offer the same pleasure as a luxurious table, when the pain that comes from want is taken away.[50]

To the Stoics lounging on their old *stoa* (porch) of the agora in Athens, trying to discover the key to "the good life" and to live it, the ethics of their rivals looking for the same thing in the Garden of the Epicureans were highly suspect, dismissing the lure of pleasure as life's goal in favor of a life of "virtue."

Stoic philosophy seemed at times an impenetrable tangle of metaphysical contradictions and dead ends. If the Stoics had stuck to their basic virtues—common sense, justice, courage, and moderation; virtues that were universally agreed upon—their philosophy might have seemed less severe or otherworldly. But since virtue was considered a state of mind, a verbal abstraction, it was easy for Stoic ethics to become opaque and at times paradoxical: "all mistakes are equally bad" or "only a wise man is rich" have the quality of a Confucian adage. As for pleasure "being rational elation," it was far more satisfying to the soul. The virtue of temperance or moderation is defined as "the science (epistêmê) of what is to be chosen and what is to be avoided and what is neither of these."[51]

The international vitality and reputation of Hellenistic philosophy soared just as the austerity of the Roman Republic was on its way out, to be replaced by imperial ambitions that fatally embraced exhausted Greece. The issue of ethics and the question of restraint, in which the symptoms of immorality were linked to luxury and self-indulgence, had a particular appeal at a time of internal political and social upheavals in Rome. Both Epicurean and Stoic philosophies attracted followers in the waning years of the Roman Republic and in the empire established by Augustus that followed. Many of the sophisticated Roman

Stoics were both well heeled and well traveled. Athens had the same cultural cachet as Rome would have for eighteenth-century England. In fact, the most complete works by Stoic philosophers that have survived are those by writers of imperial times, particularly Epictetus (ca. AD 55 to 135), the Greek philosopher who deeply influenced the writings of Emperor Marcus Aurelius (AD 121 to 180). Extracts of the philosopher's discourses first appeared a decade before the emperor was born.[52]

Seneca, the rich man of letters who, more than anyone else, became the leading Roman Stoic, outlined in his writings (particularly his essays on moderation: "On Tranquility of Mind" and "On the Happy Life") the fundamental Stoic doctrines that would become an influential strand in the thinking of the church fathers and the Renaissance humanists. He was the favorite pagan of the Church of Rome.

The Latin author and philosopher was born of a wealthy family in Cordoba, Spain, about 4 BC. Through good connections (or as he would say, "Fortune"), he was launched into a hugely successful career, amassing a large fortune by means both fair and dubious. Since then, ancient moralists and modern critics alike have had a difficult time reconciling his wealth and its shady origin with his famous advocacy of following the simple life of the Greek Stoics, since he was surrounded by and a part of opulent court life, particularly that of Nero.

When Nero's chief police enforcer and hatchet man asked his friend Seneca for advice on how to cope with the corruption and decadence of court life, the old insider laid out his philosophical guide to achieving the good Stoic life through moderation by following "the Platos and Xenophons and the famous Socratic brood." It is easy to see why Seneca's Stoic universe—"life in accordance to nature"—remains so appealing today and means much more than our common adjective "stoic" to describe our resignation to the quotidian jobs of cleaning out the attic, paying bills, or attending family reunions. "If Fortune gets the upper hand and interdicts action," he tells the victim in his essay "On Tranquility," he must take the offensive and not turn his back "and fly defenseless to seek a hiding place as if there were any place that Fortune could not reach him." The Stoic considered the whole world his school in order "to afford virtue a broader scope" and to learn how to manage the vagaries of fate—both good and bad—even if the experience is boring or disagreeable.[53]

In another passage in the essay, Seneca moves on to the old Greek problem of material possessions, confessing his "deep love of frugality" and opting for understated shabby elegance. "I do not like a couch pretentiously decked out, clothing brought out of the chest and pressed with heavy irons and repeatedly mangled to make it glossy, but prefer cheap and homely wear which does not need to be tended or worn with such care." Warming to his take on the virtue of contrived parsimony: "I do not like food prepared and gaped at by a troupe of chefs, ordered many days in advance and served up with many hands, but something handy and easy to prepare with nothing recherché."[54]

"We pass now to property," which he warns is the "the greatest affliction to humanity." (This line has always brought out the moralists, loudly shouting, "Hypocrite!" Seneca was one of the richest Roman plutocrats of the first century of the Christian era.) "If you balance all our other troubles—deaths, diseases, fears, longings, subjection to labor and pain—with miseries in which our money is involved, the latter will far outweigh the former." Therefore, Seneca argued, people with less money to lose are more cheerful than those whom fortune has abandoned. "Give this kind of security any invidious name you like—poverty, neediness, pauperism; I shall not count a man happy if you find me another who has nothing to lose."

Seneca then addresses the importance of frugality and thrift as singular virtues that have their own rewards for those who practice them. And aside from their usual tedious, niggling, hedging caveats, Plato, Aristotle, Zeno, Epicurus, and all the lauded Greek moral instructors would have concurred:

> We must learn to strengthen self-restraint, curb luxury, temper ambition, moderate anger, view poverty calmly, cultivate frugality (though many are ashamed of it), use readily available remedies for natural desires, keep restive aspirations and a mind intent on the future under lock and key, and make it our business to get our riches from ourselves rather than from fortune.[55]

3

ROME
The Road to Ruin

———— ❦ ————

*No country has ever been greater or purer than our own, or better
endowed with noble precedents. Nor has any country managed for
so long to keep itself free from avarice and luxury. Nowhere has the
simple life of frugality been held in such honour until recently.*
—LIVY, *THE RISE OF ROME*, 27–25 BC

*The world today speaks for itself; by the evidence of its decay it
announces its dissolution. The farmers are vanishing from the
countryside, commerce from the sea, soldiers from the camps; all
honesty in business, all justice in the courts, all solidarity in friendship,
all skills in the arts, all standards in morals—all are disappearing.*
—SAINT CYPRIAN, AD 200–258

Aside from an excuse to enjoy sex and violence on the screen, there is at
least one obvious purpose of the film and TV blockbusters about ancient
Rome. Judged by the casts of thousands staging scenes of "violent splendor" in
a movie lot and studio, these spectaculars were a quick way to solve the film industry's unemployment problems, just as they were in the flamboyant imperial
city of rulers such as Tiberius and Caligula.

Turned loose, Federico Fellini's production designers for the *Satyricon*
outdid even Nero's party managers' most perverse inventions. On film, Petro-

nius's prostitutes, transvestites, the denizens of fetid bathhouses cavorting in plaster palaces with lush roof gardens, hid unimaginable couplings, perpetuating the glamorous fiction of Rome's insatiable appetite for excess. A seductress takes a dip in an alabaster bath of asses' milk, while glistening Numidian slaves serve drinks, in which rare pearls have been dissolved, to wash down the platters of peacock brains and flamingo tongues. That is why Cleopatra's over-the-top gesture of drinking an extravagant aperitif by dissolving a priceless pearl in a goblet of vinegar—to win a bet (according to Pliny) with her besotted lover, Antony, that she could consume a meal worth millions—made her a favorite of the silver screen.

We hardly need comic-book movies and TV caricatures of the past with their sensational, inventions of debauched entertainment to embroider the recorded saga of Roman history. Luxury is given a fine moralizing edge in the narratives of Livy, Plutarch, Sallust, Cassius Dio, and other Roman historians who regularly acted the wet blanket to what they perceived as dangerous excesses indulged in by their authoritarian rulers. They endowed luxury with a depraved reputation that would last for millennia. Even with whole libraries of books forever lost, the surviving literature of Rome's pantheon of biographers, poets, moralists, and historians has left little to the imagination. Of course, many of the complaints of contemporary writers who deplored what they saw as perverse luxury were often expressing their own "peculiar temper and situation." Few if any observers viewing "revolutions of society" from the inside, as Gibbon cautioned, are capable of identifying "the secret springs of action" that drive the unpredictable, churned-up passions of the masses.[1] But many believed, then and later, that the temptation of luxury and indolence was a debilitating influence on human appetites, particularly of the powerful rich, a degenerative disease that played a significant role in Rome's decline and eventual deterioration into weeds, rubble, and massive colonies of stray cats.[2]

As the people of the ancient world attempted to explain the steady slippage of traditional virtues each generation seemed to detect, their frame of reference may have been largely myths used to uphold civil equilibrium; yet these reveal the subculture of Roman power at the top as well as those who dared to question it. Despite their reputation for administrative skills in most areas of government, the Romans never figured out how to establish an orderly transfer of imperial power, a systemic flaw that regularly convulsed the state. In all the manipulation and plotting to discredit a ruling emperor or a deposed former administration, enemies and critics didn't hesitate to raise the specter of decadence and corruption as a political strategy, embellishing the charges with lurid details of the presence of luxuria in high places. Historians of the day tried to identify both the strengths and weaknesses of the Roman constitution to explain the government's cycles of political revolution, often led by tyrants and their accomplices. Polybius, the worldly Greek chronicler of the second century BC exiled in Rome, concluded that "avarice and unscrupulous money-making . . . drinking and the convivial excesses that go with it" by disturbers of order provoked "envy and indignation" that led to the disintegration and collapse of the state.[3]

Greek and Roman thinkers who accepted the apocalyptic vision of abuses of concentrated power as a threat to the health of the body politic still could offer no clear explanation for the cycles of corruption that repeatedly set off upheavals. What was most troubling was that while fate was inevitable and inexplicable, the ancients still held (and we still hold) society responsible for its own moral decline from causes rooted in behavior and institutions. Frustrated and baffled, they made efforts to understand, which seemed to fall into two categories or theories: the infection was from external sources, alien values introduced by foreign wars and imperial hubris; or it developed from within, the result of the repeated syndrome of greed that had been generated internally from causes no one understood beyond human missteps that stirred up the ire of the gods.

Luxury (luxuria) and avarice (avarita) with their train of gaudy abuses, public and private, become seriously divisive political issues during the late republic in the first century BC, as it was transformed under the weight of the staggering plunder pouring in from the new territories brought under Rome's rule. In the view of Pliny the Elder, the fall from grace occurred in 154 BC, the year he pinpointed as marking the end of sexual modesty. The exotic plundered objects themselves—a gold and ivory Egyptian console or a silk robe from Persia embroidered with jewels, sculpture from Greece—were the perfect stage props of opulent excess, promoting squalor and the collapse of morals in daily life. Republican moralists of the old school kept an eye out for an addictive lust for wealth for its own sake as well as the telltale lust for power and sex, announced by luxury's subversive appearance and the onset of disorder and decay. The only appetite or desire that was tolerable was the virtuous love of honor and glory to serve the nation and the public good. It was the one human passion that would check the others; even Saint Augustine would later agree.[4]

Nostalgia for ancient rustic virtues and the praise they earned become a major theme of Roman literature, revealing a growing rift between the inherited ideals of a once sturdy, self-reliant republic and the state of affairs brought on by unexpected and unimagined success, the result of imperial adventures. Rome's rapid growth into an urban center of the empire intensified the memory that it was once an agricultural center. As Ovid the poet-friend of Emperor Augustus puts it in *The Art of Love*, "There was rude simplicity of old, but now golden Rome possesses the vast wealth of the conquered world. See what the Capitol is now, and what it was: you would say they belong to different Jupiters." The poet Juvenal also regularly exploited the vices of excess enjoyed by Rome's smart society during the Antonine ascendancy, adding mouth-watering gourmet details as metaphors of morally suspect menus: "peeled truffles," the correct "relish on mushrooms," "quail and plovers served up in their natural juices," contrary to the conventions of the traditional Roman diet.[5] To the cynical poet, money reigned supreme—"of all the gods it's Wealth that compels our deepest reverence"—even though the Romans had not yet built a temple to "pernicious Cash."[6]

The Roman matron who once "with hardened thumb" took care of the sheep and laid the twigs and logs on the family hearth now thinks of nothing more than "opulent dress, costly vehicles . . . leisure to accompany her husband to dinner parties, to visit friends, attend festivals."[7] She had strayed from the firmly gendered ancient boundaries, enshrined in the proverbial Roman woman's epitaph, *Domi mansi, lanam fecit* (She stayed at home and made wool).

According to Seneca, a sure sign of moral softness was

> when prosperity has spread luxury far and wide, men begin by paying closer attention to their personal appearance. They go crazy over furniture. Next, they devote attention to their houses—how to take up more space with them, as if they were country-houses, how to make the walls glitter with marble that has been imported overseas, how to adorn a roof

with gold, so that it may match the brightness of the inlaid floors. After that, they transfer their exquisite taste to the dinner-table."[8]

Pliny the Elder's cold eye spotted luxury in the unseemly novelty of the rare gems, artwork, and a giant gaming table made of precious stones that were part of Pompey's spoils and splendor—"the stuff of triumphs"—the conqueror paraded through the streets in Rome in 61 BC to celebrate his military victories. Jewels of such a size had never been seen in the city, and to Pliny this was proof, as it were, that the world's natural resources were being seriously exhausted. It is an early speculation on the impact of material excess on natural resources. Pompey's defeat of the enemy, Pliny concluded, was in fact "the defeat of austerity and the triumph, let's face it, of luxury."[9]

The introduction of gold and silver table ornaments to replace the family's humble earthenware and wooden pots and the loss of unpretentious manners and personal modesty, bred in a simpler age, were noted with growing apprehension. During the republic, the grander establishments had simple candelabra, with only a few made of ostentatious marble, but in the early decades of Augustus, the use of elaborate lighting fixtures, often made of precious metal, became widespread, an index of new extravagance.[10] According to this idealized reading of the past, the cycle begins with an ancient, self-sufficient pastoral society living according to austere, established traditions, which then succumbs to greed and self-interest where, in the words of Sallust, "men were reckoned good in proportion to their wealth and power to harm, inasmuch as they defended the existing conditions" of selfish pleasures.[11]

Whenever courage, temperance, frugality, and patriotism seemed to be in short supply, moralizing fingers would wag in the direction of the culprit, often someone who had fallen under to foreign influences. It was drilled into every student's head that uncontrolled appetites and greed "taught men to be proud and cruel, to neglect religion and to hold nothing too sacred to sell." These were the core vices agreed on by both the governing class and the governed of the Republic; they set the standard for Roman morality and established the critique to bring power down to earth. The American Revolutionary generation looked to the Roman Republic as the ideal republican society, filled, in the words of John Adams, with "all great, manly and warlike virtues." Rough-and-ready Gen. Charles Lee, a soldier of fortune in the American cause, told Patrick Henry not long after Independence that until the Revolution came along, he "us'd to regret not being thrown into the World in the glorious third or fourth century of the Romans."[12]

Historically, the critical factor is that, until the end of the eighteenth century and the founding of the American Republic, this "Roman response" to the disruptive power of rebellious human appetites—expressed in opulent living that destroyed once thriving, modest, independent societies—defined the debate about virtue and corruption as a political issue. Like the Romans of the Republic, the American Founders saw the country's future greatness based on their romantic notion of classical republican virtues. They themselves became, in their painted and sculpted portraits as in their beliefs and private lives, more Roman than the Romans.

But as men of the Enlightenment, optimistically buoyed by the doctrine of progress, they also knew their ancient history and were haunted by the decline of the Roman Empire, the first civilization to exhaust itself. Could they be confident that progress would continue into an infinite future and spare them the fate that had finished off Rome? If such a model civilization had collapsed, who could guarantee that it wouldn't happen again? Since art and science was the engine of progress, would not the new plural society they were building make collapse impossible? This was the experiment of enlightened "progress" that had yet to be tested.[13]

According to its own historians, the Roman Republic was established by an older, sterner breed of men who viewed most things that were un-Roman as forms of luxury, often representing the misuse and unequal distribution of wealth for strictly private, selfish satisfactions at the expense of the public welfare. Roman citizens considered modesty, frugality, and discipline to be core virtues, qualities that can easily be read into their resolute marble likenesses. Willful gratification of selfish desires indicated a flawed, destabilizing character, and it could lead to political disintegration, as when the greed of the wealthy could bring on a civil uprising after ordinary citizens finally realized they had been reduced to slaves. Expressions of self-indulgence in pursuit of sensual pleasures would also make men unwilling and unable to serve the public good when that might require personal courage and sacrifice. Like the

Greeks, morally conflicted Romans saw limitless acquisition of material wealth and concomitant endless imperial conquests as a dicey game. Both civilizations had found such suspicions "deeply embedded in Greek literature from Homer to Attic tragedy," in the words of historian Andrew Wallace-Hadrill.[14] The removal of military threat by foreign pressure opened the way to worldly temptations and vice, just as the collapse of the Athenian empire was caused, many thought, by imported Eastern decadence paid for with the plunder of war. The introduction of luxury's gross appetites and effeminate softness weakening the citizen for military service was perhaps the most vivid, well-known example of a reversal of fortune due to defective national character. For the Greeks and the Romans, effeminacy induced by the debilitating vices of excessive drinking, eating, and whoring was "evidence of slavishness, lower-class habits or the behavior of foreign barbarians"—damaging to an orderly, upright society that had to be ready to defend itself.[15]

Cicero, who had seen Pompey's conquests more than double foreign tribute to Rome's treasury, also saw public bribery become a respectable profession. Not surprisingly, he declared avarice the worst vice of politicians. Following Aristotle's warning, he saw that a nobility addicted to excess could reduce an aristocratic government from a benevolent oligarchy to a ruthless tyranny devoid of virtue when the tyrant, ignoring the interests of the state to gratify his own selfish ambitions and expensive appetites, ultimately brings about his destruction.[16]

Taking a page from Greek ethics, conservative Romans of the Republic and its historians were suspicious of spend-thrift habits and pushy manners on the part of louche politicians looking for political opportunities. Those who knew their Greek plays could quote Euripides on heedless ambition and its predictable pathology—what he called the most destructive of chaotic forces. Luxury as a personal expression of abusive power could dangerously stir up the vice of envy and produce mob rule and ultimately despotism. To preserve itself, the state had a duty to uphold some notion of public good as a superior ideal.

Plutarch's portrait of Julius Caesar shows how his "ability to make him-self liked through extravagant propaganda" masked his daring ambition to impose a dictatorship. "He spent money recklessly, and many people thought that he was purchasing a moment's brief fame at an enormous price . . . in reality he was buying the greatest place in the world at inconsiderable expense." At an early age, Julius Caesar was famous for living in a "certain splendor," throwing grand dinner parties and entertainments. As a fledgling magistrate of the city of Rome, he once sponsored an exhibition of 320 gladiators fighting in a single combat, "and what with this and all his other lavish expenditure on theatrical performances, processions and public banquets," he exceeded all other attempts by public officials to seduce the public. Having ignored all the familiar warnings of incipient despotism, "the Romans gave way before his good fortune" in war; they "accepted the bit. The rule of one man would give them, they thought, a respite from the miseries of civil wars, and so they appointed him dictator for life. This meant an undisguised tyranny; his power was not only absolute but perpetual."[17]

The ideal of the virtuous citizen, summed up in the noble Roman concept of *gravitas*, was so important it was set out in legislation. First of all, gravitas required a Roman to be a good soldier and later, when called upon, a public servant—a sober, frugal, upright man who had no time for levity in either his private or public life. He must have short hair, be well shaved, and dress in simple knee-length tunics unless he was an official. Only later when the republic was in decline would the toga become the defining dress of a Roman gentleman, a sartorial detail overlooked in neoclassical sculpture of the late eighteenth century.

Assessing the qualities of the Roman Republic, Polybius saw two elements in every political system

by which its true form and quality are either desirable or the opposite. By these I mean the customs and the laws. The desirable ones are those that make men's private lives virtuous and well disciplined and the public character of the state civilized and just; the undesirable are those that have the opposite effect. So when we see that the customs and laws of any given people are good, we can conclude with confidence that the citizens and their constitution will likewise be good; and on the same principle when we see a community in which private life is characterized by greed and avarice and public conduct by injustice, then clearly we have good reason to pronounce their laws, their particular customs and their constitution in general to be bad.[18]

There was no doubt in Polybius's mind that Rome's sudden rise to world power following the final defeat of Carthage had introduced a new "moral laxity" taking it to the edge of the abyss. And everyone of cultivation agreed that a civilized society always avoided the abyss. The changes were obvious in the everyday extravagance of imported stuff: exotic foods, spices, jewelry, perfume, and particularly silk (called "soft wool" by Virgil). Because of silk's rarity and cost, Gibbon dubbed the Eastern insects that mysteriously produced it "the first artificers of the luxury of nations." The rare and sexy material was immediately condemned by "old school" Romans for creating a "thirst for gain," setting off imperial explorations to "the last confines of the earth for the pernicious purpose," in Gibbon's chaste words, "of exposing to the public eye naked draperies and transparent matrons" so that the "turn of the limbs and colour of the skin . . . might gratify vanity and provoke desire."[19]

The historian Livy, writing from the perspective of the Augustan monarchy, agreed that the effect of luxury on republican Rome's "customs, laws and constitutions" had been seriously tested after the victory in the Second Macedonian War in 187 BC. It is a date that has become hallowed as a watershed. "Foreign" luxury arrived in wagonloads of loot, along with all manner of imported, alien temptations hidden beneath the booty." People became obsessed "with consuming all else through excess and self-indulgence.[20]

The connection between imperial conquest and the introduction of unheard of wealth into Rome was dramatized in the triumphal processions parading their loot through the streets to celebrate military victories. To those who concerned themselves with civic virtue, these vulgar displays, cheered by the crowds, effectively reduced the Roman tradition of frugality to empty hypocrisy. It was no exaggeration, Livy concluded, that "the things that began to appear in those days were no more than the seeds of the luxury yet to come."[21]

Despite exaggeration by Renaissance painters and Hollywood film directors, what's best about Livy's account of the stunning triumphs awarded to the military commanders are his rich details. The plunder paraded by Marcus Fulvius in January 187 BC after his victory over the Aetolians—112 pounds of gold carried before his proconsul chariot—is a famous contribution to the literature of the Roman triumph. The train that followed the proconsul carried 83,000 pounds of silver, 243 pounds of gold, "785 bronze statues, 230 marble statues," along with the usual armor, spears, catapults, and other war machinery. A respectable number of bedraggled prisoners were also a part of the well-staged extravaganza.[22]

The dazzle and scale of the triumph of Gnaeus Manlius Vulso with his plunder from Asia Minor a few months later in March outdid his rival, bringing, according to Livy, 220,000 pounds of silver and 2,103 pounds of gold. The celebration launches the gloomy historian into a sustained indictment of luxury, claiming that its message, delivered to the capital city by the army, introduced the foreign signs of luxury—prostitutes, gourmet cooks, fine wines, poets and philosophers. Pliny singled out couches as the ultimate symbol of indolent living: "These were the men who first introduced into Rome bronze couches, expensive bed-covers, tapestries and other woven materials, and—things then regarded as furniture of high fashion—pedestal tables and sideboards." That was not all: "This was when girls playing harps and lutes made their appearance at dinner parties, together with other entertainments to amuse the dinner guests; and more attention and expenditure also began to be devoted to the dinners themselves." The work of a lowly cook "doing menial labor became an art," a novelty costing more than the price of a good-looking slave or dancing girl.[23] Cookery as an art had been dismissed by earlier Romans and considered a waste of time. When two chefs were honored with public statues while Cato the Elder was censor, he could see what was coming. He told a well-known epicure, "While good food was celebrated, virtue was sadly ignored."[24]

The Greek sculptures and paintings that first appeared strapped to army chariots and wagons as they made their entry into Rome were a cultural shock unlike anything ever experienced before. The first big haul to bring on an attack of "consuming" curiosity was in 211 BC. Among the booty of Marcus Claudius Marcellus, after the capture of the Sicilian city of Syracuse, was the first large display of Greek art ever seen in Rome. According to Plutarch:

> He transported the greater part and the finest objects that in Syracuse had
> been dedicated to the gods, to be a spectacle for his triumph and an adorn-
> ment for the city. For before that time Rome neither possessed nor was
> it even aware of these elegant luxuries, nor was there any love in the city
> for refinement and beauty. Instead it was full of the weapons seized from

barbarian enemies and blood-stained booty, and crowned with memorials and trophies—not a pleasant nor reassuring sight, nor for fainthearted spectators and aesthetes.[25]

Plutarch added that older Romans thought the display that had included sacred objects and temple gods was a sacrilege, treating the deities "as if they were prisoners." With all the details in ancient texts, the triumph of Marcellus has been seen as a crucial moment marking a cultural revolution, now called the "Hellenization" of Rome. But for many Romans, all things Greek meant the viral growth of vice.

A taste for expensive art and high fashion was a part of luxuria (ostentatious glut, obsessive spending), and Romans who once thought of Greek artworks as corrupting and un-Roman soon began to actually buy imported Greek sculpture and paintings at grotesquely inflated prices to decorate their fashionable villas and gardens in the latest Hellenistic style. Even the lavish fishponds that became a passion with the Roman plutocracy were an imported diversion first indulged in by Greek aristocrats. The flaunting of conspicuous living of the nouveau riche lost much of its social and moral stigma. Though Cicero was considered "a new man," much of his rhetoric makes him come off as a snobbish member of the old establishment, but with a taste for the latest imported stuff. In a letter to Atticus, his friend living in Athens, he sounds like the American press lord William Randolph Hearst furnishing his mountain retreat at San Simeon:

> As to your Hermae of Pentelic marble with bronze heads, about which you wrote me—I have fallen in love with them on the spot. So pray send both them and the statues and anything else that may appear to you to suit . . . my passion and your taste—as large a supply and as early as possible. Above all, anything you think appropriate to a gymnasium and terrace. . . . while I expect assistance from you, I expect something like rebuke from others.[26]

Rome's profitable military ventures, like all successful wars, had brought about a radical redistribution and concentration of wealth disrupting the hierarchy of the established and close-knit social classes. In the wake of this upheaval, ambitious parvenues, newly rich profiteers from the provinces, and the usual hangers-on looking for any commercial opportunity floating in the confusion, injected new energy into the capital. No longer was worldly gain open to just the Roman aristocracy. Everyone understood the role of extravagant, rare possessions as definers of social standing, and the breakdown of class distinctions as the newly wealthy appropriated these established signs of rank brought on widespread anxiety.[27]

While the Roman armies were consolidating sprawling territories in all directions, the rhythms of Rome's primitive society of farmers, slaves, and powerful family clans closely tied to the state had remained unchanged for generations. In 44 BC, when Octavian (the future Augustus) rushed to Rome to be adopted by Julius Caesar, the city's "mean and narrow streets" were no match for the cosmopolitan Greek cities of the East. The old republican city had spread haphazardly beyond the walls without any plan or vision. There were few signs of a cultural life in art, architecture, and literature compared to the far more cosmopolitan Hellenistic culture centered in Athens. Philip V of Macedon ridiculed his enemy's backwardness. But after Rome's conquest of the Grecian East, all things Greek proved irresistible. The architecture of fashionable Greek villas (with fishponds), Greek art and music, wine, and poetry, carrying with them the pervasive aesthetic and philosophical traditions of what we think of as Classical Athens soon filled Rome's cultural vacuum. In Horace's famous words, "Captive Greece captured the victor." For many of the established order, this new appetite for the exotic encouraged one to "forsake one's hereditary poverty," conduct that was as morally disgraceful as squandering an inherited fortune.[28]

It is no surprise that the collision between two such disparate worlds set off internal conflict and instability in which the specter of material excess loomed prominently. "[Rome's] conquests," Plutarch wrote in his understated words, "provided it with a great mixture of customs and ways of life of every kind." The effects of Greek influence on the Roman way of life, its religion, and character were profound, even if it is doubtful that Roman soldiers first discovered sex during the Greek and Asian campaigns. That was how Sallust, who seemed to be familiar with the franker vices of the times, put it when he blamed the new decadence squarely on the effete, seductive East: "That lovely country and its pleasures soon softened the soldiers' warlike spirits. This was where Roman soldiers first learnt to make love, to be drunk, to enjoy statues and pictures and embossed plate. They stole them from private houses and public buildings; they plundered temples and polluted everything, sacred and secular."[29]

Sallust claimed that he turned to writing after becoming disgusted by the spread of Greco-Roman excesses. It was something he knew firsthand, having been thrown out of the senate on charges of corruption before he pillaged the Province of Africa Nova where Caesar had sent him as governor. A very rich man when he returned, he bought Caesar's villa in Tivoli and built a splendid park in Rome that was grand enough to later become the property of the emperors.

So Sallust's moralizing—that luxury and its influence was an imported menace capable of undermining native self-sufficiency and prudence—has to be taken as a reformed sinner's homily, with political implications. "Growing love of money, and the lust for power which followed it, engendered every kind of evil." Avarice destroyed the heroic virtues of honor, integrity, and other virtue, and encouraged men to neglect their old-time religion. His analysis sets out what he, and others with less shady credentials, agreed were unmistakable portents of Rome's degeneration. "Since that time the manners of our forebears have not only declined little by little, as was formerly the case, but have tumbled down headlong like a torrent. Young men have been vitiated by luxury and greed," Sallust lamented, repeating the sentiments from earlier Greek writers who also predicted the fall of empires. What is left unresolved in these ancient sources is whether corrupt appetites were picked up in foreign parts or developed on their own with Rome's hugely profitable military successes, which brought new prosperity and the freedom to satisfy all passions.[30]

Resisting the rising tide of the new wealth, some Romans made self-conscious attempts to hold on to reminders of the old traditions of restraint, expressing their ambiguous feelings and unease about all the changes even in the style of their tables and the food they served. At a basic level of daily life, the symbolic role of food—simple and luxurious, raw and cooked, foreign and native—offered a commentary on the homely victuals of the past compared to the oversophisticated cuisine prepared by professional chefs that was now appearing at the dinner parties of the elite. Some of the food critics sounded like members of a proto–slow food movement. Writing of Sulla after the success of his Libyan campaign, Plutarch described how members of the aristocracy thought the general was "giving himself airs," boasting of his achievements even though the age of plain and stalwart manners had long since deteriorated into shallow taste for display and fashion.

On feast days, in the middle of the imperial Roman forum, the very heart of the political and religious life of the city, a rustic farm table was symbolically laid with frugal offerings of simple country food, a ritual tribute to the rural gods Silvanus, Faunus, or Pan as a reminder of a vanished way of life. The pastoral display, its original significance probably long forgotten, was a commentary on the groaning boards of senatorial power banquets and entertainments Rome's new elite set up a short distance away. The contrast of theses extremes of the virtuous beginnings with the luxuria of an oversophisticated, overindulged city dramatized the mythology of Roman history. In literary terms, as the lively classical scholar Emily Gowers has pointed out, gluttony became the "image of the Romans' uncontrolled appetite for power, their unlicensed absorption of the world."[31]

At the beginning of Augustus's "Golden Age," people living in the stylish houses on Aventine Hill held an annual ritual of offerings of firstfruits, as if they were primitive farmers coming in from the fields of the Compagna. Or take the sacrifices placed in the temples of Vesta, Cybele, and Carba. Much like the ritual breakfasts served to the gods at the ancient Shinto Shrine of Ise, the humble, homegrown fare served up to the Roman deities—bread, bacon, cabbages, beans—was a reminder of the primeval tribal diet before it had been corrupted by imported gourmet cuisines, at least on the fashionable tables set with "bronzes, bowls and tripods," sparkling with imported glassware, where luxurious excess was believed to have appeared first.[32]

Some grand houses actually maintained private shrines to frugality, a "poor man's cell" where austere, nostalgic meals could be ritually served once a month to the well-heeled owner, a kind of rite of penance for his good fortune. Not only a symbolic reminder of a simpler life untainted by luxury, it also built character, according to the rules of Epicurus, whose philosophy taught that in times of plenty, one should prepare for unexpected reverses of fortune. "We should be practicing with a dummy target," Seneca reminded a friend, "getting to be at home with poverty so that fortune cannot catch us unprepared."[33]

In 184 BC, when Cato the Elder became a candidate for the powerful office of censor to staunch the corruption described later by Sallust and others, the Roman public at least knew what it was getting. Cato was a stickler for disciplined self-denial, and his dour, tight-fisted (some said mean-spirited) reputation was famous long before the state issued him a license to police private excesses. Generations later, Petronius would immortalize him by calling those who dismissed his satirical novel the *Satyricon* as pornography "nagging prudes of Cato's ilk."[34]

Cato exemplified the special muscular, republican gravitas that Cicero regarded as peculiarly Roman and essential for civic leadership. Even after he was given high posts by the state, Cato continued to personally work the stony fields of his small farm in the Sabine Hills outside Rome, ostentatiously following a Spartan regime: "a cold breakfast, a frugal dinner, simple raiment and a humble dwelling" with bare, unplastered walls. It was the kind of "plain living" Horace would praise in his odes nearly a hundred years later on his own nearby "Sabine" farm.[35] In a letter to his patron Augustus, Horace reminded the emperor "how times and taste have changed," how "the Romans used to like to get up early and open their doors to let the fresh air in . . . To listen to the advice their elders gave them." Now everyone was "giving in to ruinous appetites and gratifications . . . Now everyone is seized with the desire to write a poem."[36] The poet's own verse was famously full of his contempt for the pretentious life of the city's "appetites and gratifications":

> Let go the smoke and noise of Rome,
> Change brings the rich man back to earth,
> Straightforward cooking, a simple house like mine,
> This sort of poverty has often soothed
> The puckered forehead of despair:
> No need of purple hangings, gaudy carpets there.[37]

Some years before he was made censor, Cato had been defeated in his noisy fight to stop the repeal of an unpopular sumptuary law. In 213 BC, the senate had tried to resist what was perceived to be moral decline with legislation directed at women to curb their personal, unnecessary spending in the middle of the Second Punic War. With the influx of astounding wealth following the expansion into Greek territory by conquest, the Roman elite's cultural ambitions were fed by the discoveries of the Hellene world. Cato was well aware of the pull of Hellenization against attempts to restrain the conspicuous displays of imported riches.[38] But as the Romans would find, then and later, laws reining in private excess and its assimilation into a competitive setting were easier to enact than to enforce. In fact, legally imposed rules directed at unseemly consumption have been hard to police from the moment they were first instituted. Our knowledge of Roman sumptuary laws is fragmentary, however, so it is hard to say to what extent they were enforced or ignored. The details of these laws largely depend on summaries written long after they were abolished.[39]

In its recital of offenses, the hard-line sumptuary law *lex oppia*, promoted by Cato in time of war, was directed at the usual displays of wealth and instructed that no woman could possess more than a half-ounce of gold, flaunt multicolored (often imported) clothing, or ride in a carriage in the city or town or within a mile of it, unless on a religious mission to attend public sacrifices. It is not clear just what this proscription had to do with Rome's war effort, beyond the propaganda that everyone was participating in the war, like the Victory Garden and volunteer sock-knitting programs for the troops of World War II.

Twenty years after *lex oppia* was adopted, it became an irritating political issue no longer justified by a military threat. A move to repeal it was loudly supported by women who decided to take matters into their own hands through unprecedented direct political action. It was this unexpected development that fired up Cato's tirade of misogyny, representing what might be called "the family values wing" of Rome's republican politics. Livy includes in his *History* Cato's rant against repeal, adding "the Censor" to his moniker "the Elder."

Believing that foreign habits and customs, as well as new material wealth, were threatening the republic's moral fabric during the turmoil of war, the old soldier resisted the feminist uprising. He considered it his patriotic duty to cut off the head of "the hydra-like luxury and degeneracy of the age." But the women were too well organized, "presuming to accost consuls, praetors, and other magistrates with their appeal." On the day of the vote, armies of angry women—

mostly married, according to Plutarch's account, whose husbands could not keep them at home—stormed the voting hall, and the law was repealed. According to Livy, Cato was relieved to be called away for military duty to put down a rebellious Spanish garrison, a job in which he was far more successful.

Even after the repeal of lex oppia, the city of Rome continued to wage a rear-guard legal fight to restore Rome's reputation of republican virtues. The sumptuary laws that follow from the days of the republic into the reigns of Sulla, Augustus, and Hadrian invoked ancient laws to restrain the expense of elaborate dinner tables where excessive banqueting and gluttony were encouraged. Fancy cooks and highfalutin cuisine, even obesity, had always been targets of Cato's moral attacks. Conjuring the image of an overindulged stomach upsetting the body's equilibrium when desires were allowed to rule the head, Cato described Rome as "a belly without ears" to express his alarm over the mindless concentration of wealth (and population) followed by the steady decay of the state.

The collapse of the Roman Republic into the turbulence of civil war over several generations, and the widespread feeling of dislocation, seemed to confirm Cato's darkest predictions. Looking for explanations, people believed they found them in the neglect of the gods and the rejection of the traditional moral values of the "good old days." As the rustic Roman farmer who personified patriotic, austere republican virtues faded into the past, along with much of Rome's historic cultural identity, Cato's mythic image as the ideal citizen grew. But the realities of those patricians living in luxurious villas outside Rome and Naples were far removed from the imagined simplicity and piety they endowed their self-sacrificing forbears.

In the preface to the history of the conspiracy of Catiline, written not long after the assassination of Caesar, Sallust has much to say about the contrast between the virtuous Romans of Cato's day and the character of their successors. The conspiracy involved an ambitious, reckless politician, a near contemporary of Sallust, who had plotted a bid to take over the government by promising his followers a cancellation of their debts and other briberies that would have bankrupted the state.

The story provides a perfect excuse for Sallust to hold forth on Spartan republican greatness, before corruption had gotten the upper hand. Catiline was "a man of flaming passions . . . covetous of other men's possessions as he was prodigal of his own. . . . His monstrous ambitions hankered continually after things extravagant, impossible beyond his reach."[40]

Sallust concluded that the trouble began with the final defeat of Carthage in 133 BC. "It was then that fortune turned unkind and confounded all her enterprises." The sudden new wealth of conquest was more than the old military establishment, trained and hardened in battle and adversity, could absorb. "Growing love of money, and the lust for power which followed it engendered every kind of evil. Avarice destroyed honour, integrity, and every other virtue, and instead taught men to be proud and cruel. . . . As soon as wealth came to be a sign of distinction and an easy way to renown, military commands and political power, virtue began to decline." To be poor or merely thrifty became a disgrace, while riches made the new generation prey to "luxury, avarice and pride." Instead of building temples where "piety was the ornament," people were now building huge private villas on such a scale and complexity that one monstrosity looked like an entire town.[41]

The houses of the wealthy dramatized the widening gap between the rich, including the three elite ruling orders and the poor who were packed into slums. In Rome, as in the first great American oil boom of the early twentieth century, it all happened in one generation. Before 100 BC, even the houses of nobles were simple affairs. Marble columns had not been used in private buildings, so when the censor Marcus Crassus decked out his new house on the Palatine Hill with six twelve-foot columns of Hymettan marble taken from a public theater, he was sharply criticized. Yet, not to be outdone, a neighbor immediately incorporated many more columns in his atrium, some towering thirty-five feet high.

Pliny, who had a well-trained eye for excess and cultivated prejudices against it, thought this privileged splendor absurd, considering the shortness of life and the achievements of Rome's long history itself. The damage done by useless wealth and luxury was central to his *Naturalis historia*. In one refectory of a villa built by a recently freed slave, he counted thirty columns made of oriental alabaster—far too many for someone of the builder's former status. When Caesar's chief engineer threw up a particularly tasteless house built only of green-veined marble from Euboia, Pliny dismissed it as a vulgar commentary on the plunder the predator had taken from Gaul. But he had not seen anything compared to the great building boom following Augustus's triumph at the battle of Actium. Even he had to admit that Augustus's visionary effort had been a remarkable achievement, transforming the city's provincial character into that of an international capital built of marble, with an exhilarating atmosphere announcing peace, security, and growing prosperity. Ticking off the list of world-class monuments—the Forum of Augustus, the Basilica Pauli with its superb columns from Phrygia, and the Theater of Marcellus—Pliny confessed that he could not muster a single complaint of political or moral censure. Augustus's calculated strategy of establishing one-man rule by translating architectural grandeur into a positive expression of public virtue succeeded, as we know all too well, becoming a model for despots—both political and economic—down through the ages and into the twenty-first century.

Throughout history, both patriots and tyrants have used the language of architecture as a prime image-making tool: to inflate reputations, hide corruption, and build legitimacy. Successful generals returning to Rome with political ambitions lost no time in throwing up new temples and monuments to promote themselves and curry public favor. To upstage his enemy Pompey's pretentious theater and porticoes, Caesar launched his own aggressive plans to rebuild the old Forum Julium dominated by a colonnaded piazza. The sharp elbows of egos and power politics left little room for any serious, orderly urban planning.

The familiar film-and-television image of the imperial city, illuminated with its reputation for high living on a wide-screen scale, emerges when all the power of Rome is placed in the hands of a single individual. In 31 BC Octavian's celebration of the triple victories at Illyrium, Alexandria, and Actium can be seen, in retrospect, as the turning point—the first emperor's permanent achievements far overshadowing the cost of his brutal struggle for power. Before his victory, he had already changed his name from Octavian to the majestic Augustus and provoked his rival and brother-in-law, Mark Antony, into the disastrous fight at Actium on the northwestern coast of Greece. Antony's final defeat, witnessed by his lover and new trophy "wife," Cleopatra, from her own ship, sent the ambitious, ill-starred pair fleeing back to Egypt and their death, making Octavian the master of the Roman world. When word reached Rome that Egypt's storied treasures were now in Roman hands, interest rates in Rome dropped from 12 percent to 4.[42]

With the change of his name from Octavian to Augustus—"the most revered"—the founder of the empire has gone down in history as the shining protector of Roman virtue, a model of Roman rectitude and republican traditions of frugality, justice, and temperance inherited from simpler days, reinforced with the comfortable, imported Greek Stoicism, the adopted philosophy of the Roman aristocracy. In fact the Golden Age of Augustus, upholding moderation, religious family values, and civic order would be central to the "classical" image of Rome for centuries. As long as slaves did the heavy lifting and the military fulfilled its duty, it was a flexible moral creed that allowed the elite to maintain their high-minded moral principles while enjoying very profitable careers compatible with a good life of optimum leisure.[43] In the metamorphosis engineered by clever propaganda, the young thug Octavian, who could gouge out a man's eyes with his bare hands in a fight to take control of the state, reinvented himself as a model of respectable morality, an enemy of despotism.[44] Compared to the idealized traditions of Rome, the details of the extravagant, dissolute lives of Antony and Cleopatra, as when the couple "pissed in a gold chamber pot," was useful propaganda invented to highlight the calculated Augustan image of down-to-earth Roman virtues. The queen herself became a useful scapegoat as an example of the role of women in promoting "Oriental" vice. For political reasons, Augustus helped to create the mythical image of Cleopatra's extravagance and Eastern despotism to bolster his own persona as a fatherly ruler upholding old-fashioned republican values and traditions.

With unprecedented public magnificence, Augustus and his successor rulers would create a world capital like nothing ever seen before and a mythology to go with it. After decades of bloodshed, double-dealings, and brutality, a legend emerged in the dominant discourse that in all this urban grandeur, the ancient, ancestral Roman virtues would, as Augustus predicted before Antony was destroyed, somehow be revived. Romans would not require luxury in their private lives, but they would be uplifted and revitalized by the message of civic virtue radiating from the marble façades of the splendid public temples, monuments, and entertainment centers replacing the scruffy, crowded mud-brick rabbit warren that was Rome before the large-scale public investment of the first century.

According to the imperial propagandist Suetonius, Augustus carefully avoided living in a splendid palace, choosing instead a private house next to that of his wife, Livia, on the Palatine Hill. Everyone knew that he had bought this house secondhand from Hortensius the Orator. It all advanced his modest image of "first amongst equals," living a retiring, frugal life of civic-minded republican rectitude.

There is another aspect of the imperial hype and its ambivalence underlining the political message of Augustus's rejection of personal extravagance in favor of conspicuously "simple living." But, inevitably, self-righteous advocates of plain living for the hoi polloi usually wanted it both ways, claiming that a certain opulence inescapably went with their own elevated rank. Augustus actually had his "ordinary house" discreetly connected to the splendid new temple he had built nearby for his protector Apollo ("Nothing in excess") where he could hold large public receptions within its stately marbled interior. The shady entrepreneur Vedus Pollio, one of the richest men in Rome, stepped over the line when he gave his vulgar city palace to Augustus. The emperor had the house and estate razed just as he had done according to Suetonius when he discovered that his granddaughter Julia had built a lavish country villa. Such gross competitive display was not the kind of Golden Age that Augustus had in mind.[45]

Putting public magnificence at the center of his cult of moral renewal, Augustus saw this radical chic of public excess to advance the state a brilliant move to exorcise the taints of corruption and dissolution that were associated with the growing spread of private profligacy. Augustus's enormous and expensive architectural projects in the name of "moral rearmament" and in particular the unprecedented construction of elaborate buildings used exclusively for public entertainments—theaters and arenas for games and festivals—went far beyond any practical purposes. This was a significant break with the past. Ostensibly for civic order, the senate had once prohibited the construction of buildings for public entertainment, such as theaters and baths, where large crowds could gather and might slip out of the control of the authorities.

Not everyone was convinced by the Augustan hagiography in support of republican austerity produced by the poets Horace, Virgil, and Prospertius. The painting of Venus rising from the sea that Augustus had taken from a Greek temple to install in the new temple of Divus Iulius dedicated to his adopted father, Julius Caesar, and the "double doors, of noblest ivory" made in Africa and installed on the temple of Apollo did seem, to some grumblers, to violate the traditional rules against extravagance. The lavish covering of the temple's interior walls with bright cut stone, polished marble, cut glass, and mosaic (a vulgar fashion picked up in Asia) was not only bad taste, it was also immoral and set the Stoic Seneca's teeth on edge.

Rome easily holds the title as the world's preeminent slave society, a system that defined and molded every aspect of Roman civilization until its collapse. Slavery as a primary source of production and large-scale labor organization was a decisive invention of the Greco-Roman world.[46] There is nothing in the classical world—from roads and buildings to poetry and philosophy—that is not shaped by it. The luxuries of Roman domestic life, mostly inspired by Greek fashion, with all the seductive amenities and agreeable vices that were available, depended on countless slaves to generate the energy and the wealth to provide the goods and services. Scholars can only guess within one or two hundred thousand the approximate census of Roman slaves in Italy alone, but conservative estimates suggest two million. The pervasive magnitude of the system was nearly exposed when it was recklessly suggested that slaves, who looked like everyone else moving around in the streets of everyday Rome, be identified by wearing a special uniform.

From the late third century BC to the third century AD, the ubiquitous presence of slavery animated and transformed all aspects of Roman society and its character, a fact that easily invites moralizing. More than any other institution in Roman culture, slavery compounded the perceived corruption of Roman luxury with the inconceivable excesses it encouraged and supported. While only the rich and well-off owned large numbers of slaves, for those who did, it expressed their unquestioned power. One does not have to quote Lord Acton's cliché to guess the final results.

The unspoken fact was that Rome's notorious and entrenched reputation for luxury among the top tier of society was built on human slavery, ultimately harnessing much of the population one way or another to its insidious addiction, just as the West's modern consumer luxury is fatally tied to oil. While historical analogies can be misleading, wildly distorting history and taking any lessons from the past invariably out of context, one cannot ignore the parallels between Roman slavery as the vital force of imperial supremacy and our contemporary obsessive dependence on fossil fuel as a critical ingredient of international ambitions. As Sir Moses Finley pointed out in his study of ancient slavery, "there was no action, no belief or institution in Greco-Roman antiquity that was not, in one way or the other, affected by the possibility that someone involved might be a slave."[47] Disconcertingly, like modern oil cartels, the vested interests of governments, military regimes, and international slave traders colluded in order to keep the wheels turning, literally, while making huge profits.[48]

Rome's pre-industrial economy was based on agriculture. If you were rich, it was assumed that you owned both land and slaves, even if your money had originally come from trade, craft, or other less respectable activities. The ancients could not have measured the effectiveness of slavery versus coercing their independent peasantry to work for someone else, simply because slavery as an alternative source of labor was so deeply rooted in the Mediterranean world. And while slavery was not the consequence of conquest, conquest vastly expanded the system, providing a steady supply of labor from the outside that did not threaten the ordinary citizen's membership in the community. Importantly, it created the basis of larger and larger agricultural operations, the source of vast wealth of the Roman upper-class oligarchy and government. Land guaranteed high status, and slaves underpinned both the values of the agrarian society and its stylish, relaxed, civilized living. Cato the Elder, that most venerable example of republican virtue, was like most established leaders of the republic and the later empire: he operated his agricultural estate with slave labor that produced both his income and his reputation for knowing how to live. Slaves ran their masters' domestic households and often managed their businesses. Shrewd operators saw the everyday commercial value of slaves for shopkeeping, bookkeeping, trading, and banking—occupations not suitably aristocratic.

It appears that as the empire matured into middle age, slave owning was not limited just to the wealthiest members of society. Every free man who could not afford a slave dreamed of doing so one day, the ultimate measure of success.[49] Many people of lesser rank and of the middling sort could own a few, although from the perspective of the upper classes owning only one or two slaves was a sure sign of poverty. Because of their skills, many slaves were also profitably leased.

The steady expansion of the wealth of the Roman elite, including the aristocrats in the senate who dominated Roman politics, was driven by the massive growth of slavery. Wars of conquest backed by the Senate, natural reproduction, trade, and piracy meant that there was an endless supply. The quick conquest of Epirus in 167 BC brought in a hundred and fifty thousand slaves, and later, Caesar's wars brought another million from Gaul. Arguments against imperialism and warnings of its fatal link to luxury were beside the point. By the end of the first century BC, it is estimated that 35 to 40 percent of the Italian population were slaves.[50]

Most of the military conquering had been completed when Augustus died in 14 AD, but by then the institution of slavery was firmly established, and through breeding and trading the slave market appeared to be able to meet the labor demand before a decline of this internal labor supply would begin to threaten the late empire. But if current estimates are correct that the Roman Empire needed between 250 and 400,000 new slaves per year just to maintain the population level, it is hard to imagine where they all came from after the major wars of conquest had ended.

When labor became dehumanized as a chattel commodity, it could be instinctively squandered on inconceivable indulgence, including the slave's unrestricted availability for sexual relations, while those few who could afford not to work made their leisure and indolence a mark of class, "educated in idleness . . . rendered unfit to get a living by industry," in the later words of Benjamin Franklin.[51] This has been the pattern throughout the history of slave property. The Roman elites' growing standards of high living could be calculated by their extravagant employment of slaves for useless, conspicuous show, and by absurd subdivisions of labor that exceeded anything known even in the antebellum South. In some houses, slaves served as clocks whose only job was to announce the hours.

In his study of the realities of the life of Roman luxury in literary references, Jasper Griffin lists more than a hundred servants' posts in the domestic household of Augustus.[52] In common burial grounds of the slaves of Roman emperors, there are inscriptions for torch-bearers, lantern-bearers, chief sedan chair–carriers, keepers of outdoor garments, doormen to announce guests and to whisper to the host the name of someone he didn't recognize. Outside the house, the ritual of the public bath was a central part of Roman life. Not only did a grandee require a retinue to accompany his proper visit, but the bath itself required hordes of specialized slaves to keep the water running, stoke the fires to heat the water, launder the linen and towels, and to dry the clients, massage them, and anoint them with oil.

For the average Roman, the discipline of a strict routine of cleanliness, healthfulness, and relaxation was an entitlement he shared with the wealthiest citizen. By 33 BC, Pliny the Elder records 170 bathing establishments in the capital. Social historians have argued that the vast Roman water system was primarily built for public hygiene and drinking water, the republic's greatest contribution to civilization. But most Roman cities had water supplies adequate for ordinary needs. It was the enormous quantities of water required to operate the Roman baths that inspired the engineering of the aqueducts built and operated by slave labor. Keeping this luxury water flowing to the new imperial bath complex introduced by imperial policy was a serious governing responsibility. If the fountains stopped and the baths closed, political unrest was sure to follow. And more than the brilliance of Roman engineering, it was the massive scale of the great aqueducts built by slave labor and delivering an unlimited supply of water that was the envy of the world, a symbol of imperial power. The extravagant use of water—to feed the voracious appetites of the baths along with the ubiquitous public fountains, ornamental basins, swimming pools, and canals in the imperial gardens and in the villas—also softened the cold, hard lines of the official, authoritarian architecture. Only a massive water system could tame the staggering opulence of the Baths of Diocletian and Caracalla.

Agrippa sent in a slave workforce of forty thousand to build in eighteen months the Aqua Augusta, a complex system snaking more than fifty miles through the Compagna to carry the water to Neapolis (Naples), Pompeii, Hercula, Baiae, and the other smart coastal resort cities. Six years before, the emperor had built the Aqua Julia in Rome, delivering more water to that city than was supplied to the entire city of New York in 1985.[53]

Aside from the community baths, as far as the public was concerned, one of the great benefits of the material welfare produced by an oversupply of otherwise useless slaves was that the masses could count on a steady diet of public entertainment. The spectacles, games, circuses, and staged gladiator battles of blood and guts, both human and beast, required legions of slaves (or individuals who had lost their legal status as citizens) as well as shiploads of animals to mount and execute these massive productions with fast-paced action that would please the jaded tastes of the crowd. As for the aristocracy and those in power, the staged man-to-man gladiator combats reflected the Roman elite's history of intoxication with savage glory in its rawest and most debased expression.

Symptoms of imperial ambitions in the form of costly public spectacles and entertainments actually appeared in republican Rome long before its Eastern military adventures. It was Augustus, however, who set the tone for serious extravagance as public policy, by providing (so it is said) ten thousand gladiators and three thousand wild beasts to fill just one of his many arena productions, where the plebs, dazzled by and addicted to ostentatious spectacles, lost their independence.[54]

In his all-out strategy to win "the hearts, minds and stomachs" of the masses, Augustus

> distributed olive oil and salt to all, and furnished the baths free of charge throughout the year to both men and women; and in connection with the festivals of all kinds which he gave—on such a scale, in fact, that the children of senators also performed an equestrian game called "Troy"—he hired the barbers, so that no one should be at any expense for their services. Finally he rained upon the heads of the people in the theater tickets that were good for money in one case, for clothes in another.[55]

If all this public excess paid for by the state (or emperor) became a necessity of government, forcing emperors (good and bad) to spend more and more on entertainments, the proletariat—most of whom were dangerously idle and unemployed—considered them an entitlement. They were convinced that it was their unquestionable right to be entertained at public expense and on an ever-increasing scale of lavishness. As far as imperial budgeting policy was concerned, it was not unlike Hollywood movie executives forced to outdo last year's blockbuster extravaganza to meet the public's insatiable appetite for escape into more and louder screen violence and carnage.

The growth of these notorious displays supported by the state illustrates the extent to which the role of slaves penetrated political life. Slaves made possible mega entertainment events designed as a magnet to attract and hold a restless public in a manageable space for hours at a time. Slaves with the most exotic skills—gladiators, chariot drivers, actors, acrobats, and musicians—made the whole thing possible. But like an army in the field, three or four times as many support staff were needed to handle just the logistics: operating the immense stage machinery beneath the arena floor, moving the sets, chivying the zoo of lions, elephants, bulls, bears, and all the other wild animals into the arena more or less on schedule for the morning hunt. The preparations for the gladiators later in the day required a whole army of slave specialists to prepare, exercise, dress, and no doubt try to calm the nerves of the participants facing mortal combat.

In the largest recorded bloodbath ordered by Trajan to celebrate his conquest of Dacia (modern Romania), in 123 days eleven thousand animals were killed while nine thousand gladiators went at each other, leaving countless dead and wounded. The number far exceeded the thirty-five hundred beasts that Augustus boasts of finishing off during his entire lifetime. There are no estimates of the numberless slaves needed to clean up the daily carnage before the next day's ritual got under way. Slaves as stretcher-bearers, some dressed as gods of the underworld, removed the victims.[56]

In their study of Rome's Colosseum, that consummate icon of civic cruelty and indulgence, Mary Beard and Keith Hopkins have reconstructed a convincing idea of the amphitheater's standard entertainment program of lavish slaughter.[57] They admit that the familiar images of film and TV have inevitably colored the fractured, ambiguous historical sources requiring a cautious, skeptical reading. We can be fairly sure, however, that the mornings were given over to animal hunts, followed by executions in midday, and then the star attractions: the gladiator combats.

No one can agree on the "average" size or annual number of productions in Rome or in the some two hundred smaller arenas scattered throughout the empire from Northern Africa to London. Beard and Hopkins estimate that the system dedicated to the prodigal and degrading profligacy required over sixteen thousand gladiators outside Rome, while Pliny claims there were another twenty thousand in the city's training camps. The numbers were equal to one quarter of all the standing Roman legions. Without going off into all the fascinating details of the operation of this complex "gladiatorial machine" with its behind-the-scenes conscripted labor force required to make it work, this bare sketch suggests how the colossal public enterprise rested on the back of the Roman slave.

If slavery made possible the excesses of the arena, Rome's public symbol of depraved extravagance, the inevitable abuses of household slavery had a demoralizing effect on the intimacy of private life. At least among the rich aristocracy and its circle of wannabes, extravagant spending on slaves was expected. Seneca speaks of the throng of slaves in a rich man's dining room standing around watching the gluttony of the guests and leaping forward to perform any task on demand, including matters of the toilet.

Slaves and newly created freedmen took over virtually every physical function and met every basic need of the upper-class house, reducing the master and his family to helpless dependency. The surviving list of the domestic staff of Augustus's wife, Livia, was of course in keeping with her high rank, and other lists found in many upper-class establishments detail the breakdown of specialized jobs assigned to slaves. Fifty different slave jobs are recorded, ranging from clothes folder, marble cutter, and reader, to the usual footman, doorkeeper, chambermaid, masseur, and courier. Although not singled out in Livia's entourage, servants were commonly assigned even the most intimate duties, such as holding the chamber pot while the masters or mistresses relieved themselves. The decrepit consular Domitius Tullus required a slave to brush his teeth.[58]

In Petronius's sardonic masterpiece the *Satyricon*, "a book of randy satires," his novelist's eye (and imagination) doesn't miss a detail of the goings-on at the dinner party given by Trimalchio, where the silent role of obsequious slaves actually manipulate the puppets in the vaudeville tableau. The former slave Trimalchio, now nouveau riche, wallows in mindless luxury that has regularly been the target of moralists. No matter what the cost, a man of position and pretended dignity must be surrounded by his slaves. With more slaves than he can count, he personifies the coarse arriviste "so vivid that he easily survives his own satirical role."[59] Slaves were everywhere to minister to their master's whims and pleasures and those of his bored guests. Except for walking, standing, or reclining on the dinner couch, the master completed no physical act without the automatic assistance of a slave. Like Queen Victoria, who never needed to look to be sure a chair was ready to receive her, the master's every gesture was instantly read and responded to without a hitch.

Leading up to the celebrated scene called "Dinner with Trimalchio," we meet the debauched, aging host at the gym getting himself in shape for the exhausting evening ahead by "playing ball with a bunch of curly-headed slave boys." When he drops the ball, one of the slaves hands him another, saving him from having to bend or stoop. After washing his hands in a basin held by a slave, Trimalchio languidly dries them in the long hair of another young slave attendant who steps into position for the service. He returns to his house carried in a litter led by four slaves to clear the way, his favorite slave riding beside him.

At the door of Trimalchio's dining room, a slave stands guard, reminding the guests to enter the room on their right foot. Hordes of Ethiopian, Syrian, Jewish, and Egyptian slaves serve the dinner: an endless procession of exotic foods elaborately, and some erotically, presented. In the middle of a tray of cakes, the extended member of a pastry statue of Priapus holds up his apron, loaded with fruits of all kinds. If the banquet palls, troops of beautiful slave entertainers—acrobats, singers, dancers, mimes, astrologers—suddenly rush in to stir up the flagging tempo.

Petronius's caricature revels disguise his cautionary message. Trimalchio, however exaggerated, represented the Roman slave-owning class, exposing in detail its hopeless dependence on the system. Even putting aside our own ethical disapproval of the Romans' dissolution and bloodthirsty culture, they had clearly become slaves themselves in body and mind—luxury's ultimate price. Extravagance, lack of self-restraint, and corruption, made possible by the towering superstructure of slavery, paved the way for both the inevitable debility of the Roman citizen and a more sinister long-term paralysis of society itself.

4

FEAR AND LOATHING
Luxury and Christian Salvation

The alarming words of Jesus left no doubt about the connection between mammon and the snares of worldly temptations. To his followers in the dusty villages of Judea, the worship of things of this world was looked upon as fatal idolatry. This remained pretty much the official Christian position until the Protestant Reformation, when the question arose as to whether a fat bank account was a sign of unsupportable, sinful covetousness or a blessing from God. Puritans and pious capitalists would continue to wrestle with this troubling issue. Given free range, avarice could spread like a virus to other vices "to serve the insatiable undirected selfishness" that Augustine had warned against.[1]

Although their record of success was less than impressive, the Stoics of both the Greek and Roman varieties, who recognized the problem of human greed and lust, had resolved the dilemma. They concluded that mankind actually had an inner reserve of moral freedom with the capacity to lift itself up and escape enslavement to luxury and its rich congeries of deceits.

But the Christian message was clear and offered no Stoic exit. All descendants of Adam and Eve were by God's will enslaved. One could either accept bondage to God's promise of salvation or take the easy road to the "world's tyranny," the devil's gateway that would ensure temporal corruption and eventual damnation.

Throughout his life, Jesus implicitly condemned Hellenic indulgence, sophistication, and all of its renegade tastes. "The deceitfulness of riches" bred indifference to one's fellows and was an affront to God. In the eyes of the Son

75

of God, succumbing to unrighteous appetites and accumulating needless possessions short-circuited God's commands and his impenetrable plans. It was also bound to sharpen the clashes between the spirit and the flesh—"body and soul"—the well-known battlefield contestants identified by the Greeks. Recognizing a link between body and soul, both pagans and Christians believed that the health of the more elevated soul depended on restraining the body's impulsive, devious animal appetites.[2]

Whenever "riches" are spoken of in the New Testament, it is usually as an omen and a rebuke to those caught up in the pursuit of getting and spending. Jesus explicitly condemned mammon in the Sermon on the Mount and in Mark's Gospel, pointing out that it was next to impossible for a rich man to enter God's kingdom.[3] For the well off, who often used clever legal strategies to evade the spirit of God's laws and cash in their rewards here and now on earth, it was a decision that all but ensured they would be denied a place in heaven. Or as James (the Lord's alleged brother) warned in his alarming letter, the day of reckoning was near: "Come now you rich, weep and howl," for "whoever wishes to be a friend of the world makes himself an enemy of God."

This predicament of worldly wealth—the specter of luxury in all its seductive charm—posed real problems for the new religion, a struggling cult trying to find its way among older, established spiritual competitors in a culturally unfriendly environment. It seemed that the new believers were always caught up in contradictions, ambiguities, and compromises as they maneuvered the treacherous road to salvation while facing the misgivings and hard realities of everyday life. Even in the first generations of Jesus's followers, few agreed exactly on how much austerity or frugal restraint was required in the eyes of God to live an acceptable Christian existence according to his commandments. But the message Jesus preached to those living on the margins—the down-and-out, the ordinary worker, the fisherman, the slave, the ex-criminal—and his words, recorded by Matthew in the Sermon on the Mount, urged his followers to look for and expect "treasures in heaven," not on earth:

> Lay not up for yourselves treasures upon earth, where moth and rust doth corrupt, and where thieves break in and steal, but lay up for yourselves treasure in heaven, where neither moth nor rust consumes and where

thieves do not break through and steal. For where your treasure is, there will your heart be also.[4]

Money itself, stashed away in a strongbox or mattress, was not the problem. After all, coins would be useless in God's heavenly kingdom. Rather, it was the hunger to acquire all the material and sensual gratifications money could buy, beyond any human need, that kept the wealthy mired in venal bondage to false gods. Blind attachment to their possessions made it all but impossible for them to escape their vanity and pride.

The immediate background to Jesus's message of renunciation was the growing crisis in the Jewish community. Living in their rural, insolated villages of Galilee and Judea, they were surrounded by a more cosmopolitan, pagan society and its culture of Greek and Roman gods that challenged traditional, exclusive Jewish beliefs. Reduced to a province of Trajan's Roman Empire, Judea's puppet court of the dissolute Herodian dynasty supported its palaces, country estates, and pagan entertainments with heavy taxes and bribes extracted from fellow Jews. Tensions flared when pagan neighbors representing the Roman establishment dismissed the ritual of circumcision, kosher dietary laws, and all of the exclusive rites of the Jewish holidays as nothing more than naive superstition.

Many Jews were understandably distrustful of their own wealthy brethren—"the moneychangers"—who surrounded the high priest of the Temple in Jerusalem, rebuilt and expanded by Herod the Great, as the center of the Jewish faith. They held on to their tenacious belief that a messiah would soon come and free them from Rome.

Among the anonymous poor living on the fringe who were drawn to the gatherings and sermons of Jesus, there was more than a suspicion that the Temple crowd was profitably colluding with the Roman occupation. Not long before Jesus was born, some two thousand Jews had been crucified in Galilee for rising up against Rome. During the first century BC, the Essenes had moved out of the increasingly debauched Jerusalem to protest its pagan materialism and moral pollution. Like the Desert Fathers later, the ascetic group's self-reproach led its members to renounce both sex and private property while they prepared for the final holy war. In their bleak refuge hidden in desert caves overlooking the Dead Sea, they waited for the battle of Armageddon to begin any moment.

After the experience of his retreat into the wilderness where he rejected the temptations of the devil, who offered him all of the kingdoms of the earth, Jesus emerged convinced that the long-expected day of judgment was at hand when the world would be turned upside down. To prepare for the coming new age, when the last would be first and the first last, Jesus demanded and expected extraordinary sacrifices of his followers, the "despised and dejected." They would, however, be shortly rewarded when they literally inherited God's kingdom.

Jesus directed the small circle of his twelve disciples—"the salt of the earth" who were to spread out through the Roman Empire and gather up "the lost sheep of Israel"— to live and travel without money, food, sandals, or even an extra tunic. A knapsack or staff would be superfluous. Any sacrifice required of the faithful would be limited by the timing: God's kingdom was at hand. "Blessed are ye the poor, for yours is the kingdom of God," Jesus declared in Luke's version of the famous sermon:

> Blessed are ye that hunger now: for ye shall be filled.
> Blessed are ye that weep now, for ye shall laugh . . .
> But woe to you that are rich: for ye have received your consolation.
> Woe unto you that are full, for ye shall hunger.
> Woe unto you that laugh now, for ye shall mourn and weep.[5]

In an age of crisis, stirred up by worrying about humdrum details of living, what to eat and drink or what clothes to wear, Jesus delivered his best-known stricture, using the ancient Aramaic word "mammon," meaning the desire for those unnecessary things, mostly casual and hedonistic. It was also a symptom of wanting too much earthly power, something the Greeks had earlier identified. Moses himself had rebuked Aaron for allowing the Israelites to sculpt a calf of gold, the Old Testament metaphor for mammon and the personification of the idolatry of the power of wealth, contrary to God's law. The message of the carpenter's son to the "army of the disinherited" was unequivocal: "Ye cannot serve God and mammon."[6]

The Christian battle line between God and mammon was drawn, and the thrust of the war was directed to the individual sinner: mammon's iniquitous implications were tied to personal morality and denial. It confirmed once again the Latin notion of luxuria (conflated with luxus), "the lust of the flesh and the lust of the eyes and the prideful life." But unlike the pagan concept of luxury, inducing a chain of vices that could threaten the community's social and political equilibrium, mammon's link to ostentatious consumption did not have a political dimension of concern to Jesus or to the early church.

After the Crucifixion, with the Second Coming expected at any moment, useless pleasure and spending was no longer a clear and present danger to the soul. Paul had lifted expectations by warning that "the appointed time has grown very short."[7] The denial of worldly delights by the faithful would be short-lived.

Paul was the first of Jesus's followers to express the philosophical goal to achieve detached, Stoic contentment in this life while waiting for the next: "and they that buy" do so "as though they possessed not, and they that use this world, as not abusing it: for the fashion of this world passeth away."[8] If one believed the prediction of the imminent Second Coming, it was easy enough to incorporate the Stoic principle of the frugal life focusing exclusively on the state of one's soul while waiting for the fulfillment of God's promise.

"If you would be perfect," Jesus advised the rich young man who begged for guidance, "sell all you possess and give to the poor, and you will have treasure in heaven." His directive seemed unambiguous; a true follower must give up all covetous passions—sex, money, ambition, possessions—but as for a metric notion of exactly where to draw the line when God's blessings were at stake, one could only guess. Jesus's other well-known aphorism on the limits of wealth is no help: "For what does it profit a man," he asks, "if he gains the whole world, and loses his soul?"[9] It is the New Testament's toughest question. In order "to have one's cake and eat it too," our modern materialistic consumer society would find an answer by transforming consumption into a middle-class virtue of market economics to advance the GDP in the name of progress.

In his words on the subject of wealth and its corrosive consequences, Jesus does not invoke images of Roman excesses, so vividly described by contemporary pagan moralists and historians, the decadence of Rome's upper classes—their retinues of slaves, the boatloads of stuff pouring into the Roman commercial centers throughout the Mediterranean, the gourmet foods, the gluttony, the steaming baths with their oils, perfumes, and pornographic murals reeking of iniquity. Instead he invokes the pastoral village life shared by his disciples.

But wherever anyone turned, images of pagan gods with their licentious carryings-on were reminders of the deities' ubiquity, interwoven into the fabric of the community of the first century. From coins, civil contracts, and public buildings to official holidays, literature, and art, all expressed sentiments of what passed for acceptable, quotidian civic and religious piety. Much of the daily business went on in and around pagan temples, and pagan references figured in most business contracts. Christians were "offended by the fumes of idolatrous sacrifice." It was, in the words of Edward Gibbon, impossible to escape the "elegant forms and agreeable fictions" of the deities, "without at the same time, renouncing the commerce of mankind, and all of the offices and amusements of society."[10] The images of Apollo, Jupiter, Mercury, and Hercules were brought out to celebrate Rome's repeated triumphs over its enemies presiding over the vast plunder represented by the gold, silver, ivory, and rare woods signifying the empire's power and greatness.

The gap between the "world" of the pagan cults of Rome and the commonplace existence of the devout authors of what would become the New Testament reflected in the simple homilies and parables of the Gospels and Epistles was so wide that they had little firsthand experience with such a sophisticated, complex society. The Christian idea of a "conversion" or "calling"—a conscious, personal decision to embrace a new way of life of denial—was without precedent, making it inevitable that new "converts" would be further isolated and seen as an alien threat to public order. Since all ordinary pleasures of eating, drinking, transacting business in shaded arcades, or celebrating bacchanalian initiations and holidays involved acknowledging the mysteries of an entire cosmos of gods, the Christian's profession of faith in one god required that he stay aloof and indifferent to the earthly temptations of pagan society. "You do not go to our shows," one puzzled Roman complained, "you take no part in our processions, you are not present at our public banquets, you shrink in horror from our sacred games."

This deliberate segregation by Christian congregations, bound together by a rejection of all things of this world while waiting for the next, may explain why the Gospels and Epistles do not lace their monochrome narrative with colorful pagan images of Roman indulgence. Writers like Suetonius, Tacitus, and Livy, who came from the upper ranks of Roman society and understood the subtle nuances of the permissive life of the rich, were unknown to the simple, provincial Christian multitudes. When Jesus turns his rage on the moneychangers in the Temple because they had converted the sanctuary into a profitable full-service bank to pay for gold rings, rich embroidered robes, extra tunics, and obsequious slaves bought on credit, the apostle misses the opportunity to add a touch of earthy detail to his account.[11]

Paul might have made his case against the temptations of the flesh—"the folly of the body"—more credible if he had known and quoted a few perverse lines of Ovid or included Petronius's description of Trimalchio's dinner party.[12] Tacitus's narrative of Petronius's decision to commit suicide after being dismissed by Nero as his "arbiter of elegance" would have been a salutary vignette of a sin against God. In high Roman style of Stoic death condemned by Christians, Petronius opened his veins and then bound them before returning to a raucous party of friends, according to Tacitus, so he could surreptitiously reopen them and expire while listening not to "theories of philosophers, but light poetry and playful verses."[13] It would have served as another cautionary example of Rome's spiritual degradation and predictable collapse, so useful to the early Christian preachers.

When Jesus called upon his disciples to abandon their material possessions, it was God's command, not just a recommendation to practice personal self-denial or accept the Stoic ideal of simplicity to achieve a serene earthly existence. Greek philosophers five hundred years earlier had decided that all the work and worry that went with earthly accumulations interfered with mental health and contemplation, the only commonsense rewards on earth. For the Christian, the promise of eternal life to be delivered at any moment made possessions useless. In that famous image of the impossible, a camel had a better chance of squeezing through the eye of a needle than a rich man, blessed with this world's goods, had of reaching heaven's gates.

The repeated counsel of Jesus to resist the pursuit of fleshly gratifications without regard for the consequences was an old Jewish theme. Its roots reached back into Israel's early history, but no one had viewed the accumulation of ordinary material goods—land, cattle, slaves, houses, barns, and all those things that made up the agrarian economy—as a damning spiritual handicap. After all, wealth or a windfall of riches could be a sign of God's blessing. It could also be the result of God's inexplicable wrath and revenge that you might get what you wished for. To the Israelites, Yahweh was the creator of all things, including wealth and the power it bestowed. This gift was a covenant that could be abused or violated only at one's peril. Those who repeatedly reached for more than they needed—out of avarice, trickery, or deceit just to feed unclean, unquenchable desires and passions—would bring down God's vengeance.

In many of the wailings found in the Psalms, the "rich" are associated with wickedness and corruption, while the poor, weak, and downtrodden are viewed as righteous and godly. "For the wicked boasts of the desires of his heart," in the words of Psalm 10, "and the man greedy for gain curses and renounces the Lord," while "the hapless commits himself to thee." As for the man who forgot the source of his good fortune and "would not make God his refuge, but trusted in the abundance of his riches," the vengeful God of Psalm 52 will uproot him and banish him "from the land of the living."

The dangers of these earthly attractions labeled with the devil's very marketable logo, were ever present, leading to both the sins of the will and the sins of the flesh. Those who cannot resist the "many senseless and hurtful desires" invented by the devil "plunge men into ruin and destruction."[14] "The love of money is the root of all evil; it is through this craving that some have wandered away from the faith and pierced their hearts with many pangs."[15] Variations on this counsel—to jettison all of one's possessions in order to safely navigate the reefs of wealth and greed and arrive in God's kingdom—convey the unambiguous message of the early church. And this admonition still haunts and conflicts the faithful, leaving them feeling somewhat less Christian if they fail to follow the Gospels' commands to choose God over mammon. More than one rich man's zeal in search of eternal life cooled when he was told, "Sell what you possess and give to the poor."[16]

For the most dedicated converts, the practice of poverty and ascetic living, reflecting an inner detachment from all the headaches and temptations of the world, would itself sustain the demanding discipline and reap its own inner rewards. The neurotic self-reproach by the early Christian hermits living in the desert focused on the classic Greek dichotomy of the soul and body, with the resented flesh, "a filthy bag of excrement and urine," receiving most of the abuse. If the body's life were corrupted by demoralizing luxury at the expense of the soul, Christian salvation required that the body be subdued and mortified, not just simply "trained," as Plato and Aristotle recommended.[17]

This was the path followed by the Egyptian convert later known as Saint Anthony, who gave up a sizable inheritance so he could "attend to his soul," as Jesus instructed. The discomforts of "cold, heat, thirst, hunger, plain food, hard beds, avoidance of pleasures, and endurance of suffering" would strengthen both his body and his soul. Struggling for mastery over desires of the body and mind, Anthony fled to the isolation of the Egyptian desert and lived in solitude without a single possession, becoming the most famous spiritual hermit, the dean of the Desert Saints to later inspire the monastic movement of the Middle Ages.

For the relatively few well-to-do among the early Christians, unable to join men like Anthony in his deathlike austerity (he once lived in a tomb), there seemed to be no "equal justice under the law." For them, the prosperous and socially established, it appeared that they had been unjustly singled out and condemned to virtual exclusion from the Promised Land. The scriptures made clear that the rich and poor weren't on a level playing field, where each had an equal chance of reaching the kingdom of God. The traditional ladder of social distinctions was turned on its head when Jesus announced that the elite, who enjoyed the material comforts of this life, would go to the end of the line, while the poor and downtrodden would enter the heavenly precincts first.

Long before the Romans, the culture of Greece had established a humane foundation of pagan mythology that did not unduly burden mortal sensibilities. People could enjoy themselves. There was no creed, revealed beliefs, or system of doctrine to establish conduct along the lines of Christianity. Throughout the Roman Empire with its adopted Hellenistic tradition of living well—its villas, gardens, libraries, theaters, spectacles, gymnasia—the rich upper classes set a high standard of pampered domestic existence. It was an exclusive society at the top, largely hidden from the peasantry of fishermen, carpenters, farmers, tent makers, laborers, and slaves who were first drawn to the Christian message. The baptism of slaves was restricted, and they could not be admitted to full brotherhood without the approval of their Christian master. As one Christian leader advised, a far greater hardship for a slave would be to become enslaved to lust and passion.

To the contemporary Roman and Hellenic elite, observing "pagan" (a fourth-century Christian coinage) religion meant to be able to live without too obvious means of support, beyond one's investments and productive estates run by managers and slaves. The ideal of moderation was upheld within reason according to class. Moneylending, of course, had its financial rewards and could be done discreetly. Those in "trade" or market hustlers—forerunners of modern financiers and entrepreneurs—remained outside the inner circles of power where the shots were called. The conspicuous rewards enjoyed by the cosmopolitan smart set had nothing to do with reaching the heaven Jesus described or with the lives of his poor, insignificant apostles and followers. But beyond these humble masses, if the ranks of the Christian community were to include the urban elite, strategies would have to be found to accommodate their enviable lives to an acceptable creed of prudent denial without too much hypocrisy.

The dispiriting prescription for salvation that Paul delivered on his ambitious missionary trips was not an easy sell. First of all was his relentless language proclaiming the only way to salvation: the war of the spirit against the flesh; the conflict of the body and soul. The disciple's notion of the flesh embraced all those human weaknesses that resisted the will of God. By democratically reaching out to the pagan and Jew, the free and the slave, the rich and the poor to come together in new assemblies of faith, this Christian ideal of social leveling opened up many daunting new issues of traditional boundaries established by caste and class. Ancient tribal marks of social hierarchy—in dress, style of living, diet, personal adornments—had to be stripped away. "For many of you who were baptized into Christ have put on Christ," he wrote to the Galatians, "there is neither Jew, nor Greek, there is neither slave or free, there is neither male nor female; for you are all one in Jesus Christ."[18] For the sensitive businessmen and their ostentatious wives with their variegated necklaces and plump arms compressed with circlets of gold living in the wealthy port cities Paul visited throughout the commercial Mediterranean, this social mixing and leveling was particularly difficult. It was a daring experiment in living that required more than just getting rid of the material superfluities in one's daily life. In his first letter to Timothy, Paul tells the young missionary to set an example and dress conservatively when he preaches and to remind the congregation "to adorn themselves in modest apparel, with shamefacedness and sobriety: not with braided hair, or gold or pearls or costly array: But which becometh women professing godliness with good works."[19]

Remarkably, when Paul arrived in places like Antioch, Smyrna, Rhodes, Athens, as well as Rome, where the luxury trade made the wheels of international business go around, there were already a few Christian cells hidden away and ignored beneath the dust, din, and frenzy of the market arcades. In the streets and neighborhoods of these cities, God's newly chosen minority, "resident aliens" who had to rub elbows and do business with "this world's" pagan establishment and its excesses, had only a brief window of opportunity to carry out their mission before the imminent return of Jesus. In his letter to the Hebrews, Paul puts the strains of ordinary existence in these circumstances into perspective: "For here we have no continuing city but we seek one to come."[20]

By the end of the second century, the Christian message had reached many of the polyglot empire's richest communities of Jews, Greeks, Asians, Africans, and Romans, as it spread like a virus throughout the Mediterranean. It is interesting to see how the pastoral "Christian" theme based on the simplicity of Judean life idealized in the Sermon on the Mount was taken up and successfully acclimated to the environment of these large commercial centers in order for the cult to survive the economic realities of a competitive commercial society. Around AD 200, the North African convert Tertullian wrote from Carthage that

> the outcry is that the state is filled with Christians—they are in the fields; in the cities; in the islands; [pagans] lament, as for some catastrophe that people of both sexes, every age and status, even those of high rank, are passing over to the profession of the Christian faith.[21]

For these new converts, the issue of wealth combined with the distracting, divisive eruptions of temptations cultivated by relaxed pagan morality raised many questions. There were, however, more than a few individuals who had worked out a way in their own minds to assimilate their prosperity without undue conflict or guilt. But some of the more orthodox reinforced their self-righteous fervor by adopting the message of the Sermon on the Mount, to further distance themselves from their pagan neighbors. "We who used to take pleasure in immorality, now embrace chastity alone," the Greek convert Justin wrote to the emperor Marcus Aurelius. "We who valued above everything else the acquisition of wealth and passions, now bring what we have into common ownership, and share with those who need."[22]

It is a fair assumption that the total possessions of the "multitudes"—the earliest converts—were far too Spartan to be classed, like the Sadducees, as "wickedly" rich. But it is easy enough to suppose from a number of references in the New Testament that, among the converts who first joined, there were a number who were prosperous enough to set something aside for those of their less fortunate brethren. This Christian charity was an important contribution to the members of the struggling cult who had, according to Paul, "risked their necks." For all of Luke's idealized morality of a peasant economy, it was obvious that continued economic support was going to have to come from those among the faithful who were better off than Judean shepherds, carpenters, and lowly fishermen. It was not an easy balancing act. There are several biblical references to how the sudden defection of a rich member, who had underwritten much of a struggling church's operations, could demoralize a small Christian community. His large house might be closed to meetings, his generous support of the poor cut off, and the cost of putting up itinerant missionaries no longer be afforded.[23]

Hospitality was an esteemed virtue in the Middle East, so that it was high on the list of Christian virtues, even though it cost money, is not surprising. The first clandestine meeting rooms for worship were usually in the houses of more successful members of the community. In fact, buildings used exclusively for Christian worship seemed not to have appeared much before the middle of the third century. Because most inns and hostels often served as the local brothel or were infested with thieves, traveling missionaries depended on the hospitality of the more affluent brethren. As an example of the kind of underground network of travel services ready to advance the cause, Paul writes to alert the cell in Rome that on his way to Spain he expects to enjoy its generosity, food, wine, and lodging. After a much-needed rest and "filled with" their company—sinful recreations of the flesh were out of the question—he would move on to the next stop.

Instead of Spain, the evangelist might have headed for Alexandria, a fabulously rich and more challenging center of pagan immorality in which to fish for lost souls. Not long after Alexandria was founded by Alexander the Great in 331 BC and, in E. M. Forster's words, "made so magnificent an entry into history,"[24] Palestinian Jews were quickly attracted to its markets, as were Greeks and Egyptians. It was a sure sign that the place, encouraged by its Macedonian Ptolemy rulers, was on its way to becoming a commercial success. The city's position and deep harbor ensured that it would become the greatest cosmopolitan center of the Hellenistic world, offering, as one contemporary writer put it, "wealth, power, public spectacles, philosophers, pretty boys, women galore, the Museum, vintage wine." Or as the scholar Peter Green hit the nail, "Long before Thorstein Veblen, the Ptolemies were into conspicuous consumption."[25]

Cleopatra, with her mythical charms, presiding over Egypt's fabled wealth in her capital would lure both Julius Caesar and Mark Antony into high-stakes schemes of conquest—of the queen herself as well as her empire. As an expression of its power, the Ptolemy court used every form of ostentatious show as an essential tool of the royal trade. Roman visitors were both fascinated and shocked by its Eastern luxury. Nothing summed up Alexandrian excess more directly than the corpulent bodies of Ptolemies VIII, IX, and X, representing generations dedicated to gluttony and sexual license. Ptolemy IV celebrated his spectacular obesity by wearing filmy, see-through robes. All of this set the tone of the port and its burgeoning stews.

By the end of the second Christian century when Clement of Alexandria, the new religion's first theologian, addressed the rich man's dilemma of achieving salvation, the commercial and intellectual panache of Alexandria surpassed Rome as the center of Hellenistic culture. Above all, it was, in the words of the Russian poet Joseph Brodsky, a "marketplace of creeds and ideologies." The cosmopolitan city of marble, more Greek than the ancient capital of Athens, presented a particular challenge to the Christian promise of deliverance from the sins of the world, in which luxury figured both literally and metaphorically. His congregation representing the Greek diaspora was for the most part "yesterday's pagans," some who continued to enjoy living the good life: the theater, chariot races, extravagant festivals. Clement's timely homily contradicting the Gospel was called "The Rich Man's Salvation."[26]

The cleric's genius was to "approach with circumspection the souls of the rich" and to offer a guide to daily living of disciplined demeanor that was Christian, though Clement accepted the humane pagan notion of moral nuance. The world had not yet succumbed to Christianity's heavy taboos and respectability. Hellenism still seemed alive. "Listening in an off hand way" to the Lord's parable of the camel passing through a needle's eye, Clement explained to his audience brought up in the Greek mysteries, might cause the well-to-do convert to despair. But he cautioned his congregation not to take the Lord's "words literally but with due inquiry and intelligence."[27] The theologian, according to Forster, arrived at the "comforting conclusion that Christ didn't mean what He said." It was a message that appealed to the city's would-be converts of sophisticated men and women.[28]

The traditional story is that Mark the Evangelist introduced Christianity into Alexandria, where he converted a Jewish shoemaker in AD 45. The missionary was later martyred for refusing to worship the god Serapis, a hybrid deity shrewdly concocted by the ruling Macedonian Ptolemies to support their new dynasty as well as serve the city's eclectic taste for richly spiced religious consommé. Ptolemy I's Serapis looked very much like Zeus. Representing kingship, healing, fertility, and afterlife, the all-purpose god became a big success throughout the Greek and Roman world. He ensured that the Nile would deliver its annual flood of fertilizing waters. As long as Alexandria remained the imperial granary and conspicuous piety was avoided, the new deity, supposedly designed by a committee of Greek and Egyptian priests, posed no problem when Octavian later reduced Alexandria to the capital of a Roman province.

In the beginning, the monotheistic Christian sect was no competition for Serapis; it remained déclassé and obscure, drawing little attention until it insisted on continuing to practice the exclusive religious rules of worship laid down by the Apostle Mark. In fact, the idea that one religion was false and another exclusively true is essentially a Christian notion. It had never occurred to the Egyptians or Greeks trying to live side by side in reasonable peace in a sprawling, crowded urban center.

When the annoyed emperor Hadrian wrote a letter from Alexandria in AD 134, he seems to have lumped Mark's followers with other local troublemakers among the Hellenes and Jews: "Those who worship Serapis are Christians, and those who call themselves bishops of Christ are devoted to Serapis. . . . As a race of men they are seditious, vain, and spiteful; as a body wealthy and prosperous, of whom nobody lives in idleness." Their one god, he complained, was wealth "which all Alexandrians zealously worship."[29]

Hadrian's letter gives us a glimpse of the cultural and economic complexity of Clement's cosmopolitan congregation of Christian converts. In the face of the predicament of the "rich young ruler" who would have to give up everything in Jesus's parable, Clement did not hesitate to take up the thorny question of how to persuade urban pagans of means to follow Jesus's teaching, tempering it with ministrations of familiar Greek philosophy and opening a few extra paths to heaven.

Clement's wide learning—revealed in his sermon on "The Rich Man's Salvation" and his remarkable guide to Christian conduct, the *Paedagorus*—suggested that there had been money and plenty of leisure in his own background, enough to pursue his travels and independent studies, most probably in Greek libraries. His passionate attachment to culture was paraded in his elegant Attic style, a language that was the antithesis of Christian simplicity. This must have been reassuring to the more educated members of his congregation. He was deeply impressed by Plato and suggested that some of the Greek philosopher's speculations might have been inspired by the Psalms. His writings were peppered with quotations from the tragic plays of the fifth-century playwright Euripides on the desperation of the human condition. These ecumenical references to pagan literature were of course tailored for the manners and customs of a community steeped in Greek learning and aware that it was a civilization that had exhausted its spiritual capital. Besides, it was much better, as one malicious pagan critic put it in another context, than a dull sermon designed "to convince only the foolish, dishonorable, and stupid . . . only slaves, women and little children."[30]

Clement adopted the strategy of turning the luxuriously depraved pagan gods with all their human needs and passions, often identified with emperors, into slapstick demons to contrast with the noble virtues of his own newfound faith. Among the Greeks and Romans, there had been a long tradition of cutting the pagan gods down to size with a touch of burlesque and comedy. Revealing an acquaintance with the randier side of the deities' lives, Clement genially mocks them with titillating examples of the risqué, amorous adventures of Apollo and Daphne, or Venus's affair with Mars. The inventive tricks of Zeus's love life—appearing to Danae in a shower of gold, as a lusting swan to Leda, a shining bull ready to carry off Europa, or as an older lover to the unsuspecting boy Ganymede whom he abducts and rapes—were hardly models of conduct for humankind. In Alexandria, not only had Hadrian turned his young dead lover, Antinous, into a god with his own temples and rituals to memorialize their affair, many people, Clement reported,

> depict in their houses the unnatural passions of the demons. They decorate their bedroom with paintings hung there regarding licentiousness as religion; and lying in bed, in the midst of their embraces, they see Aphrodite locked in the embrace of her lover. . . . Such are the theologies of arrogance [hubris]; such are instructions of your gods, who commit immorality with you.[31]

Clement boldly launches his inquiry into the dilemma of wealth and its corrupting consequences with the discouraging passage about the unlikelihood of the rich ever reaching heaven, according to the Gospel of Mark. It was the biggest of all stumbling blocks for the more prosperous classes of Alexandria. But moving with knowing confidence, Clement is reassuring. It was a morality tale on the proper use of wealth that did not, of course, require the literal liquidation of one's assets. The issue of wealth and the fixation on sumptuous houses, piles of silver table service, a retinue of redundant slaves, and chests of jewelry was really a private matter for the soul to deal with in private prayer. If the soul is endowed with Christian virtue and obsessive desires convincingly sublimated or hidden, material riches can be put in perspective and safely juggled. If God is the sole focus, earthly things become morally neutral—here Clement paraphrases the anodyne doctrine of the Stoics, clinching his argument—"Can you . . . rise superior to your riches? Say so, and Christ does not draw you away from the possession of them."[32]

In his moral instructions for the rich, Clement's goal is to describe a Christian way of life that would be tailored to the sensibilities of the classical pagan upper crust. Moderate self-sufficiency should be the Christian model. With "divine and mystical wisdom" and inner detachment from wealth's temptations, requiring as few things as possible, one's outer life would automatically reflect the same qualities of simplicity. Wearing plain clothes and shoes, eating plain food that takes little or no preparation, and putting away distracting things like gold and silver vessels announced one's righteous serenity. As servants of God, their "food and drink [and] adornment" should be appropriate for a sudden departure to heaven at a moment's notice.[33]

Given the convenient ambiguity of the Gospels, Clement's arguments are not always consistent. No doubt aware that there were ambitious Alexandrian matrons in his congregation who liked to flaunt their jewelry and fine imported robes, he assured them that "the wearing of gold and the use of softer clothing" was not entirely prohibited as long as it did not stir up the sin of envy or lust. But pushy, overdressed women who also insisted on a role in the worship service strictly reserved for men would be brought up firmly and told "to be silent," in the words of Timothy, an early church bishop.

Clement was far more diplomatic than his contemporary Tertullian, a zealous convert in Carthage who bitingly complained that earthly luxury might physically slow down the trip to Christian martyrdom: "I fear the neck, beset with pearl and emerald nooses will give no room to the broadsword!" And those who are enjoying this world too much might be tempted to unduly delay the ordeal of torture and mortal sacrifice. Like other church fathers, Tertullian believed that woman was allied with the devil and her very physicality enhanced with art and ornamentation was a mortal threat to the soul. This growing concern of church leaders for luxurious fashions in women's dress, hairstyle, and makeup not only suggests that issues of a society preoccupied with modish style were evident in the early church, but also that such display acted "by their softness and effeminacy to unman the manliness of faith."[34]

After his assurances that with willpower the rich could slip through the "needle's eye" into God's kingdom, which was only a metaphor, as it were, to remind the successful to maintain appearances of frugal Christian decorum, Clement offered another avenue to salvation: the giving of alms to those in need. In other words, the rich could keep their property as God-given bounty remaining at their disposal, but before it was too late, it was their duty to distribute some of it to those less fortunate. Clement's warning was a much more barbed paraphrase of the Gospels' bland advice that it was "better to give than to receive."

Two millennia later, transformed into institutional charity by generous tax laws for the wealthy, the philanthropic foundations of our late capitalism still make offerings of redemptive generosity on behalf of the most recent tycoons—a kind of secular salvation for themselves and their descendants. The Alexandrian's message offering a quid pro quo, however, made more sense to the earlier nineteenth-century moguls, such as the troubled Baptist John D. Rockefeller and the Scotch Presbyterian Andrew Carnegie, who knew a bargain when they saw it and whose moral sentiments reflected their God-fearing Protestant belief in heavenly salvation through good works. They would also have been reassured with the words of Tertullian: "By the help of riches even rich men are comforted and assisted; moreover by them many a work of justice and charity is carried out."[35]

In his sermon on "The Apparel of Women," Tertullian laid out the earliest Christian dogma governing the dress of Christian women.[36] A desire for luxury was "a vicious passion of the mind" of both sexes. Men were not excluded from God's command that modesty in all things was an essential proof of salvation. Men were not to cut their beard too sharply or "disguise its hoariness by dyes," or use a "womanly pigment" as a means to "voluptuous attraction." As for women, anything that went beyond humility and chastity was a sign of "womanly" ambition or even prostitution. He condemned false hair—"you may be putting on a holy and Christian head the castoffs of hair of some stranger who was perhaps unclean, perhaps guilty and destined for hell"—and colored garments—"what legitimate honour can garments derive from adulteration with illegitimate colours?" The slightest sign of "luxurious absurdities" or fashion amounted to giving in to the world of the devil. Public entertainments—"the frenzies of the racecourse, the atrocities of the arena, the turpitudes of the stage"—were to be avoided as blasphemy. The influence of Tertullian's severe pronouncements was widely influential and his argument would be regularly repeated for centuries. It would establish a long church tradition and attitude toward conspicuous consumption later reinforced by both Augustine and Saint Jerome.

With Emperor Constantine's approval of Christianity in AD 313 (a date confirmed much later by church historians), the Christian movement was no longer a "deadly superstition," in the words of Tacitus, but now had the political backing of the state. And if the emperor was a Christian convert, most of his troops as well as his subjects throughout of the empire were not. Sin, suffering, and errant passions still survived. As the supreme head of an ambitious "moral minority," however, he could advance the cause of the church with unprecedented favors and privileges, not to mention a string of divinely ordained military victories. Recognizing the shift of the empire's center to the East, he founded a New Rome he named Constantinople in the Greek colony of Byzantium. The formerly persecuted Christians were given a new legal and exclusive theological status throughout the empire, receiving huge gifts of money, tax exemptions, and political power. As for complete "Christianization" of the empire, that was a condition, "like full employment" in the words of the historian Robin Lane Fox, "which is always receding." No longer the administrative center of an expanding world to the East, Rome remained the spiritual center of the Western church, and it was in the post-Constantine era that the visible pomp of the Vatican ceremonial, with its lavish Roman panoply of theater, increased, putting earthly wealth and grandeur at the service of God in the name of his followers. In the eloquent words of the historian Peter Brown, this celebration of God's mercy created by the Christian community (and orchestrated by the curia) was "what any thrusting institution needs—a sense of a future on earth touched by the shadow of eternity.[37]

Both John Chrysostom and Augustine were born around 354 and grew up in an empire that was nominally Christian, where the tensions between the church and the state had all but disappeared. The transition from a pagan to a Christian society moved with irresistible speed. In wealthy cities like Antioch, where Chrysostom was baptized, and Constantinople, where he would become bishop in 398, the magnificent Eastern splendor of the churches had completely changed their character and that of their congregations, which were now made up of nominal converts recruited wholesale, often by decree or fiat. As bishop, he had inherited a heroic vision of the church going back to its harassed, persecuted beginnings when the catacombs were the center of worship. The austere traditions of the early church were lost in the hubbub, laughter, and extravagant dress of Chrysostom's increasingly secular congregation. Pickpockets plied a profitable trade as if they were in the market or at the theater, far removed from his idealized image of a place of worship or his early life as a hermit.

Unlike Clement, who worked to find just the right balance of faith and greed in order to convert the pagan, the new bishop of Constantinople confronted a congregation that had, because of its excessive power and tradition of luxury, been seduced by "the tyranny of wealth" with all of its evils. How to overcome this worldly power and the introduction of luxury into the life of a Christian became a central theme of Chrysostom's sermons and homilies. How was it to be done was the typical rhetorical question he addressed to his restive, profligate worshippers.

> If you consider that as long as you are rich you will never cease thirsting and pining with lust for more; but being freed from your possessions you will be able to stay the disease. Do not then surround yourself with more, in case you strive for things unattainable, than all, and be incurable and more miserable than all, being thus frantic. . . . If you consider how these things affect the soul, how dark and desolate and foul they render it, and how ugly; if you reckon with many evils these things were acquired, with how many labors they are kept.[38]

The bishop found that while the church had expanded into the world, the world had successfully invaded the church, now run by a bloated bureaucracy carried away with its own "lust for authority." The dissolute private life of the clergy was particularly alarming; it also became a target of Chrysostom's wrath. He was outraged to find that the Bishop of Ephesus was charged with melting down church silver and giving the proceeds to his son. The ambitious bishop had also removed pillars from the church to redecorate the private dining room of his palace, where he staged elaborate banquets, and he used marble from the entry of the baptistery to refinish his sybaritic bathroom.

Unlike the words of Clement of Alexandria, who felt that the choice was up to individuals to exercise their free will to preserve and maintain the church's moral authority, Chrysostom's reforming zeal and message were not wildly applauded in the voluptuous Byzantine city of Constantinople or the imperial court that had increased luxury's reputation of depravity. For his efforts, the reforming bishop was finally exiled to the far eastern end of the Black Sea, where he was martyred.

The moral freedom of the individual to choose good or evil, which Clement preached and many Christian converts of the first three centuries viewed as "gospel," ended in the late fourth century when Augustine insisted that all men, as Adam's heirs, were forever enslaved to sin. Augustine's ascetic theology—he would ban the unspiritual desires of sex from his own life after he became a Christian—set the future course of Western Christianity. (As late as 1900, the Bostonian Henry Adams remarked that "any one brought up among Puritans knew that sex was sin.") The future bishop and saint, with a tumultuously passionate nature revealed in his *Confessions*, ranked the Christian sins according to their increasing severity and threat to the soul. He put luxury, the seed of all other sins with its pungent, ancient odor of both physical and metaphysical transgressions, in the place of honor. Knowing his Greek and Roman history, he believed the ravages of lust were an immutable fact of life. In his *City of God*, what came to be the church's definitive censure of luxury, Augustine's first lesson repeated the classic genealogy of greed and luxury born of prosperity, followed by the deadly appearance of avarice, "the root of all evil . . . wanting more than is enough."

Growing up in a half-pagan world, and not giving in to Christianity until he was nearly thirty, more than any other Christian writer, Augustine kept alive the ancient classical condemnation of luxury's licentious ways and its dreaded, primordial influence. As an aspiring young professor of classical rhetoric, he was thoroughly grounded in the Greco-Roman traditions, and he had no trouble using the writings of Seneca, Cicero, Sallust, Aristotle, and Plato to bolster his growing case against luxury's deadly curse as a part of his new theology:

> Are the pleasures of the body to be sought, which Plato describes, in all seriousness, as "snares and the sources of all ills[?] . . . The promptings of sensuality are the most strong of all, and so the most hostile to philosophy. . . . What man in the grip of this, the strongest of emotions, can bend his mind to thoughts, regain his reason, or indeed concentrate on anything . . . ?

Throughout the Renaissance and down to the modern era, Augustine would be cited as the source of the assumption that luxury's appearance in all of its familiar forms announced the death throes of civilization. Paraphrasing Sallust's narrative, Augustine warned that Christians must never forget "the calamities which befell Rome and its provinces" through luxury and impiety. Material wealth and luxurious corruption were spread by avarice, enslaving mankind to a hunger for worldly possessions and bringing on the inevitable destruction of society founded on simple virtues of frugality and self-discipline. Luxury's definition was counterposed with measured self-control, an elusive boundary that had not been securely fixed by the church fathers.

A chapter in Augustine's first book, called "That those who complain of Christianity really desire to live without restraint in shameful luxury," argued that the besotted pagans of contemporary society were as much of a threat to the Christian faith as Nero was to Rome. "First concord was weakened, and destroyed by fierce and bloody seditions; then followed, by a concatenation of baleful causes, civil wars, which brought in their train such massacres, such bloodshed, such lawless and cruel proscription and plunder, that those Romans who, in the days of their virtue, had expected injury only at the hands of their enemies, now that their virtue was lost suffered greater cruelties at the hands of their fellow citizens." The lust to rule took over and advanced with ruthless greed. "But unscrupulous ambition has nothing to work upon, save in a nation corrupted by avarice and luxury," a nation caught up in original sin.[39]

Realizing his depressing conclusion that all of mankind was enslaved by original sin might be a stumbling block for the young church, Augustine finally offered in his writings and sermons a way out of the dilemma by making luxury (or luxuria) the generic carnal lust of the individual, egalitarian and experienced by all. Other than private confession, no affirmative action to balance the scale was required. The political dimensions of the classical attack on luxury as leading to tyranny were ignored. According to Augustine, it was the *serpent* that tempted Adam with the lure of freedom of choice, something that God never intended, introduced only as a test. By allowing Adam to sin, forever tainting his descendants, God demonstrated in the Garden scene that absolute obedience to him came first, and in the natural order of things, the same obedience to his earthly agent—pope or emperor—followed. The ordained imperial Catholic hierarchy was fixed for centuries. Breathtaking extravagance in church architecture, church theater of rituals, and in the splendid costumes and stage props of the principal actors, rivaling any Eastern court, was not seen as sinful, decadent, or worldly. It was a physical manifestation and celebration of God's visible supremacy on earth.

In the drama of the soul's salvation orchestrated by the church and driven home with all the powerful multisensory tools then available—banners, tapestries, paintings, engravings, sculpture, music, incense, above all the high theater of the mass itself—men and women of luxury are tempted to their doom by ambition, the lust of the eyes and flesh, self-indulgence, and lechery. The saved chooses the straight-and-narrow through ritual, regular confession, and divine forgiveness, finally entering the City of God.[40]

With a strategic shift of emphasis on personal welfare and conduct, the classical battle against luxury became a routine policy administered exclusively by the church. Insidious as it was, luxury eventually underwent a makeover along with the other Deadly Sins, measured by degrees, pardonable exclusively through the office of the church.

By the Middle Ages, the soul on its pilgrimage confronted luxury in three forms: the beginning of the cause of Adam's original Fall; followed by fundamental carnality symbolized by the flesh—a weakness for useless, temporal things; and finally the devil's use of luxury to violate God's laws. Both Gregory the Great (Calvin called him the last good pope) and Thomas Aquinas agreed that luxury (with or without that label) was a sure sign that the devil was around and at work, delving into his bag of irresistible tricks to promote the world's most all-inclusive sin.

While the name and number of sins have changed over the centuries and from writer to writer, the agreement on luxury's primacy is remarkably consistent. Lust, the generic term for earthly desires, and luxuria were often interchangeable, and by implying excess beyond life's necessities in the definition of luxury, it endowed the notion with a powerful element of Christian opprobrium. In the earliest lists, luxury usually ranked as the chief sin, but sometimes luxury and pride shift positions from first to last and vice versa to suggest the dreaded circular results that luxury will evolve into pride and pride into luxury, the cause and effect.

Aquinas consolidated Augustine's teachings with an exhausting examination of luxury expressing the most sinful desires, the consequence of the Fall. In creating his airtight system of sin and salvation, the priggish Dominican relied

heavily on luxuria's hoary all-purpose reputation. Recognizing that earthly society was made up of sinners, a legal and political system was required to deal
with the fallen multitude who needed order and unquestioned direction. In the
realm of eternal salvation through the molding of the thoughts and wills of humankind, the church had no competition. To challenge it would be to challenge
God's purpose and his design of man's sinful nature. As for the church's relationship with the secular state, the separation of obligations followed Christ's
injunction: "Render therefore to Caesar the things that are Caesar's, and to God
the things that are God's."[41]

Aquinas reaffirmed the ancient principles of necessity and hierarchy. Before the Fall, man was free to choose according to God's law, but having been
driven from the Garden, he is forced to accept his place and function in the
scheme of things to avoid the inevitable chaos that would be created by universal sinfulness. In the name of order, the Christian must give his free will and
his body over to the power of the higher authority of the church. So unruly
desires, particularly sexual—always an obsession of the church—are subject to
the church's commands regardless of the rules and laws of the state. Using the
whole battery of enforcement tools, long applied by the state—threats, edicts,
penalties, physical power—the power of popes and bishops came from their
claim that they were acting "in God's place."

The church's ability to bestow heavenly status on the faithful did not depend on its claim that spiritual matters were far superior to worldly success. At
least for a time, the charms of material values infused with luxe—the trappings
of grand houses, personal finery, fancy clothes, lavish entertaining, splendid
equipage, the insatiable pursuit of pleasure—were subordinated to the values
expressed in the lives of saints who shunned all worldly things of this life. With
the power of its treasury, the church's patronage and direction was able to exalt
those virtues it revered, with a transcendent albeit "material" beauty created by
painters, sculptors, architects, musicians, and writers, to an unprecedented level.

While the opulent gold, silver, and rare jewels in places of worship would
have been the envy of Nero's court, the church declared that they were solely
for the glory of God. Artists and craftsmen whose talents were once directed to
promoting the worldly values of royalty, generals, and the rich now turned their
talents to honor the nobility of Jesus's lowly birth in a stable, the rags of Lazarus,

the giving of alms, the caring for the weak, the gestures of humility as in the scene where Jesus washes the feet of his disciples, the humble and contrite recognition of one's dependence on God as seen in the lives of the saints celebrated in countless portraits of piety and gruesome scenes of their martyrdom. The aesthetic importance of this extravagance of sensual riches, which would have been viewed as a sign of earthly corruption if it had been directed to hedonistic pleasures of excess, was transformed by its spiritual message celebrating the City of God.

Given the enormous wealth and power concentrated over the centuries in the Church of Rome ruled by a Christian emperor in its capital, it would inevitably reach its symbolic peak in the architectural complex of the Vatican, centered on St. Peter's. It is also no surprise that ambitious and clever men driven by a lust for status and power would be drawn to Rome. It was, after all, predicted by Saint Augustine, who recognized that all were sinners before God. The idea of an exclusive, visible "church of the pure," made up of only a few individuals who, having once received salvation, lived blameless lives untainted by worldly thoughts and desires, was an illusion. Now that Christianity was the official religion of the Roman Empire, devious, wicked men—an "enormous multitude, that almost to the entire subversion of discipline, gain an entrance, with their morals so utterly at variance with the pathways of the saints"—were able to "line the walls of our places of meeting" and take the reins of the church into their own sinful hands. Since "all may sign themselves with the sign of Christ's cross; all may answer Amen and sing Alleluia; all may be baptized, all may come to church," nothing in their outward appearance or behavior betrayed whether they were among the "elect" or the damned.[42]

The centuries following the era of the early church fathers witnessed a growing parade of talented, if often unscrupulous, men who saw the church not only as the gateway to heaven but also as the high road to riches and political advancement. The opportunity to use the church to indulge in and flaunt all the seductive possessions of this life—countless palaces and servants, artworks by the best artists, expensive mistresses; still the accouterments of unimpeachable status could not be resisted. Any biblical, moral, or theological prohibitions raised only minor issues of hypocrisy, which could be overcome and forgiven as standard, everyday human sinfulness. To Augustine, who with his wary eye saw it all coming, the very insolence of the flood of new members looking for gain and temporal advantages gave their game away:

> One has a business on hand, he seeks the intercession of the clergy; another is oppressed by one more powerful than himself, he flies to the church. Another desires intervention in his behalf with one with whom he has little influence. One, in this way, one in that, the church is daily filled with such people. Jesus is scarcely sought after for Jesus' sake.[43]

If lust and avarice, hell-bent at full throttle, are at the heart of the classical and Christian notion of luxury, one could say that the church, in all its Renaissance and Baroque glory, is luxury's supreme monument. Excluding the church as a supreme expression of faith in God's mysteries, beyond secular, material metrics, Rome's very grandeur, beauty, and endurance, commissioned by a new Brahmin caste, challenges luxury's besotted reputation. The city-makers of Renaissance Rome—Bramante, Sangallo the Younger, Michelangelo, Raphael, Peruzzi, Bernini, Borromini, and around them hundreds of painters, sculptors, garden designers, decorators, and hydraulic engineers—were drawn from all over Europe into the job of memorializing and celebrating the power of their patrons.

Following the Great Schism and the papacy's long holiday in Avignon, Catholic Christendom was reunited with the election of a Roman nobleman, Martin V, a member of the ancient Colonna family, as pope in 1417. The great papal families with their nepotism, an ancient, familiar tool of power, established themselves in the Eternal City as the papal court. The della Rovere family, who supplied two popes, Sextus IV and Julius II, provided the blueprint for other families to unite spiritual and secular grandeur.

The exclusive Roman oligarchy would dominate Italian politics and Roman life for 150 years, from the late fifteenth century and early sixteenth century, carving out princely hereditary domains for themselves in the Papal States. The focus of their new wealth was on luxurious splendor that would change the face of Rome and its surrounding Compagna, building, in the words of Emile Zola, one "colossal, sumptuous, deadly dwelling" after another. Without a hint of humility, modesty, or Christian meekness, the families of Colonna, Barberini,

Farnese, Borghese, Pamphili, and Chigi, with their *nipoti*, provided the major architectural set pieces of sovereign pomp—grand staircases with low steps, intimidating gilded salons, endless corridors lined with portraits, glorious fountains—that still dominate the city. Like the newly rich in any age, the parvenu, self-declared elite worked hard to find things on which to spend their money.

Undaunted luxuria, panting after more and more to indulge insatiable fantasies without apology, consumed both the fabulous riches and energies of these families and their protégés for generations. Unlike northern Europe, which remained in comparative poverty, Italy enjoyed wealth over many centuries, producing thriving, civilized cities—centers of extravagant culture. The pattern of infectious dissipation of the papacy and its entrenched court, however, pointed to what appeared to be the final dissolution and collapse of the church's foundation, confirming classic predictions of decline and fall. But as notorious as their excesses and vices were, the Italians had an instinct for exploring all the sensual possibilities of luxury with such imagination, fancy, and refinement, both the beautiful and splendid. The results, serving both God and mammon, were far too overwhelming to allow any moral or theological questioning of where it all might lead.

Putting aside the endless galleries hung with portraits of church princes and patrons, many that capture the corruption and cupidity as well as the recurring charm of these extraordinary figures, they are at the center of what we call the Renaissance, Western civilization's Golden Age. A German historian has summed up the exemplar of the type in his description of the character of Pope Sextus IV's favorite nephew, Pietro. The pope had showered his nephew with papal largesse, one lucrative beneficence piled on another, making Pietro in one year, a cardinal, the patriarch of Constantinople, and archbishop of Florence all at the age of twenty-six:

> He was intelligent and cultivated, courteous, witty, cheerful and generous, but his good qualities were counterbalanced by lust [for] power, a boundless ambition and pride, and a love of luxury which rendered him utterly unworthy of the purple. . . . He seemed to vie with the ancients in pomp and grandeur—and, it may be added, in vices. Instead of the habit of Francis [of Assisi] he went about in garments laden with gold, and adorned his mistress from head to foot with costly pearls.[44]

In the material magnificence of sixteenth-century Venice, the center of international trade with the East, the celebration of luxurious Renaissance hedonism reaches its splendid noonday moment in the paintings of Paolo Veronese. A more unapologetic celebration of wealth and its fantasy pleasures cannot be imagined. In his treatment of sacred Christian themes, such as the Baptism of Moses, the Marriage at Cana, and the Annunciation, Venetian hedonism is frankly acknowledged and feted in dazzling colors, fabrics, and theatrical lighting, while the scenes are managed with heroic dignity.

Veronese had been commissioned by the monks of the Basilica di Santi Giovanni e Paolo to create an enormous painting representing the Last Supper of Jesus with his disciples in the house of Simon, a reasonable subject for their refectory. The posh monastery's wealth that paid for the commission had undoubtedly come from the profits of the city's luxury trade in the sensuous silks, laces, velvets, and jeweled ornaments the artist brilliantly celebrates in the soft Venetian light. Measuring 18 by 42 feet, it is one of the largest paintings of the Renaissance. Because the canvas was so huge—the scale itself was a blatant statement of excess—he had to fill it up with whatever dramatic props and operatic stage business he could imagine, or so he claimed.

The finished work transformed the mise en scène of the first Eucharist taking place at the house of Simon, described in Mark's austere text, into the revels of a Venetian banquet of theatrical sumptuousness. Jesus is seated, surrounded by his disciples, at the center of a three-arched Palladian loggia packed with glamorous women, loitering soldiers, exotic servants, and stage extras, holding aristocratic dogs and birds and crowded around a table piled with gold and silver tankards and platters. Without any apparent moral apology or the restraints of the scriptures and Christian tradition, Veronese selected the most expensive, chic, luxurious materials gathered by Venice's trade with the Levant, India, and China to decorate the setting for the Gospels' central rite. The ensemble that so appealed to the sophisticated, extravagant Venetians assimilated classical paganism into their lavish world and surrounded the rites of their urbane religion with gloriously humane sensuality.

Veronese had also painted the portrait of the notorious Roman emperor Vitellius, one of the three emperors who had quickly followed Nero and been removed by murder or suicide during one year of the civil war of AD 69, watching the ritual of salvation as he stands by the right column framing the scene. Vitellius's porcine features (Suetonius said that he was easily recognized by his red face and bloated belly, proof of his flawed moral character) were likely drawn from the ancient marble bust that had recently been excavated in Rome and presented by Cardinal Grimani to the city of Venice.[45] Cassius Dio's portrait is even more lurid, the very symbol of "luxury and licentiousness." There seems little doubt that the introduction into the sacred setting of the Last Supper of the glutton Vitellius, who was famous for vomiting during banquets in order to increase his capacity to consume, delivered its own condemnation of contemporary Venetian excess.

When members of the Holy Office of the Inquisition saw the painting in 1573, it did not take them long to smell heresy. It was not only the physical details of elegant, long-necked women dressed in stunning imported silks and velvets hung with long strands of oriental pearls and surrounded by men even more richly dressed in smart capes and doublets that upset them. The problem was also the tasteless presence of the dogs, cats, midgets, German soldiers, and the irrelevant drunken characters sprawling on the stairs. And what about the buffoon with the parrot on his wrist and someone picking his teeth with a toothpick?

On July 18, 1573, Veronese was brought before the Inquisition and charged, in the words of the Counter-Reformation, with "heretical irreverence" and accused of introducing into a sacred subject, "lures of impurity and lasciviousness . . . drenched in shameless beauty." As a result of the successful religious revolt led fifty years earlier by reformers like Martin Luther and John Calvin against Rome, the church had begun its own program to clean up its tarnished image. Following the Council of Trent, simple examples of faith in ritual, architecture, and church decoration became official church policy.

With intimidating sarcasm, one of the Inquisitors asked the artist, "Does it seem suitable in the Last Supper of our Lord to represent buffoons, drunken Germans, dwarfs and such absurdities?" Most leaders of the Protestant Reformation would also have been appalled by the painting's brazen celebration of unabashed hedonism. For the next three hundred years, the stern moral values of Lutheranism, Calvinism, and Puritan churches would try to eliminate "shameless beauty" and any other forms of the devil's carnal temptations from the lives of their members and places of worship.

After pleading a guileless motive rooted in ancient aesthetics claiming the artist's freedom of imagination as "that of poets and jesters," Veronese declared, "My art is joyous and praises God in light and color." As for the presence of Vitellius, the artist claimed that the figure richly dressed in stripped silk brocade was merely a maître d' or a "steward who I had imagined had come there for his own pleasure to see how things were going at the table." Following the trial the artist eliminated all taint of heresy by ingeniously renaming the painting, *The Feast in the House of Levi.* The Last Supper was transformed into a secular Venetian banquet where the luxury of exotic food and wine served in gold goblets and plates—even the entertainment of buffoons and dwarfs—would not have offended the Lord's scruples.

There are at least two possible readings of the artist's real motives: he simply wanted to record a familiar Venetian scene of luxe, his favorite painterly subject; or he wanted to not-so-subtly confront his decadent patrons and audience with the painting's hubris and hypocrisy, both symptoms of luxury's deadly effect since ancient times. The profile of Vitellius—one of the few imperial portraits in the painting identified with reasonable certainty—seems to underline the artist's last word on the wages of sin.

5

UNINTENDED CONSEQUENCES
Indulgence and the Reformation

Despite the torrents of cold water doused on luxury by the early church fathers, profligate spending gradually became a part of the job of the Vicar of Christ. By the fifteenth century the papacy and its network of princely families that controlled the College of Cardinals, vested with the power to elect the pope, adopted magnificence as an important strategy for the advancement and authority of the church. The values of this world overwhelmed those of the next. It is not hyperbole to call the sumptuous pontificate of Leo X, elected pope in 1513, a "Golden Age." No one considered his example of sacred opulence a sacrilege or his dependence on a litany of self-indulgences a mortal transgression. And no one could foresee the unintended consequences of Leo's brilliant, reckless bequest of lavish imprudence so important to the civilizing triumphs of art, architecture, and literature, first called "the Renaissance" by Jules Michelet in 1855.

The classic (and Christian) virtues of prudence, frugality, and self-restraint certainly played no part in the shaping of the character of the first Medici pope. As one contemporary put it, Giovanni de' Medici, was "by nature given to ease and pleasure" with an "overweening grandeur," hopelessly "estranged from practical affairs." After all, his bankrupting taste for the princely pleasures of art, music, poetry, and architecture was a part of his family's Florentine breeding. But to his German nemesis, Martin Luther, who had taken a vow of poverty as an Augustinian monk seven years earlier, Leo's love of luxury summed up the papacy's reputation of decadence and profitable vice, paid for by brazen financial extortion of the faithful, and periodically redeemed by conspicuous repentance.

For the faithful north of the Alps, it was not enough that their pope was the premier patron of the arts in Europe. Worship, according to the church's rules, had become choked with elaborate ritual, symbolized by material opulence in its rigid punctuation of daily offices and calendar. This self-fulfilling theater had little to do with the Christian narrative unfolding in a meaningful way in the lives of ordinary people. The growing anxiety over excessive ceremony among the devout, far from the Vatican, underlined the unseemly hypocrisy of what became the Reformation, expressing this deeper concern over the way the historic biblical story had been transformed by Rome's materialism. In its last undivided hour, it would be this Medici pope's legacy to reap the retributions for the church's long record—and sensational rumors—of scandalous administrations of excess, setting off Luther's revolution.

In addition to his own cultivated extravagance and sophisticated tastes, which strained the church's vast resources, Leo had inherited the staggering financial commitment to carry on the construction of the new St. Peter's, designed to replace Constantine's decrepit old basilica, consecrated in AD 326. Started by Pope Julius II, the della Rovere pope had dreamed of turning the weed-covered ruins of the city of the Caesars into a sumptuous New Jerusalem, a papal palatinate capping the Vatican's hill. With "vaulting ambitions," and more sins than even an imperial basilica of marble and travertine could atone for, Julius, in 1507, laid the cornerstone for the building in the former gardens of Agrippina, the mother of Caligula.

The new basilica was only the largest of the many monumental Vatican projects supported and encouraged by Leo as he enthusiastically worked his way through the Vatican's dwindling treasury. Huge amounts of money had disappeared down the sinkhole of St. Peter's construction site and into the pockets of the corrupt network of contractors and builders. But the succession of banquets, elaborate hunting parties (his favorite sport), and festivals that consumed much of his time had forced him to double Julius's papal household budget, further swelling the debt. His only fiscal policy was to make sure that his mounting bank loans covered his bankrupting spending.

The thirty-eight-year-old Medici pope was a born epicure, turning more often to the rules of Castiglione's *The Book of the Courtier* for guidance than to the letters of Paul. "Avoid the Epistles of St. Paul," Leo's papal secretary, the bon vivant Venetian humanist Pietro Bembo, advised, "lest his barbarous style should spoil your taste."[1] As the second son of Lorenzo the Magnificent, destined for the church, Leo found his early religious experience to be impressionably sensual and utterly devoid of a sinner's guilt or of self-denial. Dressed in rich jewel-encrusted brocade robes to celebrate the increasingly elaborate rituals, he was transported on his spiritual journey by the sounds of consoling choirs and Gregorian chants, and surrounded by heavenly visions created by Raphael and Michelangelo. He could not tolerate long, droning sermons on morality and God's grace. The name of Jupiter in a sermon was more comforting than Jehovah: the question of the immortality of the soul became an open topic of debate.[2]

Leo's father, Lorenzo, had managed to set the boy up with fabulously profitable church benefices, assuring the future pope that he could live in opulence without any thought of "practical affairs" or balancing a budget. He was tonsured at the age of six, given an archbishopric at seven, and his father had badgered a cardinal's hat for him just before he turned fourteen. Although patience was not a Medici trait, for appearance's sake, Lorenzo agreed to wait three years for the child to actually take his seat in the powerful College of Cardinals as a prince of the church.

A restless impresario, Leo saw boredom as the eighth deadly sin, to be avoided at any cost. Aside from the slaughters in the Colosseum and other gross public entertainments, many of the more tempting venal excesses of ancient Rome, detailed in the newly rediscovered works of Plutarch, Livy, and Suetonius, became the inspiration of Leo's reborn city. To eradicate any hint of tedium with every distraction that luxury could conjure became the objective of the Leonine papacy. Intent on incorporating all elements of life and power into the new Rome, Leo appropriated antique ritual and theater, classical temples, and pagan gods into the church's elaborate ceremonies and papal court. One of Leo's favorite places to stage grand dinner parties was in the Castello Sant'Angelo, the emperor Hadrian's magnificent mausoleum of the second century that now served as the Vatican's fortress, treasury, and prison. Its stone terraces high above the Tiber, where the archangel Michael had once appeared to announce the end of a plague, made the perfect setting for a papal dolce vita.

Just as Rome's imperial rulers had collected, as a conspicuous privilege, rare fauna gathered from remote corners of the empire to represent its exotic geographical dimensions, the Medici pope created his own menagerie of lions, cheetahs, leopards, monkeys, bears, and birds. The pope's elephant was brought from Cochin, India, as a gift of the king of Portugal. It was the first pachyderm to be seen in Rome since the days of the Antonines, when the great beasts were featured in public ceremonies and triumphs. Among the openhanded payments recorded in Leo's household accounts are the gold ducats he gave the man who brought lions from his family's zoo in Florence, the generous salary for the leopard trainer, and a small fortune of eighteen gold ducats paid "to the Hungarians for the bears."[3]

Leo left balancing the budget to higher powers, assisted by the international bankers like the Chigis and Fuggers, who were more than willing to bankroll any shortfall in the pledges of the faithful to cover the mounting expense of the papal pomp and circumstance. When Leo died in 1521, his debts amounted to nearly a million gold ducats. The Vatican's treasury was empty without even enough money to pay for a papal funeral. Second-hand candles from a cardinal's funeral a few days earlier had to be recycled. The jewels of the sacred crown were removed and sold.

Leo X is rightly celebrated for his remarkable patronage of arts and letters, and of music and learning, although Michelangelo, Donato Agnolo (called Bramante), and young Raphael of Urbino had actually begun working at the Vatican under Julius's patronage. At the very moment when the papacy's finances teetered on the brink, Giovanni de' Medici's inspired generosity knew no limit. For the artists and skilled craftsmen, or for talented musicians who staffed the seven choirs ready to perform in the sacristy or papal apartment on a moment's notice, entertainment itself became a luxurious art, radiating unparalleled creative power and pretensions. With his Medici reputation for an exalted appreciation of the arts—Michelangelo had been a part of his family circle in the cosmopolitan city of Florence—and a genuine appreciation of music, theater, and poetry, hordes of artists and poets had followed him to Rome, offering their services. Leo's pudgy frame settled comfortably into the Chair of Saint Peter, his soft, delicate hands folded in his lap. For all of his common place looks and aura of decadence, at that moment in history he was central casting for Saint Peter's throne. His papacy would be the culmination and the end of one of the most brilliant—and most lavish—epochs any world capital had ever seen.[4]

After a hundred years of work to pull itself out of the insignificant village of decay huddled around the rubble of the Colosseum, the Baths of Caracalla, and Trajan's Column, Rome had entered a new era of speculative prosperity. Extravagant palaces with rich households for the arriviste power players who had crowded into the city sprang up in all directions. Rome had become the center of international wealth, art, and fashion. Cardinals were expected to live a life of grandeur with retinues in the hundreds. The pope led the way in financial speculation when he reduced his debts in 1517 by peddling thirty-nine new cardinals' hats, adding more than 500,000 ducats to his coffers. Leo had lost no time in tearing up the papal bulls Julius had issued at the Fifth Lateran Council, which he had called to reform the church everyone knew was paralyzed with corruption. The bulls banned the sale of any church office, and if Julius had been successful, Martin Luther's more sweeping reforms might have been avoided. Leo more than doubled the number of venal offices to over two thousand.

While attempting to raise money to pay for the Vatican's new imperial grandeur and his own epicurean tastes, Leo was also driven to complete St. Peter's. With Leo desperate to find a way to finance the staggering costs of the papal "palace," a wildly profitable traffic of another order of indulgence offered a solution.

By the end of the Middles Ages, the church felt confident enough in its power to forgive or remit penances imposed on individual sinners following confession and the absolution of sins, offering to "indulge" the contrite for good works, including monetary contributions to sacred projects. By the 1470s, the church went one step further, offering indulgences for those who had already died but still languished in purgatory.[5]

With the monopoly of the Eucharist serving as an engine promoting eternal life, it soon developed that a monetary value could be put on any of the church's blessings, pardons, and interdictions, particularly for carefully graded personal sins, in exchange for an indulgence or remission, usually certified by a piece of paper. In his papal bull of 1515, *Sacrosanctis salvatoris*, Leo declared that the faithful could renew their indulgences as a literal "stairway to heaven," or *scalas ad aulae coelestis*.[6] Such a system would inevitably lead to abuse. Later, the timely invention of Gutenberg's printing press allowed the mass-production of these heavenly fast-track pardons, which would turn the scheme of papal forgiveness—originally documented by labor-intensive hand-inscribed notes—into an international business.

Until Martin Luther challenged the church's power head-on, it held absolute and sanctified access to Christian forgiveness. So it didn't take long for the profitability of "fines for sins" to become an efficient kind of ecclesiastical-secular tax system, and the Holy See and the Holy Roman Empire divided the proceeds based roughly on the familiar modern principle of revenue sharing. The credible quid pro quo offered by the papal authority was merely the extension of an established part of the church's central role in the life of the faithful, holding salvation and morality under its profitable control. And at the beginning of the luxury-obsessed twenty-first century, secular indulgences have been resurrected to ensure the environmentally guilt-ridden their passage into a green paradise, absolving those who leave a sinful trail of carbon footprints leading to global climate change. A travel co-op in England now sells "carbon offsets," allowing customers to buy a clean conscience every time they fill up their SUVs or fly off to some remote spot for a holiday, their jets spewing carbon monoxide into the atmosphere. The proceeds from this convenient ecological atonement will be invested in the developing world—probably their holiday destination—on ecologically friendly projects like wind farms and animal waste management systems.[7]

Although his extravagance was carried out with better taste and sophistication than earlier popes, Leo was nevertheless accused of "immoderate avarice and insatiable ambition"—not particularly original shortcomings throughout Rome's history.[8] His financial advisers calculated that he spent more than eight thousand ducats a month on private gifts to favorites and on gaming. An unapologetic hedonist, Leo reportedly told his younger brother Giuliano de' Medici at the time he was elected that "God has given us the Papacy—let us enjoy it."[9] Leo's borrowing at usury rates barely kept pace with his spending. Chigi was conveniently there to advance the funds for Leo's coronation, a loan secured by the gold beehive crown of the Vicar of Christ. The banker's clients also included Leo's inner circle of friends who were looking for ways to support their own spendthrift life of endless pleasure. A number of them were aspiring humanists as well as good company, encouraging classical research and collecting ancient works of art. They were men who knew how to carry their scholarship lightly as they investigated antique Roman traditions and archaeological evidence to reinforce the papacy's claim to imperial succession.

From the moment Constantine saw the cross in the sky and embraced Christianity on behalf of his kingdom in AD 312, while successfully defending Rome with his army at the Battle of the Milvian Bridge, it would not be too long before faith was caught up in the turmoil of big-time European power politics. As everyone knew, for those in control of matters both temporal and sacred, it would take more than moral discipline and the fear of eternal damnation to resist the temptations of all the worldly luxury that this supreme power would bring to those who managed to hold it.

An implicit agreement between the church and the state evolved over the centuries after Constantine's epiphany, giving both establishments, and their representatives, the right to express their God-given authority through public magnificence and splendor. It was a power system that had undreamed of earthly rewards for the newly elevated class of noblemen managing secular affairs and for Christ's ordained servants, who benefited from gifts of huge sums of money to carry on the work of the church. Together, ambitious feudal lords, aristocrats, and a grateful papal bureaucracy, along with bishops and abbots, had a common interest in amassing worldly lucre while maintaining society's carefully structured ladder, where everyone had allegiance to someone else above him in a measured ascent toward heaven.

The church had long worked to construct an elaborate theater of ritual and tradition to explain and advance the Bible's mysteries in the eyes of the awed, unlettered masses. Waves of solemn music announcing triumphant salvation, massed candlelight, and incense produced a dreamy mixture that became an essential part of the Christian pageantry of worship. But the image of this extravaganza, paid for with sacred revenues, raised critical questions about the place of the arts in religion and added further propaganda to Luther's uncompromising message of church reform that included teaching the faithful to read the Bible in their own language without the help of 'visual aids.'

The crisis reached a critical moment when Luther issued his Ninety-Five Theses, allegedly nailed to the church door in Wittenberg in the fall of 1517, disputing the power of papal indulgences. In Thesis 55 of Luther's indictment, even the most obtuse German peasant could grasp the church's histrionic, overpowering abuses: "The pope cannot help taking the view that if indulgences (very small matters) are celebrated by one bell, one pageant, or one ceremony," Luther slyly argued, "the gospel (a very great matter) should be preached to the accompaniment of a hundred bells, a hundred processions, a hundred ceremonies."[10]

For the Renaissance and the rediscovery of humanism, exalted man became the measure of all things—a startling conclusion for the wielders of divine power. Nothing was too exaggerated, too extreme, too expensive to be thought about under the patronage of the papacy in the pontifical city of Rome. As Aquinas had argued, ostentation and the elaborate use of finery were legitimate in ecclesiastical ritual, as long as they advanced the worship of God.

By the end of the fifteenth century, medieval Europe had been transformed by two developments. The first was the opening of Europe to the world by exploration, bringing staggering new wealth from Africa, Asia, and the Americas. The second was the religious and growing intellectual upheaval leading to the Protestant Reformation, eventually becoming the root of protracted political and military conflict. By the time of Columbus's landfall in the Caribbean, Europe had been torn asunder by the tremors of the oncoming Reformation.

As the Mediterranean became more and more a war zone between Christians and Turks, the center of European trade moved first to Portugal and Spain, then north to England, the German states, and particularly to the Low Countries. Imperial exploitation of foreign continents and populations to supply Europe's new luxury trades in silk, spices, precious metals, and jewels was propelled by rising consumer aspirations among the nobility and aristocracy. An endless train of riches stretched from Africa, the Americas, and the Far East to the capitals of Europe. In 1307, some two hundred years before these seismic shifts in the church's European hegemony, centered on the ruins of Augustan's capital, the papacy was moved from Rome to Avignon, bringing about the loss of its lucrative Italian estates. The popes, now all French, scrambled to find every plausible scheme to extract revenue from the faithful to fill the papacy's once again exhausted treasury. The strategy of their exploitation was a spectacular financial success, producing an annual income three times that of the king of France.

It has been suggested that the Avignon papacy invented the first "modern court," establishing a tone of acceptable official splendor that later centuries called court society. This new society was made up of two types of people that would become important fixtures in the court machinery: cultivated noblemen with polished savoir faire, whose only job was to spare the court from boredom (an occupational hazard) by creating a distinctive atmosphere for luxurious, sybaritic living; and beautiful women "distinguished in deportment and spirit," giving court life its striking character of "sumptuous worldliness."[11] All this concentrated personal extravagance originated with the frank pursuit of sensual pleasure. "Any thing that charms the eye, the ear, the nose, the palate, or the touch" found its perfect expression in the daily objects of court life and court display. Material magnificence would become the model for ecclesiastical and secular courts throughout Europe, and particularly in France as it became greater and richer than all the Italian principalities combined.

After the Avignon schism was solved and the papacy returned to Rome in 1378, the Roman popes quickly regained their former spiritual and civil power, launching the most brilliant period of papal history in Rome "a pagan spirit pervaded the city, with the theatrical splendor of ancient imperial times. Secular pomp became a necessity of the papal government. The pampered populace called for festivals, and the festivals were given with abundance."[12] With the growth of his authority in the fifteenth century, the pope was now head of a city-state backed by an international financial system able to fulfill the papacy's wildest dreams—extravagance on a scale that would have been the envy of the Augustinian emperors of the Roman Empire. On Saint Mark's Day in 1476, a tournament held in the Piazza Navona drew more than a hundred thousand people. Not only the selling of indulgences but also the selling of high church offices became big business. While the Borgia pope Alexander VI may have had more mistresses and illegitimate children and is reported to have sold a cardinal's red hat for fifteen thousand gold ducats, Leo outdid him by raising the price of a cardinal's throne to a princely twenty-five thousand.[13]

The pope's rich, money-loving city of Florence was also the home of the firebrand evangelical preacher, Girolamo Savonarola, who was deeply troubled by the money culture of commerce and its network of international banking houses. An industry of hundreds of merchants, craftsmen, and artists was ready to supply the upper crust with the latest fashion of luxe. The largest industrial city in Italy, with more international bankers than any other in Europe, its oligarchs took seriously their wealth and the right to display all the stuff of grand living they could lay hands on. A craze for palace building, of course, went along with the city's growing economic power.

In the 1490s, the mystical, charismatic Savonarola—a "puritan" before there were Puritans—began to recruit armies of Florentine children to take on the Sisyphean task of turning Florence into a godly city. Corrupt finances and sex were at the top of his agenda. His attack was, first of all, a religious protest; second, it was directed against the city's voracious appetite for wealth and display; and third, it aimed at the corrupt political establishment. His blistering sermons, nourished by a fundamentalist reading of the Bible, indicted the easy targets of the "thieving priests," as well as the church establishment reaching to the pope and the powerful business interests that extracted taxes as a form of stealing from the poor. Inflamed with apocalyptic images from the book of Revelation, his message for Christians was "to give up hunting, hawking, fishing and . . . pursuing other vain and disorderly pleasure." Above all, he commanded, remain "sober and quiet, as well as prudent and moderate in all your approved amusements, stick to your God-fearing habits."[14]

With his condemnation of luxury, greed, and worldly decadence, the Dominican friar's incendiary warnings looked back to the early days of primitive Christianity, assuming the voice of a desert prophet: "Repent! The kingdom of God is at hand." While Savonarola was not a revolutionary genius like Martin Luther, the thrust of the Florentine's attack on excess, pride, and corruption anticipated both Luther and Calvin. His timing was fortunate. When Alexander VI was made pope in 1492, it seemed that the bottomless abyss of papal corruption could comfortably accommodate the entire church. The Borgia pope has come to personify the perverse side of the Renaissance papacy—particularly its profligate excesses of sex and greed.

In 1496 the threat of plague and famine in Florence had managed to transform what had been a pagan-inspired spring carnival into a summer of violent cleansing to purge the city of the sins of luxury—gambling, gluttony, "pagan" revels, self-regarding pride, arrogance, and the flaunting of all "superfluities." In his public battle to clean up the church, the friar had not only exposed the selling of church offices (called simony), he had also singled out for special censure tepid faith, greed, fornication, and sodomy—luxury's more conspicuous quotidian vices in Florence at the time.

Savonarola's army of scores of teenage enthusiasts, called the *fanciulli*, were ordered to scour the streets and search every house and villa for "instruments of vanity" and pleasure. The theology behind the reformer's message was straightforwardly directed at pride. With its roots in ancient Hebrew, pride—"a haughty spirit"—now headed the revised list of cardinal sins because it turned the believer away from God. Luxuries and vanities were not only a sign of pride, they also promoted the sin itself. A long laundry list of anything that might short-circuit a Christian's higher spirituality and cause him to lose his way—dice, cards, mirrors, cosmetics, jars of "lascivious scents," silks, mirrors, musical instruments, paintings of nude women, "dirty" Latin books of "pornography" (particularly the familiar works of Boccaccio, Dante, and Petrarch), gold-threaded satin and velvet cloth, feathers, lace, jewelry—were to be taken and burned in public bonfires. The largest of these bonfires (becoming a metaphor to celebrate vanity's fate) was built in the civic square of San Marco on Carnival Day, February 16, 1496. Beneath all this public recrimination directed at any sign of public or private excess, there was also a radical political message directed against Medici tyranny and the family's abuse of power. It was a message that would later confirm Leo X in his implacable dedication to his "ease and pleasure" whenever it was threatened by wild-eyed priests calling for reform. That peasant priest Martin Luther was dismissed out of hand.

As the wealth of the state grew throughout the late middle ages in Italy, France, and Spain, the increasing number of decrees and laws dealing with the problem of excessive consumption indicated a concern more for maintaining the established social hierarchy than for dealing with any metaphysical anxiety over extravagance in style of living. The latter was fine, so long as it fit one's station and class. Controlling the use and exploitation of luxurious commodities was a matter for the secular arm of governments rather than the church.

Oddly, it was not the despots of authoritarian regimes but their counterparts in the more or less republican governments of Venice and Florence who initiated the most legislation to manage luxurious consumption. These were also the two international centers of the commercial luxury trade throughout the Renaissance. Long before Savonarola's army of "elected children of God" burned the "vanities" of Florence, the city would pass more than sixty ordinances, and Venice some forty laws, attempting to control, if not eliminate, the spread of luxury. The preamble of the sumptuary law of Padua in 1504 lays out a misogynous indictment against the evils of female luxury—a common proscription—and how it had undermined Padua's economy, rather than, as Adam Smith would later argue, making things boom:

> The nature and condition of the female sex, full of vanity through sloth, cause of many ills, and the lack of prudence of those who badly weigh their affairs and the harmful expenses made for new fashions and superfluous ornaments, lead this poor city of Padua to great misery, scandalize the minds of the good, who desire to live well, and, what is worse, disturb many marriages which would have been made, if it were not for these lascivious and excessive luxuries, which are displeasing to God and to the world and are of bad example. And this occurs because no one wants to appear inferior to his companion, and many are constrained to spend more than their condition can support; and in this way the city is filled with poverty.[15]

Exploring the nexus between luxury and capitalism, Werner Sombart in his *Luxus und Kapitalismus*, published in 1903, identified a change in sexual values that began sometime in early modern Europe: sex and love, in which women played the decisive role, became secularized. In the chapter called "The Secularization of Love" in the 1922 English translation, his argument went like this: Around the thirteenth century or a bit later, a "hedonistic aesthetic conception of woman" began to emerge that was in irreconcilable opposition to the religious and institutional restraints limited to procreation, to which love had been subjected in former times. "Free love" appeared on the medieval scene, liberating a new class of women known by such names as *courtisane, maîtresse, grande cocotte, cortegiana*. Think of Titian, Giorgione, Ariosto, and Rabelais. According to Sombart's labels, these terms designated women who served "as objects of illicit love" and who played a powerful part in shaping the future pattern of the age of capitalism. Suddenly these new, liberated women

UNINTENDED CONSEQUENCES 117

began to decorate the courts of Europe, large and small, introducing not only liberated sex but also a taste for wealth, glitter, conspicuous consumption, and grand entertainments. The concentrated demand for fine design, rare materials, and craftsmanship to serve the cultivated tastes of courtiers and their circles established the foundations of the elite European luxury trades. Inevitably, the bourgeois wives of bankers, merchants, and government dignitaries followed the taste for fashion and extravagance set by the court and carried it into the more inhibited society at large, the beginnings of consumerism, however limited in its market. "In the last analysis," Sombart wrote, "it is our sexual life that lies at the root of the desire to refine and multiply the means of stimulating our senses, for sensuous pleasure and erotic pleasure are essentially the same. Indubitably the primary cause of the development of any kind of luxury is most often to be sought in consciously or unconsciously operative sex impulses."[16]

This brief sketch barely cuts the surface of Sombart's suggestive interpretation of the sexual dynamics of luxury that he then connects with the genesis of capitalism. Making the pleasure of sex and sensual gratification the operative impulse for the origin of modern luxury, he then takes the next bold step:

> For this reason we find luxury in the ascendant wherever wealth begins to accumulate and the sexuality of a nation freely expressed. On the other hand, wherever sex is denied expression, wealth begins to be hoarded instead of being spent; thus goods are accumulated, especially in such abstract forms as precious metals, as in more recent periods.[17]

In his final chapter called "Capitalism: The Child of Luxury," Sombart moves to the eighteenth century and the countries in which the capitalist consumer system was beginning to expand. Here he found that the liberal friends of "progress" and the capitalist philosophy were also the strongest advocates of material luxury, which in turn stimulated industry. He also argues effectively to establish at this stage the critical influence of women on the growth of market capitalism through their tastes of style in houses, furnishings, theaters, restaurants, shops, travel, and luxury hotels. The only anxiety of the new capitalists was that this spending on trinkets and baubles might jeopardize the accumulation of capital on which the system was built.

Adam and Eve did not make even a cameo appearance in Sombart's *Luxury and Capitalism*. But there was no dispute between the church of Saint Augustine and the church of Savonarola, Martin Luther, John Calvin, and John Knox that it was Adam and Eve who had introduced disruptive sex, a penchant for needless worldly pleasures, and enjoyment of the luxury of the weed-free Garden of Paradise without working or suffering puritan guilt. (After all, the notion of capitalism and its connection with sex through luxe would not arise until the early twentieth century.) Their original sin, according to Christianity's orthodox interpretation, famously led to the "great chain of vice"—inexorable luxury of unrestrained sensual pleasure, corruption, and death.

The First Couple, and all parents that came after them, transmitted their genetic weakness for sensuality and the portmanteau of other sins that followed in its train. Unpredictable, ambiguous, elusive, luxury as a metaphor for corruption, lust, avarice, ambition, and pride was "so universal, so old, so deeply rooted in the minds of men," it could no more be eliminated than death or taxes. The established medieval church concluded that to do God's work it needed the institutions of government to maintain civil authority, helping to preserve order and defeat the devil's repeated interference. Instead of eliminating luxury, managing it and assigning its uses according to position and office was the realistic, practical strategy to come to terms with the world's imperfections.

The church drew up canons to support civil legislation—protection of property, including slaves, and the separation and preservation of classes—while governments gradually took over the church's moral functions, condemning excessive spending, gambling, swearing, drunkenness, and disorderly conduct.[18] Both institutions recognized and embraced what they believed to be the fixed hierarchy of society. With established rules of conduct and behavior according to rank, freedom of consumption, comfort, and magnificence were reserved for the most elite circle of power, wealth, and prestige. Even if holy war was not overtly made against luxury's threat, everyone recognized that if the wrong sort indulged in unseemly excess, they would invite God's punishment. Both church and state saw serious violations of this rule as akin to heresy, and men and women were exiled, beaten, fined, locked up, and even executed if they violated the agreed-upon hierarchy of consumption.

Before the Reformation, sumptuary laws, enacted by the secular state, were administered by ecclesiastical courts that regularly enforced "consumption by rank." This church-state cooperation was particularly close in trying to maintain social harmony while controlling consumption—both institutions had a stake in the stability of the existing hierarchy. The city fathers of Bologna saw signs of status in the details of women's dress, so they decreed that only wives and daughters of knights could wear full dresses of gold cloth and that gold sleeves were only allowed for those of notaries and bankers. Sleeves of crimson would be adequate for women representing the lesser order of society. Patricians of the city of Nuremberg, Germany, were restricted by law as to the number of out-of-town guests attending a wedding, as well as the cost of wedding presents. In sixteenth-century Augsburg, Germany, laws carefully calibrated the amount to be spent on wedding rings according to class: a hundred and fifty gulden for patricians, seventy-five for merchants, and only three for ordinary workers. Similar rules also addressed graduated expenditures on funerals.

As the leaders of the radical Protestant revolution consolidated their gains against Rome, the metaphor of "luxury" became an integral part of their moral vocabulary attacking all manner of human sins—particularly the excesses of the clergy, along with the papacy's princely, hereditary court that dominated the church and its inner workings. The rejection of epicurean Rome, its traditional religious aesthetics, and its nonchalant dissipation became a useful strategy to advance the audacious Protestant doctrine. It was also an opportunity for Protestant faith to concentrate the spiritual imagination of the masses as it sought perfect communion with the Holy Spirit without external assistance stimulating the bodily senses. This policy involved a moral difference, not just a difference of sensual indulgence to manipulate unpredictable emotions and tainted thoughts. Aesthetics originated in sensual pleasure, leading to desire and temptation, on to sin and damnation. In the history of Christianity and of Islam, as Jasper Griffin has pointed out, there has been a recurring tension between the appeal of beauty, "dangerous to look upon" (which may or may not be "luxury" in the orthodox sense), and the contradictory commands that desires and energy must be focused "on values which should be ascetic, spiritual and ... explicitly anti-aesthetic."[19] According to the new doctrine of reform, Christian worship—in words, gestures, and the space where it was conducted—had to be cleansed and "purified" by removing all those sensual distractions of beautiful paintings and sculpture; the glorious sounds of choir, organ, trumpets, and bells; the intoxicating smell of incense—not only in worship but also in all aspects of life—that could arouse the unruly senses. The most zealous Protestant reformers encouraged the destruction of churches, religious art works, images, statues, pipe organs, and clerical regalia, setting off a wave of iconoclastic urban riots throughout northern Europe in the sixteenth century.

The medieval church had already dealt with Adam's sin of intellectual pride in his quest for knowledge—"the original sin"—by turning it into a sexual sin, symbolized by the temptations of the bodies of women, beginning with Eve. Theology and common sense proved that women were the source of spiritual and sexual peril. This shift, allowing regulation of consumption by both canon and secular law in the name of morality and physical modesty, would remain a part of the background of moral legislation into the twenty-first century.[20] It is not surprising that in carrying out God's laws of morality amidst the temptations of luxurious indulgence in fashionable clothing and ornamentation as expressions of the sins of pride, lust, and envy, legal and theological battles could take place over the precise amount of flesh a woman was permitted to expose between her neck and breast or the number of rings she could wear. This attempted control of luxury by law directed at women and their right of self-expression becomes a part of the history of gender wars.[21]

Women's necklines, which might plunge into indecent exposure, seem to be a particular obsession of sumptuary laws. In 1498, the city of Milan legally limited the amount of flesh that could be revealed above the neckline of a woman's dress to the width of one finger placed sideways below the collarbone. There are records of members of the clergy carefully measuring a woman's exposed flesh above her collar before she could join in the Eucharist. This erotic area was, of course, the main place to display jeweled treasures of rare and expensive luxe, surrounded by soft, diaphanous silks or rich velvets to stress the sexual tensions between exhibitionism and modesty, voyeurism and fetishism. At the height of the glorified female nude in Renaissance paintings, the naked body's potency is increased by the surrounding voluptuous and expensive fabrics. Elizabeth Taylor instinctively and unapologetically understood this ancient, magnetic attraction when she displayed in her alluring, deep cleavage the fabulous 33-carat Krupp diamond Richard Burton had given her.

The Reformation debates over wealth, led by John Calvin and his followers, drew their sumptuary code from a literal reading of the Bible. It was the duty of the church elders to act as *custos morum* (guardian of morals) of the community in the strictest fashion. Many of the more moderate reformers, however, would come to agree with the comfortable words of the more pragmatic Italian cleric, that riches in themselves were neither good nor bad: it all depended on how they were used. When the Dutch faced their own "embarrassment of riches" in the sixteenth and seventeenth centuries, they came to the same conclusion. This was in spite of John Calvin's warnings that "wealth is generally the mother of extravagance" and a serious breeder of sin.[22] But in the historical circumstances of great prosperity through commerce and thrift, the native sensibilities of the solid, rich Protestant Dutch burghers allowed them to go further in creating an enviable civilization of commonsense balance and enlightened moderation that seemed to avoid any uncomfortable burden of guilt over getting and spending. To self-satisfied Dutchmen, "it was a 'demi-paradise' of freedom and affluence."[23] An important voice in shaping Dutch Protestantism's attitude to salvation and worldly riches was that of the theologian Jacobus Arminius. Contrary to Calvin's hard doctrine of predestination, he argued that God's "irresistible grace" did not conflict with material achievement through hard work and frugality. This linking of economic success with virtue was to have a significant influence on Charles and John Wesley. Their preaching the Methodist evangelical gospel of "profitable virtue" and a "zeal for good works" would in turn profoundly shape American Protestant fundamentalism.

The astonishing Dutch civilization of the seventeenth century had emerged in little more than two centuries, and many members of its parvenu ruling class looked to the superior, more sophisticated Baroque manners and style of France, turning their back on their own provincial, rough-hewn traditions. It was, however, Dutchmen of strong Protestant convictions with a moralistic bent who delivered the most severe criticism of what appeared to be a departure from the virtues of enterprise and thrift that could lead to ruin. Foreign manners and rampant materialism, it was claimed, were already sapping the nation's strength.[24] It would take the mad speculation of tulipmania when on February 5, 1637, affluent burghers abandoned all self-control and bid up a single tulip bulb to 5,200 guilders, twenty times the average annual wedge of urban workers. Within a week, the bubble burst the climax of the country's fifty years of a booming economy and ready money to burn.

The historical background of this more independent society, with fewer signs of rigorous political, social, and ecclesiastical hierarchy, was that feudal, seigniorial controls had never been firmly established among the Dutch peasantry. By 1500, as the historian Jonathan Israel has written, the greater part of the Low Countries comprised owners of small fee-simple holdings, whose values were far removed from the aristocratic institutions of church and court in most of Europe.[25] In their heterogeneous composition, the citizens of the United Provinces created a capitalist consumer society out of religious toleration and individualism born of the Reformation's disputes over God's truths. Reformed Protestantism never became the established church or worship made compulsory. To the Dutch, faith was a private matter of individual choice. It would set the country apart from other states and nations of Baroque Europe inspired by the church's Counter-Reformation, where a vast wall between the powerful rich and the majority still appeared impregnable, even after all of the catastrophic human and financial costs of waging war for God. For more and more people in the seventeenth and eighteenth centuries, particularly those in the British colonies of North America, the Dutch model seemed the lesser of two evils.

The Dutch struggle for independence from authoritarian Spanish rule began in 1566 with violent assaults on the Spanish occupation underpinned by the Catholic Church. Spain retaliated with ruthless military efficiency leading to a war of liberation that would last—with interruptions—until the 1640s. Upon the conversion of William of Orange to the Reformed Confession, the more progressive Calvinists of the northern provinces transformed the war into a successful campaign against the reactionary Spanish church and the hated Inquisition.

This protracted political and economic struggle leading to the establishment of the Dutch Republic gave the evolution of the Calvinist Dutch church a distinctively different character, reflecting its particular past and willing to compromise with the realities of secular Dutch society. The theologically orthodox Genevan Calvinism (with its morality courts to enforce and supervise conformity to the language of the Bible interpreted by John Calvin) did not fit the religious (and cultural) eclecticism of all Protestant reformers. As a result, the unique Dutch experience with its humanism—along with Calvinism's individual fundamentalism as it was expressed and encouraged in Switzerland, Germany, France, England, Scotland, and New England, each with its own defining character—makes it difficult to put those who called themselves "Calvinists" under the same theological umbrella.[26]

A more flexible, commonsense interpretation of the scriptures appealed to the country's colorful mixture of Calvinists, Lutherans, Remonstrants, Mennonites, and Jews, along with significant enclaves of Catholics, who managed to live side by side with a reasoned ecumenical restraint. Despite Calvin's admonitions on the moral dangers of material excess and conspicuous consumption, the Dutch worked out rules and conventions that accommodated their love of comfort, and the pleasures of the table and the flesh encouraged by their extraordinary prosperity. Instead of tempting perdition, most Dutchmen praised their earthly blessings as part of God's mercy.

In the best Dutch tradition, Hollanders continued to celebrate with earthy, provincial exuberance the growing profusion of the things of this world that poured into their port cities and booming trade. By the seventeenth century, the Dutch Republic had become the dominant commercial center of Europe, so it is no surprise that the old tensions among materialism, luxury, and morality faded or were reinterpreted. The idioms of scriptural piety and Calvinist fundamentalism flowing from the pulpit more often emphasized historic Dutch patriotism and traditions supported by providential guidance according to a divine plan than it acted as a divisive force over what and how to consume in the marketplace. Foreign visitors were shocked by Dutch society's hearty egalitarianism, its lack of respect for the monarchy, nobility, and established lines of social and ecclesiastical hierarchy. In the highly urbanized society of the Dutch Republic, the old, rigid format of an aristocratic hierarchy ruling a servile peasantry was no longer relevant. The new free-market forces of commerce, banking, and the financial institutions could be managed in an orderly, humane manner for the benefit of all.

The Dutch version of Lutheran piety was inclined, in Max Weber's words in his treatise on the Protestant ethic, "to leave the unrestrained vitality of instinctive action and uncomplicated emotional life undiminished," without constant self-examination and regimentation.[27] This did not mean that there was no wariness of repeated excess resulting from the country's abundance that could bring on the calamities of excessive luxury and wanton self-indulgence. Prosperity, with its psychological impact of well-being, would continue only so long as divine laws and the doctrine of grace were obeyed, although no one seemed to agree on a clear list of infractions, or who exactly had authority to adjudicate offenses, or which theology provided the most acceptable rules. As Simon Schama put it, "What was needed was a set of rules and conventions by which wealth could be absorbed in ways compatible with the godly purposes for which the Republic had been created."[28]

Alcohol and tobacco were both very profitable to the Dutch Republic and the excessive abuse of both had deep cultural roots. Though they were traders and producers, their own addictive consumption of these products greatly contributed to Dutch prosperity, no matter how much the moralists disapproved. The Dutch reputation for hard drinking reached back into the dim medieval past. In Amsterdam alone in 1613, there were 518 alehouses.[29] The country was also famous for its gin, regularly drunk in excess with the usual results of brawls and domestic troubles.

The old ebb and flow between feast and fast, set by the pre-Reformation religious calendar but reaching into ancient Netherlandish culture, was preserved into the republic and enthusiastically observed in the face of militant Calvinist condemnation. In his pre-Reformation painting called *The Battle of Carnival and Lent*, a comic-serious tableau, Pieter Bruegel the Elder documents in earthy detail snozzled pagans—the common people—cavorting around the allegorical character of Carnival, sitting astride his cask waving a skewer of roasted capons. Community feasting on inordinate amounts of food was an ancient Dutch tradition that remained undaunted by Catholic or equally militant Calvinist reformers. Later, humanist painters such as Jan Steen, Pieter Aertsen, and Joachim Beuckelaer, who addressed both popular and religious themes, produced many pictures of hearty Rabelaisian kitchen scenes and prodigious market stalls piled high with luscious fruits and vegetables, which presented a realistic but enigmatic cultural terrain "in which humanist moralizing is set in the here-and-now jostle of contemporary life."[30]

The popular picture of the Dutch described by foreign travelers was one of a tight-fisted people with an instinctive aversion to luxury and conspicuous consumption. Many believed that this tradition of frugality and a naturally austere way of life created the foundation of their material success. More critical travelers who held to aristocratic refinement were not impressed by the bourgeois Dutch civilization with its parsimonious signs of material luxury designating rank.

But by the 1660s, some observers believed that prosperity was being squandered on vain luxury by a falling away of old habits and manners. Dutch moralists begin to sound like Roman stoics complaining that sybaritic pleasures were replacing native republican virtues. It is doubtful that the self-satisfied burghers and merchant classes paid much attention to the sporadic diatribes from the pulpit. Even if their discreet houses lining the canals of Amsterdam looked puny compared to the palaces of Florence or Genoa, they were five or six times as deep as they were wide, providing plenty of room for conspicuous display of grand furniture, tapestries, Turkish rugs, china, and silver surrounded by walls and walls of new Dutch paintings. For a society of new money, Rembrandt's paintings, with their rich, encrusted surfaces, smacked of luxe and appealed to the voluptuous stoicism that was peculiarly Dutch. One thinks of Rembrandt's late self-portrait with the artist's resigned yet rugged face above his burnished gold Middle Eastern gown tied up with a dashing red silk belt, his head covered with an exotic black beret from another era.

While most writers on the subject of economy believed there were connections between frugality, prosperity, and civic morality, there were those who thought that the gratification of desires was in the national interest of commerce, compatible with its good fortune. Luxury itself entered the discourse on trade and commerce. Defending the morality of luxury, Bernard Mandeville of Rotterdam, whom we will meet again in London, dismissed as humbug the theory that Dutch austerity was key to the country's economic achievements. "The Dutch may ascribe their present grandeur to the virtue and frugality of their ancestors," he wrote in his satire *The Fable of the Bees*, published in 1714 "but what made that contemptible spot on earth so considerable among powers of Europe has been their political wisdom on postponing everything to merchandise and navigation [and] the unlimited liberty of conscience that is enjoyed among them." History, reason, and humanism rather than Calvinistic piety and zeal supplied the answer. Above all, the peace they achieved through "the hardships and the calamities of war" allowed the Dutch to develop a comfortable and humanely sensual society, not their careful attention to the strict ethics of the Calvinist Protestant religion:

> In pictures and marble they are profuse; in their buildings and gardens they are extravagant to folly. In other countries you may meet with stately courts and palaces which nobody can expect in a commonwealth where so much equality is observed as there is in [Holland]; but in all Europe you shall find no private buildings so sumptuously magnificent as a great many merchants' and other gentlemen's houses are in Amsterdam, and in some of the great cities of the small province; and the generality of those that build there, lay out a greater proportion of their estates on the houses they dwell in than nay people upon the earth.[31]

In his mischievous exaggeration, Mandeville was not comparing the public buildings and merchants' houses of Amsterdam, The Hague, or Rotterdam with Versailles or Blenheim Palace; rather he was making the point that a small, cohesive, commercial society could establish its own rules of personal consumption and balanced standards, enjoying the republic as a consumer's middle-class emporium for life's civilized pleasures without giving up the Dutchman's religious dedication to savings and investment.

The symptoms of conspicuous consumption, spreading with the unprecedented and wide availability of desirable things as well as necessities, become the hallmark of Holland in the late-seventeenth and eighteenth centuries. The French philosopher and mathematician René Descartes, who spent his most productive years in the country, was astonished to find the congenial atmosphere of Amsterdam's booming economy "an inventory of the possible." Where on earth, he asked, "could one choose where all the commodities and all the curiosities one could wish for were as easy to find as in this city." A decade later, the English traveler John Evelyn marveled at the "Assemblys of Shipps, & Vessels which continually ride before the Citty, which is certainely the most busie concourse of mortall men, now upon the face of the whole Earth & the most addicted to commerce."[32]

The testimony of these visitors to the astonishing "embarrassment of riches" undercuts the clichés of sobriety and asceticism of the protocapitalist ethos of the early modern culture of the Netherlands disciplined by military and environmental hardship. "There were more mysteries of the flesh and spirit at work in Rembrandt's Holland," Schama has observed, than are allowed in all the standard platitudes on austere Dutch culture, or for that matter in the rich milieu of Johannes Vermeer's calm Delft interiors. The men and women who inhabit Vermeer's whitewashed rooms represent a kind of sensibility that manages to unite their very being with the tactile satins and brocades of their elegant skirts, the lace, pearls, and imported blue-and-white porcelain, above all with the lengthening silver light shining through tall windows. Take, for example, the red-coated officer in a grand felt hat casually posed with the richly dressed, amused young woman in the Frick Collection's *Officer and Laughing Girl*, or the lady standing before a window with the light caressing a pale green curtain featured in *Young Woman Reading a Letter at an Open Window*, now in Dresden. These are hardly celebrations of the work ethic of Calvinist faith. All the conventional arguments over the morality of the epicurean pleasures are transcended by the sensual beauty and serenity the artist has bestowed on the stuff of this world.

6

PLAIN LIVING AND HIGH THINKING
Piety and Prosperity in the American Colonies

⎯⎯⎯⎯ ⚬⚭⚬ ⎯⎯⎯⎯

Their limited resources dictating the terms of survival, the first wave of Puritan settlers developed their own inner state of grace through a "less is more" determination to endure life's burdens and meager earthly rewards. Anxious about one's status as an elect of God, the most inspired Reformed Protestants embraced an "inner asceticism" reflected in hard work, self-discipline, and austerity. According to the tenets of Puritan self-restraint, enduring the harsh reality of New England climate and soil they confronted became an act of daily obedience to God's will. The Puritan myth would linger on as an increasingly ambiguous part of the larger, complex narrative of national purpose long after sheer physical endurance was no longer a major challenge and undreamed American prosperity began in earnest in the nineteenth century.

What Max Weber called "ascetic Protestantism" was a wholesale rejection of all things of this world magnified in the lives of the first generations of New England immigrants. This renunciation (exaggerated in the endless retelling of the saga) became an element of the moral, economic, and political character of the seventeenth-century transatlantic experiment. Calvinist, Quaker, Puritan, nonconforming—whatever label that was attached—this "Protestant character" was expressed not only by what people said and did and how they lived, but also by what they hoped to become and how spiritual values would shape their spare existence. In domestic life, sober, pious concerns proclaimed the Protestant household's godly identity. Without the slightest feeling of deprivation, passions were to be buttoned up with good Calvinist buttons, and bodies dressed in drab clothes were to rest in stiff chairs and hard beds. In many ways the radical Protestant rejection of "luxury," although far more severe, still faintly echoed something of the Apollonian ideal of the ancient Greeks who regarded excess as a dangerous retreat from rational order and moderation into chaos.[1]

The God of John Calvin demanded that the true worshiper, recognizing his own "total depravity," reflect on God and his transcendence alone, without any physical images, objects, ceremony, or sensual pleasures to deflect the scriptures' central message that there is but one God who demands total and absolute concentration. As Calvin wrote in his *Institutes*, "Those whose eyes rove about in contemplating idols, betray that their minds are not diligently intent upon this doctrine."[2] Any form of distraction from God's message was to be banished. Identifying "sin" with "the sins of the flesh" became a part of the fundamentalist Protestant theology.

The more rigid Protestant thinking held that since wealth and its dangers were always with us in this world, any striving after it was pointless—a waste of time in the face of God's promise of life everlasting. If there was to be rest, it would be found in the next life and not in idle pleasures of looking at art, listening to music, watching a play. Gossip, soft living, and sleeping too long were morally reprehensible. Time was something to be esteemed and dedicated to God's worship, Richard Baxter wrote in his popular book *The Saint's Everlasting Rest*, first published in 1650. Not only was time money but spending time on small talk or "unprofitable company" embezzled it from meditation on life in heaven.[3]

As Calvin's reforming followers (most intensely the Puritans) struggled to explore the mystery of God's presence, their desire to live simple lives, appropriately dressed according to the Word of God, shaped an aesthetic sometimes called the plain style. In the very plainness of their worship, their churches, and their houses and domestic lives there was an attempt to express transcendent values not of this world. The paring away of all superfluities and rejection of useless ornaments, images, and comfort beyond bare necessities was the very essence of the Protestant imagination, which revealed the "longing to see the world remade, restored to its Edenic purity."[4] Even the dark, earthy colors of their clothes and household linens and their natural coarseness, the rag carpets recycled from worn-out shirts and dresses, the abstract plainest of furniture served as the perfect backdrop to the pilgrim's internal search for salvation by continued examination of his sinful inadequacies and surroundings.[5] It was, as the Elizabethan historian Patrick Collinson put it, "a society suffering from visual anorexia."[6]

What comes through in the early Puritan sermons, diaries, and journals is the preoccupation and obsession with the body—particularly the female—and everything related to it. Any concession to the body's needs beyond survival could be traced to the flesh and lust, summed up in the metaphor of luxury. If the Puritans were not exactly ascetics, opposed to all earthly pleasures, they at least believed the pleasures of the flesh must be subordinate to the greater glory of God and never stray into excesses of lust.

Just what made up the simple life and when it exceeded acceptable boundaries have been as hard to determine as luxury's shifting, elusive qualities. The dictionary defines the noun "simplicity" as "direct, clear; free of pretense or guile; free of vanity, ostentation, and undue display; free of secondary complications and distractions." Protestant immigrants would have no problem with this definition, but given all the opportunities for material success if they worked hard according to the Gospels, living a simple life was not easy, and it was full of ambiguity. The fight was not against wealth and profit but against the lusts of the flesh and lust for possessions that prosperity inevitably brought with it. For the "true warfaring Christian" it was a lifelong battle, but the rejection of sin and the temptations of the world by the faithful was well worth the struggle because "a transcendent realm of plenitude" was said to exist for those mortals whose character could overcome their human weaknesses.[7]

The Puritans regularly proclaimed that while they were forced to live in this world, they must be "dead" to its disorderly intrusions, or at least view it with a "weaned affection" so as not to be diverted from the higher calling of the spirit. In his study *Visible Saints: The History of a Puritan Idea*, Edmund Morgan's metaphor of "visible" is useful in considering the Puritan world and its rejection of all outward signs of excess. Anything hinting at the superfluous—elegant colorful clothes, sumptuous houses, refined tastes—was a sign of greed, lust, pride; the worship of wealth and prestige amounted to a "spiritual felony," an affront to genuine Godliness according to the Commandments. By developing an inner discipline and putting strict moral bounds on what people desired or actually needed, Puritanism "was as much a practice of restraint through temperament," the poet Robert Frost sensibly observed, as it was living by rigorous, literal, moral principles of conduct.[8] Or to put it in its historical context, the Protestant asceticism that would become an expressive part of the American character was in fact deeply rooted in European origins and shaped by European culture and European quarrels—not uniquely American or of an "exceptional" American quality, as some have claimed.[9] Wave after wave of these Protestant groups with all manner of theological and ethical shadings of "faith" would move to the American colonies looking for a place to worship freely.

Although similar in many ways to the Puritans, the Religious Society of Friends known as Quakers was a movement of Christian believers who in the mid-seventeenth century England drew their strength by attempting to follow what the Puritans' considered the radical belief in the individual's "inner light of Christ." To many, Puritan sobriety was being stretched and worshipped in a way that went beyond Christian "plainness." The Quakers' austere manners and houses, sober dress reduced to a uniform, and plain speech, shorn of all lexical ornament, told the world around them that they had taken control over every detail of their existence according to the dictates of their inner beliefs: "Where is our acknowledgment of God," Calvin asked, "if our minds be fixed on the splendour of our garments?"[10] This meant, regardless of the Lord's bounty, a resolute exclusion of anything that might be seen or judged as self-indulgence, introducing its undoubted train of sins. Their moral inhibitions instinctively rejected all consumption except things of utility—the fruit of hard, productive work. In the portraits of Puritans, Quakers, and their descendants, we see repeated the same hard, pale, thin-lipped, northern European face of Protestant denial, a stereotype of the tenacious features of the Revolutionary leadership, the adventurers of the western frontier, and the nineteenth-century industrial buccaneers of steel and railroads who would turn up in American history books as long as WASP morality remained in the ascendant. Acquiring wealth merely to live a life of pleasure and indolence was out of the question. So was any moral questioning of the source or purpose of earthly riches; they were God's blessings and the generosity of nature. It would be several generations later, in the nineteenth century, that the American-made "genteel tradition" would emerge in all its respectable banality and become obsessed with co-opting the new material abundance and undreamed of "luxury" in the name of "truth and beauty," most of it with roots in European traditions. Unsurprising, it failed to invigorate and transform, in the words of the historian of American letters Vernon Parrington, "a timid and uncreative" native culture.[11]

For Quakers as well as Puritans, sustaining a common idea of sin required a very high degree of psychological and political control with a premium on community approval. But the Puritans were more relentless in monitoring and condemning their sexual desires than they were in insisting on plain speech or the most ordinary dress. It was a sexual asceticism that differed only in degree with the monastic austerity of the early church and the Desert Fathers. In his tract *A Garden of Spiritual Flowers*, published in 1616, Richard Rogers drew up an impressive list of subtle violations of the flesh that could lead to even more unthinkable transgressions (anticipating the inventive censures of the Hollywood's Hays Office of Censorship or more recent alarm over exposed breasts on television). "There are nine fore-runners of [the sins of luxury]," Roger darkly intones, "voluptuous eating, scurrilous talk, a discovered dug, a naked breast, frizzled hair, artificial painting, costly perfumes, a rolling eye, and unchaste foot." Eating, in all of its pleasurably indulgent forms, could lead to more serious temptations, "for when men have filled their bellies and crammed their paunches as full of good cheer, wine, and strong drink as their skin can hold, what are they meet for, or what mind they else but adultery and uncleanness. . . . Except they be abstemious in diet, they will be much troubled with lust." Even one's dreams were not beyond scrutiny and suspicion. While "dreams are neither good nor sinful simply in themselves, because they are not rational and voluntary, [still] they may be sinful by participation. And the acts that make them sinful are either such as go before or such as follow."[12]

The most uncompromising among them in their zeal—particularly the Quakers—anticipated by three hundred years Adolf Loos's indictment in 1908 that "ornament was a crime," one of the clichés of modernist aesthetics. Although for other reasons, the Austrian architect (at war with late-nineteenth-century vulgarity of the Viennese bourgeoisie) would have agreed with the Quaker maxim that simplicity in all things was the ultimate "truth." When the

Pennsylvania Quaker preacher John Woolman detected a decorated panel of "sundry sorts of Carved work and imagery," outside his cabin on the ship he had taken to England, he immediately moved his quarters to steerage in order to avoid the sin of looking upon such disturbing luxury.[13] A country Quaker minister refused to cross the threshold of the elegant house of a wealthy Philadelphia Friend when he saw the rich oriental rugs spread out on the polished floor of the entry hall.

The moral responsibility of American followers of Calvin to make every thought, action, and choice serve God would be overwhelming. Even as growing abundance drove an increasingly complex society, and the virtues of consumption replaced the early colonial vision of a community of saints, the national character continued to reflect a conflict and contradiction between the historic promise and the reality of a booming market of temptations.[14] Moral pronouncements delivered with Hemingway terseness against idolatrous material culture increasingly fell on deaf ears. The predictable categories of "superfluities, necessaries and conveniences" presented a language of quicksand that discouraged a common interpretation. The Puritan spoken and written language itself was carefully scrutinized, scorning all similes, metaphors, and fancy tropes unless they were biblical. Colored adjectives and adverbs could stir up sinful thoughts and stimulate the imagination; they had to be dropped, even if the pruning impoverished the language.

The Pilgrims on the *Mayflower*, sighting land off the coast of New England on a blustery November day in 1620, and the Puritans, arriving ten years later on the *Arbella*, framed the moral dilemma they had first encountered in the expanding economy of seventeenth-century England. How were they to preserve the Christian piety and virtue they brought with them if, through God's grace, plain living, and hard work, their untested experiment turned out to be an unintended commercial success producing prosperity and useless excess— all those temptations they had rejected in the home country? Resolving this unsettling tension between piety and prosperity was uppermost on the minds of these first generations of New England settlers.

Well aware that it would be hard going in the beginning, John Winthrop, the first governor of the Massachusetts Bay Colony, believed that following the Calvinist life of denial would pay unexpected spiritual dividends in the long run: "God will by this means bring us to repent of our Intemperance here at home, and so cure us of that disease, which sends many of us to hell."[15] But only two months after arriving, Winthrop fatalistically saw the devil already organizing "his forces against us . . . so that I think here are some persons who never showed such wickedness in England as they have done here."[16]

From his "very wild, and dissolute youth," Winthrop, a member of the English gentry, understood the ubiquitous specter of worldly indulgence as a cliché for the all-too-human temptations preying on the life of the spirit. But there were also the contradictory requirements for the self-righteous Puritan that he do whatever job or "calling" that was set before him to the best of his ability and accept as God's mysteries whatever rewards came his way. Beyond putting together the essentials of everyday living—food, shelter, clothing—the ethics of work would produce its own spiritual reward. It was to achieve, as Max Weber underlined in his study of Protestant ethics, "the eradication of *uninhibited* indulgence in instinctive pleasure.[17] But any unexpected worldly prizes produced by hard labor were not to be taken as a signal of heavenly approval. Since God had withheld any signs of who had pleased him and who had fallen short, most people were left with an agonizing uncertainty hanging over them whether they were headed for "eternal glory or eternal torment."[18]

Determined that he could resist all the worldly temptations without literally retreating into a monk's cell, Winthrop fortified himself by requesting of his Puritan God to "crucifie the world unto me, that though I cannot avoyed to live among the baites and snares of it, yet it may be so truly dead unto me and I unto it, as I may no otherwise love, use or delight in any the most pleasant, profitable, etc, earthly comforts of this life, than I doe the ayre which I continually drawe in, or the earthe which I ever tread upon, or the skye which I ever behould."[19]

The Puritan contradictions regarding the "baites and snares" of this life were also very much on the mind of the Reverend John Cotton, who arrived three years after Winthrop to become the colony's chief spiritual voice. Echoing John Calvin's conclusion that "riches are a means to help the needy," Cotton came up with a measured formula of balancing piety and unexpected prosperity as a practical Puritan standard of worldly ambition in the new "city upon a hill" built in the wilderness: "We may desire wealth from God, partly out of necessity and expediency, and partly to leave our posterity. . . . But we are never to desire more than we can make good use of."[20] Any surplus beyond everyday requirements was to be given away to the poor and needy as a Christian duty. The idea of "waste" was dismissed in the motto "Waste not want not."

Sustaining piety in the midst of prosperity has been an unresolved paradox in the American experiment from the beginning to the present. Although very different in background and motivation, many like those who signed the Mayflower Compact and the leaders, divines, and magistrates of the Bay Colony not only intended to create a kingdom of the saints but a place for immigrants to take advantage of God-given opportunities. "This is the place," the poet Edward Johnson announced, "where the Lord will create a new Heaven, and a new Earth in new Churches, and a new commonwealth together."[21] But in this vision of an Edenic garden, others saw unlimited economic possibilities—gold, furs, fish, timber, and land—for all who could grab it at the first opportunity, not unlike John Smith's fellow adventurers planning a colony in Virginia. Smith wrote in 1616, "I am not so simple to think that ever any other motive than wealth will erect there a Commonweal [sic]."[22] These two contradictory perspectives—the pursuit of earthly happiness measured largely by material success on the one hand, and the search for spiritual contentment on the other—have remained entangled throughout American history.

In the eyes of English Puritans during the first quarter of the seventeenth century, the moral environment had seriously deteriorated into "intemperance of all excess of riot." With the burgeoning wealth brought in by the aggressive empire and ruled by the dissolute, amoral Stuart monarchy, English society had slipped from Spartan, primitive simplicity into moral decay and luxury, compromising contemporary civilization. If the average Puritan had not experienced worldly goods directly, most knew John Bunyan's *The Pilgrim's Progress*, published in 1678, where he lists the things of "vanity" temptations promoted at the Vanity Fair. His list is all-inclusive: "houses, lands, trades, places, honours, preferences, titles, countries, kingdom, lusts, pleasures, and delights of all sorts, as whores, bawds, wives, husbands, children, masters, servants, lives, blood, bodies, souls, silver, gold, pearls, precious stones, and what not."[23] There were no limits to getting and spending at mammon's smorgasbord. It was the Christian pilgrim's duty to confront it but show the moral conviction not be

drawn into the house of horrors of Hell's shopping mall. It was a cautionary tale intended to cure any incipient shopaholic. Only those who remained
above temptation and survived with their virtues of moderation, faith, hope,
and their pocketbook intact would receive their reward of peace in the Land
of Beulah.

In his famous sermon called "The Model of Christian Charity," preached
to the passengers on the *Arbella* sailing for Massachusetts Bay in 1630 (or in
the port before they left), Winthrop warned that among the "trials and temptations" they were about to face would be unexpected economic opportunities that could cause them "to embrace the present world and prosecute our
carnal intentions, seeking great things for ourselves and our posterity." But it
became apparent that the devil had lost no time massing "his forces against
us." Within four years, and after endless sermons and warnings on the subject,
"new and immodest fashions" from London shops arrived in the colony and
were flaunted among all ranks, violating the basic Puritan ideal of simplicity.

The *Mayflower* had brought its exhausted passengers to a rocky, unpro-
ductive landfall on the Massachusetts shore not suitable for cultivation beyond
bare subsistence, so the settlers' attention quickly turned to the financial possibilities of the fur trade, specifically beaver pelts, to sustain their initial domestic needs. Pelts quickly became the colony's chief source of income. However,
the obvious economic opportunity presented by this international market was
deeply compromised by moral ambiguity because it was driven by the burgeoning European demands for the very expressions of the fashion trade denounced by the colonists.

At the beginning of the seventeenth century, stylish Europeans had become obsessed with elaborate, expensive hats and headgear demanded by not
only the aristocracy but also the military and clergy. Enterprising New Eng-
landers (and Indians) trapping, skinning, baling, and shipping tons of beaver pelts to Europe knew what they were intended for: to serve the corrupt,
decadent Old World appetites that they had rejected by their immigration for
religious reasons. The irony, needless to say, was lost on them. Whatever the
Lord's plans to elevate the moral judgment of the faithful in the New Jerusalem, the elect ignored the implications and dilemmas presented by profitable
beaver skins so that they might survive, quite aside from any abstract moral
complexities of the beaver hat markets of London and Paris.

Alarmed by signs in the streets of Boston that the pursuit of easy wealth was being driven by age-old avarice rather than Christian charity, the General Court of Massachusetts tried to outlaw the excesses. "No person, neither man or woman" the court ordered, shall make or buy clothes of "great, superfluous, and unnecessary expenses." When this directive was disregarded, detailed prohibitions were spelled out banning "immoderate great breeches, knots of ribbon, broad shoulder-bands and rails, silk rases, double ruffs and cuffs" because they were useless luxuries that only added to "the nourishment of pride." Beaver hats were not mentioned. Those who had prospered beyond their neighbors were not to flaunt their good fortune by showing off extravagant equipage, furniture, or houses or clothing. The law also ordered selectmen in each village to "take notice of apparel of the inhabitants of their several towns respectively; and whosoever they shall judge to exceed their ranks and abilities in the costliness or fashion of their apparel in any respect, especially in the wearing of ribbons or great boots (leather being so scarce a commodity in this country) lace, points, etc., silk hoods, or scarves," was to be fined accordingly. Winthrop was deeply disturbed by the lavish, un-Puritan addition and decoration Thomas Dudley, the deputy governor, was making to his house, telling him that "he did not well to bestow such cost about wainscoting and adorning his house, in the beginning of the plantation both in regard to the necessity of public charges and as an example."[24]

If some New England Puritans saw wayward extravagance in a well-crafted molding, a touch of lace at the throat, or a great boot of polished leather as both a theological flaw and a threat to the social order, a few generations later William Penn's Quakers banished all forms of sensual attractions from their lives in favor of utility and sobriety. As far as what constituted sufficient "plainness" and what represented an outward sign of spiritual abuse, the Bible, particularly the books of the Prophets, Proverbs, and the letters of Paul, along with God's inner revelations, provided all the guidance that was needed. In the pilgrimage of life, the beauty of holiness was the only aesthetic purpose and end; it required nothing else. As Penn laid out in his moral tract *No Cross, No Crown*, "The Cross of Christ . . . truly overcomes the world and leads a life of purity in the face of its allurements." Both Puritans and Quakers saw worldly "allurements" as the work of the devil's incorrigible imagination, "the forge of villainy . . . the warehouse of wickedness . . . the Sea of all abominations, which overflows into the senses." It was the duty of all who hoped for salvation to curb their appetites and avoid being snared by the world. But the fundamentalist Quakers went further in expressions of humble austerity to reach the "simplicity of Truth."[25]

Penn's rejection of the immorality and debauchery of the court of Charles II in favor of a life of modest self-denial had all the fervor of a convert overcoming a life of indulgence and luxury, something he had actually known firsthand. Penn was born in the midst of the English Civil War in 1644, the son of Adm. William Penn, the conqueror of Jamaica and a friend of the restored Stuarts, Charles and brother James, Duke of York. The younger Penn received a humanist education grounded in the classics as a gentleman scholar at Oxford. Penn then traveled widely on the continent with several friends, "persons of rank," and returned to London in 1664 where Samuel Pepys saw him and concluded that the young courtier had "a great deal, if not too much, of the French garb, and affected manner of speech and gait."[26] In appearance and style—high-heeled shoes; enormous, full-bottom wigs; lace; silver buttons; perfume—Penn easily assumed the role of a Restoration rake. But in three years, he would become a member of the Society of Friends and one of its most impassioned leaders.

Expounding the Quaker gospel and appealing to the examples of the "holy men and women" of the Bible, Penn, like a reformed addict, hoped to wipe out all dependence on superfluous luxuries among the Friends:

> How many pieces of ribbon, feathers, lace bands and the like had Adam and Eve in Paradise or out of it? What rich embroideries, silks, points, etc., had Abel, Enoch, Noah, and good old Abraham? Did Eve, Sarah, Susanna Elizabeth, and the Virgin Mary use to curl, powder, patch, paint, wear false locks of strange colors, rich points, trimmings, laced Gowns, embroidered petticoats, shoes and slip-slaps laced with silk or Silver lace and ruffled like pigeons' feet, with several yards, if not pieces of ribbons?[27]

To confront head-on any sign of excess within the households of members, particularly those who had been unwittingly successful in business, the elders of one meetinghouse issued a remarkably detailed guide to plain living:

As to chests of drawers, they ought to be plain and of one color, without swelling works. As to tables and chairs, they ought to be all made plain, without carving, keeping out of all new fashions as they come up, and to keep to the fashion that is serviceable. And as to making great moldings one above another about press-beds and clock-cases, etc, [they] ought to be avoided, only what is decent according Truth.[28]

Enforcing the Quaker aesthetics of interior decoration could not be relied on, even with such specific advice given out at meetings. In grand houses it required a pitiless clearing away of all accumulated excesses and even family heirlooms of questionable taste, much like Edith Wharton's all-out war on the suffocating bad taste of Victorian houses in late-nineteenth-century New York, New Port, and Boston. The morality of plainness was serious business, and the issue was sometimes turned over to special committees to "inspect and visit" every Quaker family to make sure that nothing was overlooked—no hidden breaches of bold "chimney pieces" or "twisted banisters." Joseph Pike, a well-to-do English Friend, recalled just how far the policing of luxury reached in his "deconstruction" of his once stylish house:

Our fine veneered and garnished cases of drawers, tables And stands, cabinets, scrutoires &c, we put away, or exchanged for decent plain ones of solid wood without superfluous garnishing or ornamental work; our wainscots or woodwork we painted of one plain colour. Our large mouldings or furnishings of paneling, &c; our swelling chimney pieces, curiously twisted banisters, we took down, and replaced with useful plain woodwork &c; our curtains with valences, drapery, and fringes that we thought too fine, we put away or cut off; our large looking glasses with decorated frames we sold or made them into smaller ones; and our closets that were laid out with many little curious or nice things were done away.[29]

Explicit Quaker restraint went further than the typical New England Puritan's in reaching for the direct divine experience or at least a glint of the Inner Light. Quakers created a radical, austere form of worship by adding prayerful silence to reinforce the visual purity of their bare meetinghouses, stripped to a structural abstraction evoking the Zen aesthetics of the seventeenth-century Villa Katsura outside Kyoto, an icon of early-twentieth-century Bauhaus.

The plain style of the Quaker meetinghouse rejected all ecclesiastical references—steeples, pulpits, altars, paneled pews—as well as decorative ornaments or fashionable details taken from the latest architectural pattern book. No highfalutin seat cushions or swelling balustrades were allowed to interfere with direct communion with God. The meetinghouse itself was built of common, local materials, construction techniques, and vernacular craftsmanship—the same that was employed in building their houses and other domestic structures—representing a visible protest against other religious building traditions of established faiths. In this physical setting of self-conscious sensory deprivation, the Quaker search for guidance of the Inner Light would not be distracted "by the pleasures of the ear, the eye, and the imagination." Its utterly functional simplicity represents the ultimate statement of Protestant standards of internal beauty.[30]

Penn's *No Cross, No Crown* spelled out the Friends' preoccupation with "the lust of the eye, the lust of the flesh and the pride of life"—all part of luxury's immoral legacy reaching back to the Greeks and Romans. His list of things to be denounced and banned from the sensible, sober life of a Quaker was both imaginative and exhaustive. Since any spare time or leisure was restricted to doing good, the innocent pleasures of gardening, bowls, parties, even "chess, riddles and drollery" were on the forbidden list. Penn combined the Gospels' command to renounce the world with the pragmatic utility unburdened by useless bric-a-brac, and customs, particularly of courtiers and people of rank:

> Several sober reasons urg'd against the vain Apparel and usual recreations of the Age (as Gold, Silver, Embroyderies, Pearls, precious Stones, Lockets, Pendants, Rings, breaded and curl'd Locks, Painting, Patching, Laces, Points, Ribonds, unnecessary change of Cloaths, superfluous Provisions out of state, costly and useless Attendence, Rich Furnitures, Plays, Parts, Mulbery and Spring-Gardens, Treats, Balls, Masks, Cards, Dice, Bowls, Chess, Romances, Comedies, Poets, Riddles, Drollery, vain and unnecessary Visits, &c) by which they are proved Inconsistent with a Christian life and very destructive in all civil Society.[31]

The first Quakers had appeared in a rustic corner of northern England. They were mostly yeoman farmers, craftsmen, and ordinary workers far removed from the sinful purlieus of Stuart London, where Penn had grown up in an established family. An orthodox Friend had no idea what a "beauty patch" on a cheek or chin was and had never been near a "ball" or "masque" or indulged in "drolleries"—such conspicuously "city" foibles did not exist in isolated provincial Quaker societies—so any rejection of these sinful signs would have required little or no effort. Like Thomas Jefferson's yeoman exemplar of his ideal republic, William Penn had envisioned that his society in the new American colony would also be made up of hardy farmers, willing to create and live a self-sufficient life of unassuming moderation where social differences were ignored or at least flattened. Like Jefferson, Penn called them "natural aristocrats," settlers capable of eliminating both "want and excess," ready to "promote good Discipline and just Government among a plain and well intending people."[32]

The size of Penn's grant of some forty-five thousand square miles of virgin territory made him a major real estate developer in the colonies. One of his first steps was to publish a promotional tract "to give some public notice" of Pennsylvania "to the world" as a place for people to settle. Since he was well known as a Quaker, "Some Account of the Province of Pennsylvania" made no mention of his religion or his plans for a holy experiment. Instead, he led with a vigorous defense of the policy of colonization as "the very seeds of nations," not only using the scriptures but also raising the classic specter of luxury to buttress his argument that it was morally right to leave the decadent Old World for the innocence of the New.[33]

Penn pointed out that some of the wisest men in history, such as "Lycurgus, Theseus and those Greeks that planted many parts of Asia," believed that they should set an example of disciplined moderation, and reminded his readers that the Roman Republic had actually "moralized the manners of the nations they subjected," conquering their barbarity rather than allowing themselves to be conquered. Nor was it the colonies that brought corruption to the empire. "For the cause of the decay of any of those states or empires was not their *plantations*, but their *luxury and corruption of manners*. For when they grew to neglect their ancient discipline that maintained and rewarded virtue and industry, and addicted themselves to *pleasure* and *effeminacy*, they debased their spirits and debauched their morals, from whence ruin did never fail to follow to any people."[34]

In the definitive summary of Quaker beliefs written by Robert Barclay in 1676, while the essence of meetinghouse testimony included the renunciation of vanities and luxury, the strict ideals were relaxed for rich converts, members of the ruling class. Penn and other Quakers of rank were allowed to define their own style of modest dress and inconspicuous living. "We shall not say that all persons are to be clothed alike," Barclay wrote, "because it will perhaps neither suit their bodies nor their estates. And if a man be clothed soberly, and without superfluity, though they be finer than that which of his servant is clothed with, we shall not blame him."[35]

Self-conscious frugality for the masses was the Quaker rule. But for the few at the top, the measured, enlightened gentility of luxury—wine, books, manicured gardens, and elevated conversations over glasses of imported rum—was not self-indulgence but rather a model of a pious, civilized model for all to admire and respect.

Samuel Fawconer's *Essay on Modern Luxury* expressed his horror at the "distemper," "frenzy," and "madness" spreading from London throughout the country, even to the colonies. While Aristotelian principles of necessity and hierarchy might still permit splendor and elegance for the ruling class to give them dignity and announce their authority, the "depraved taste" for excess remained a treacherous "intestine foe":

> Luxury is the natural parent of indolence, pusillanimity, and effeminacy, which it introduces and diffuses over the whole moral world. It unnerves the whole system of the human fabric, and breaks the force of our several powers, both of body and mind enfeebling the strength and hardiness of one, and enervating the vigour and activity of the other. So powerful is its blandishments that it works the strangest of alterations in our nature: softens the rough, makes cowards of the brave, renders the active indolent and the industrious idle.[36]

As we will see, throughout the eighteenth century the moral, political, and economic argument in which the specter of "luxury" is the ethical measure of a consumer society would continue to escalate in the colonies as well as in England and Europe. Former luxuries were beginning to be relabeled as "rich, new, innovative, curious fine, polite and imported" as the market expanded.[37] It seemed to one critic that "a whole nation habituates itself to look upon the most superfluous things as the necessaries of life and thus every day brings forth some new necessity of the same kind." Whether it was sustainable or not in the long run (and by our standards of the twenty-first century), the material, psychological reality in a nutshell was that when "Industry has furnished any Person with the indispensable Necessaries of Life, such as *Food, Raiment,* and *Lodging,* he rests not there, but proceeds to *Luxury,* the *Bane* of Wealth, to create new Wants, which are so far real, as they prompt and excite us to Action and Industry; without it, Life would be tasteless, and a heavy Burden."[38] The words sum up the dilemma and paradox of a consumer society whose course seemed blessed, in the nineteenth-century words of "America the Beautiful," with limitless "spacious skies . . . amber waves of grain" and "fruited plains," but with this stern Protestant caveat added, that "God mend thine ev'ry flaw, confirm thy soul in self-control, thy liberty in law!"

7

THE AGE OF ANXIETY
Luxury and the Eighteenth Century

———— ❦ ————

Their taste for physical gratifications must be regarded as the
original source of that secret disquietude which the actions of
Americans betray and of that inconstancy of which they daily
afford fresh examples. He who has set his heart exclusively upon
the pursuit of worldly welfare is always in a hurry, for he has but
a limited time at his disposal to reach, to grasp, and to enjoy it.
—ALEXIS DE TOCQUEVILLE, *DEMOCRACY IN AMERICA*

In the ongoing tension between the virtue of republican moderation and desires, religion and consumer materialism, the specter of luxury's excesses continued to exacerbate feelings of unease throughout the eighteenth century. To many, the threat of demotic surfeit in whatever disguise seemed to herald the breakup of society's moral fabric woven of religion, tradition, and authority. Despite their diversity and violent resistance to one another, these three strands, inherited from antiquity, had held Atlantic civilization together for millennia. For Americans, the question was focused on whether a new society and government attempting to embrace cacophonous customs, habits, and manners could be firmly put in place in time to shape an unknowable future.

This anxiety was by no means an American phenomenon, and as the debate grew over both its cause and its effect, some of the most curious minds in England and the Continent became connoisseurs of the subject. On both sides of the Atlantic, fear of "luxury" and its ominous metaphors of imminent threat punctuated newspaper editorials, political tracts, speeches, sermons, debates, philosophical essays, poems, plays, and novels to signal its message of society's collapse. New arguments joined the old prophesies of dissolution, linked to reckless human appetite with few restraints. Edward Gibbon's six volumes on the *Decline and Fall of the Roman Empire*, published in 1776, made the idea of the disintegration and collapse of a society an inevitable element of history's cycle. "From the eighteenth century onward," the classicist G. W. Bowersock has pointed out, "we have been obsessed with the fall: it has been valued as an archetype for every perceived decline, and, hence as a symbol of our own fears."[1] Men of the Enlightenment, with their optimism and faith in progress, could look critically at the past, and some began to question where things might be going wrong. And if, as in the case of imperial Rome, it had allowed itself to be conquered by the barbarian, why couldn't it happen again? It was this gnawing uncertainty that prompted the more thoughtful political thinkers to consider in their diagnosis that perhaps "a secret disease" had induced the collapse of civilizations. Close analysis of ancient texts suggested that a lack of self-control leading to decadence may have played a key role.

Some critics also saw luxury as the cause of contemporary economic and political inequality, particularly in the great urban centers of London and Paris. Others condemned its role in depopulating the countryside, encouraging people to favor the base attractions of the cities over the pastoral virtues of courage, honor, and patriotism. Those who were more class-conscious in the large anonymous urban centers, complained that it was becoming more difficult to identify the hierarchy of rank in clothes, equipage, houses, and personal ornaments, which could now be easily counterfeited and devalued in a mass market. This led to troubling, unnecessary confusion in ordinary social intercourse.

Much of the debate over the growing evidence of luxurious consumption implicated the new economic system that had been created through the use of national and public debt by the sophisticated financial market of England in the early eighteenth century. As Catherine Ingrassia writes, "New institutions, the types of negotiable paper available, proliferated: lottery tickets, stocks, bills of exchange, and letters of credit were among the numerous forms of 'credit'-able paper in circulation."[2] This economic and political revolution, so volatile, raised fundamental questions about the true value of material objects that could be manipulated by the system of paper finance—"a strange new account of physical substance as something that could be changed, suddenly and seemingly effortlessly."[3] No one could possibly imagine that the traditional production of consumer goods or services as a source of private wealth might one day be displaced by unheard-of fortunes made principally by mysterious financial transactions, themselves independent of other economic activity or public benefit.

In a subversive recognition of the new disturbers of the peace as positive economic benefactors serving the public good, Bernard Mandeville, a free-minded Dutch doctor living in London in 1714, launched his popular challenge to the traditional perception of luxury as a moral issue. Before he proceeded to question luxury's moral premise in his scandalous satire, *The Fable of the Bees*, Mandeville restated the "receiv'd Notion"

> that Luxury is as destructive to the Wealth of the whole Body Politic, as it is to that of every individual Person who is guilty of it, and that a National Frugality enriches a Country in the same manner as that which is less general increases the Estates of private Families . . . . What is laid to the Charge of Luxury besides is, that it increases Avarice and Rapine: And where they are reigning Vices, Offices of the greatest Trust are bought and sold; the Ministers that should serve the Publick, both great and small, corrupted, and the Countries every Moment in danger of being betray'd to the highest Bidders: And lastly, that it effeminates and enervates the People, by which the Nations become an easy Prey to the first invaders.[4]

Mandeville then moves on, in ironic doggerel, to challenge luxury's negative influence, claiming for it a positive contribution to the economy of human welfare. Prodigious spending of the rich, in fact, made the wheels go round, providing jobs for the poor. It is hard to fully grasp the hostile and sustained response his famous "grumbling hive" would elicit among the thinking classes when they read:

The root of Evil, Avarice
That damn'd ill natur'd baneful vice
Was slave to Prodigality
That noble sin; whilst Luxury
Employ'd a Million of the Poor
And odious Pride a Million more.

The book was condemned to the bonfire in France and denounced by Bishop Berkeley. As far away as Tidewater Virginia, the staunch republican Richard Henry Lee was heard sixty years later ranting against "American Mandevilles" like Alexander Hamilton "who laugh at virtue."[5]

The moral outrage was detonated by the Dutchman's subtitle, *Private Vices, Publick Benefits*, suggesting that mankind had overlooked the profitable commercial possibilities of wasteful luxury, avarice, vanity, pride, envy, and even spendthrift recklessness. Most startling, his sardonic attack questioned what had long been accepted as the source of wealth and progress, a novel theory that was to have far-reaching implications. Contrary to centuries of economic assumptions, Mandeville argued that it was not the working classes that were at the root of national wealth, but just the opposite. It was the vain, fickle, and hard-hearted rich, spending their (mostly paper) money on absurd tawdry fashions, trinkets, and useless stuff—often to their detriment—that actually provided employment for the laboring lower classes, who in turn generated society's essential capital. In his hard, cold economic rationality of enlightened policy, the workers after all "have nothing to stir them up to be serviceable butt their wants, which it is prudence to relieve but folly to cure."[6]

Many complained that the new affluence of eighteenth-century London had overwhelmed the city's streets and alleys with mountains of garbage, waste, and all manner of castoff detritus—the residue of the mania of greed—making daily life a nightmare. Mandeville, however, saw the noisome dirt and filth Londoners had to confront a positive sign of prosperity—"money in the bank"—for which everyone should be grateful,

when once they come to consider, that what offends them is the result of the Plenty, Great Traffick and Opulence of that mighty City, if they have any Concern in its Welfare, they will hardly ever wish to see the Streets of it less dirty.[7]

Most Americans in the eighteenth century living with the bare rudiments of what the Old World considered "civilization" had never heard of Mandeville or read his "libertine screed." Wholesale luxury and its cluster of vices—and the urban litter Mandeville sardonically praised—was far removed from their sober, backwoods lives. From their rustic, isolated perspective on the fringes of Europe, any social refinement, let alone an aesthetic pleasure, was perceived as something alien and remote. Except for a small gentry—men and women of pretension indulging in spending beyond necessities—most colonists saw luxury and corruption as a condition mainly thriving in their popular, negative image of urban centers like London, the capital of worldly power, and of course in the decadent royal courts of Europe.

While the Puritan God's condemnation of mankind's predictable indifference to frugality and moderation appeared less strident as the century wore on, the Revolutionary generation's political readings in classical literature led them to discover a parallel pessimism embedded in the seemingly unalterable diagnosis confirming the fall of republics as well as empires. "Every page of the history of the great revolution of Rome," declared one Philadelphia editorial, "shows some instances of degeneracy of Roman virtue, and of the impossibility of a nation's continuing free after its virtue is gone." All seem to depend on the unrelenting cultivation of personal moral rectitude that would insure the "moral health of the civic individual."[8]

Around 1750, the French had coined the word "civilization" to identify this advancing evolution from a state of rudeness to a society of refinement in which the arts—music, dance, painting, poetry—were no longer seen as expressions of excess but "the animators of empires and the comforter of the human race." This new, abstract notion of a "good society," a product of the Enlightenment repeated a year later by the English moralist John Brown, seemed to create a realm where the arts and luxury could be viewed as common human interests, signs of human progress, sources of vitality and renewal. But citizens of a healthy society would have to find a way to reap the benefits of commerce and growth while checking and controlling its harmful effects—to have their cake and eat it too.

In his article on "Luxury," published in 1762 as an entry in the *Encyclopédie*, the marquis de Saint-Lambert seemed to endorse luxury's progressive advocates. "Luxury does not make the character of a nation," he declared, "but takes on that character" of a nation's government—bad or good.[9] Luxury itself could be good, by producing "worldly happiness," or bad, as extravagance promoting sensuality and capricious lack of self-control. The trick was to find a way to mitigate luxury's ill effects without derailing its contribution to economic and cultural progress. During the financial crisis leading up to the French Revolution, Charles-Alexandre de Colonne, Louis XVI's finance minister, was accused of urging on the king a policy of luxurious spending as a pump-primer, the source of the country's prosperity to get the economy rolling, a positive, proto-Keynesian public works program. Any moral hazard was beside the point.

To Americans, focused on their far-from-proven experiment, the crisis over the balance between corruption and republican virtues, in which the definition and function of luxury—wealth and commerce—was central, and became an important part of the heated controversy. Not surprisingly, the American debate was more about politics and morals than the latest philosophical quandary gripping Paris drawing rooms. The accelerated move toward a more complex, unstable, commercial society raised many questions and contradictions with few agreed-upon answers, threatening the core political ideology of the Johnny-come-lately republic.

Put simply, did the incipient commercialization of society represent moral and social progress for everyone, or did it accelerate the irreversible degeneration and cyclical decline, like a disease hidden in its DNA? Were the dynamics of commerce compatible with America's Revolutionary, republican ideals of liberty and the promotion of virtuous citizens necessary for a republic? Where did the self-sufficient yeoman farmer figure in this "empire of goods" brought on by progress? And how could the issue of equitable distribution be addressed in a society in which the quest for material gain reigned supreme over any other moral issues involving the public welfare?

By the middle of the eighteenth century, a consumer frenzy fed by the growing supply of British products from its "new empire of things" pouring into the colonies seemed to have already transformed what had been a simple, well-ordered society into a free-for-all bazaar.[10] One did not have to be a die-hard reactionary to see that these changes represented a dramatic and dislocating break with the past as it was generally understood. Material temptations were stirring up new appetites for things that far exceeded any commonsense definition of "necessities." Even worse, they were inciting a taste for things most people couldn't afford. And by encouraging indolence, popular indulgence in luxuries even gave the old half-forgotten sin of sloth new life. "Commodities sent thither," the successful London publisher Robert Dodsley wrote in his book on trade and commerce, "besides Linen, Silks, India Goods, Wine, and other foreign Manufactures, are Cloth, coarse and fine Serges, Stuffs, Bays, Hats, and all Sorts of Haberdashers Ware: Hoes, Bills, Axes, Nails, Adzes, . . . Knives, Flour, Stockings, Shoes, Caps for Servants and in short, every Thing that is made in England." Regardless of whether anyone could separate the "good" luxuries from the "bad" on Dodsley's list, making Americans dependent on these foreign commodities raised fundamental doubts and anxieties about the republican political economy.[11]

When the Continental Congress announced in April 1776 the opening of all American ports to international commerce, only the most cynical or depressed thought they saw an empire of trade in the making. It was simply a military necessity to get supplies from Europe. But while few would admit it, the move also symbolized the new republic's faith in the obvious benefits of international free trade. Yet as the more jaded Greek and Roman historians had pointed out, empires of trade (or military arms) were not necessarily compatible with republican ideals of virtue or economic and political firmness.

The success of the Revolution had given way to a postwar economic boom of new wealth and prosperity, bringing the inevitable "destructive tendency to luxury." Everyone seemed to be living beyond his means, caught up in a scramble to buy superfluous foreign products, goods on credit that had been denied during the conflict. Contrary to the ideals of Revolutionary rhetoric proclaiming freedom and self-reliance, America's postwar economy seemed to be built on runaway consumption with all kinds of strings attached. Foreign goods were not only flooding the households of rich merchants in the port cities but also reaching the most humble country families with temptations of new consumer merchandise. To the more austere, this sudden appetite for more and more all appeared a shade second rate.

Some of the old Revolutionaries, such as Samuel Adams in Boston and George Mason on his plantation in Virginia, saw that the victory of the war carried with it a high price, confirming their earlier doubts about whether people would be willing to give up their individual self-interest for the good of all. Plain, instinctively frugal Adams found extravagant Bostonians with their "Decoration of the Parlor, the shining Board of Plate, the costly Piles of China," a betrayal of older republican (and Puritan) values.

The central issue that kept the debate going was where to draw the line between virtue, still defined by classical standards, and the protean power of compulsive, laissez-faire consumption, with its hidden Malthusian price tags. The paradox was that despite the rhetorical attachment to the ancient, anti-commercial ideal, the survival of the republican experiment also required vigorous, commercial growth to support its emerging population. "Freedom and luxury have always been thought to be incompatible," Hannah Arendt shrewdly observed in her essay on revolution, "and the modern estimate that tends to blame the insistence of the Founding Fathers on frugality and simplicity of manners" they inherited from "the Puritan contempt for the delights of the world" overlooks their deep concern for "the fatal passion for sudden riches." In the former colonies the condition was inevitably introduced by the poorest classes that were beginning to arrive in waves. The future masses of destitute immigrants from Europe, attracted by the prospects of "a promised land" of "milk and honey," would push the pursuit of abundance and unchecked consumption—always the ideal of the poor and wretched—ahead of the Revolutionary notions of *public* happiness and *political* freedom before solid barriers could be put in place capable of resisting "the futile antics of a society intent upon affluence."[12]

For the traditionalists who saw economics in moral terms, luxury stimulated the unprincipled pursuit of gain through the deliberate exploitation of sordid human appetites. Such a society inevitably became greedy, hedonistic, and selfish, concerned only with wealth and comfort. But under the pressure of what Samuel Adams called "the deceitful dream of a Golden age," which transformed luxuries into necessities and "decencies," individual choices according to taste and comfort would give luxury a new meaning.[13]

Luxury's early maverick defenders in Britain would later be joined by intellectual leaders of the Scottish Enlightenment, such as Adam Smith, David

Hume, and Henry Home, (Lord Kames). As the construct of capitalism grew, gradually the argument shifted away from the question of luxury's morality and its threat to liberty, and the study of economics itself became the dismal "science" of modernity. Luxury, now drained of much of its religious or philosophical content, lost its aura of guilt and apprehension. The pleasure of "luxury" goods became just a part of social and economic progress expressed in the morally neutral workings of the capitalist marketplace. Transmogrification was under way; metamorphosis into the banal would shortly follow. The notion of luxury was becoming merely a useful marketing ploy to advance a more relaxed, egalitarian, domestic approach to how people chose to spend their money. A radical new law of economic progress emerged; "progress" should be measured by popular, limitless consumption restrained only by the virtuous consumer with the strength of character to avoid buying more than he needed, could afford (credit cards would not appear until 1950), or cause harm to anyone else. Liberalism's "no harm principle," defined by John Stuart Mill, would ultimately spell out the only real limit. In his classic *On Liberty*, Mill's maxim held (and still holds) that "the only purpose for which power can be rightfully exercised over any member of a civilized community against his will, is to prevent harm to others." It was assumed that harm would be direct, immediate, and obvious, requiring action by the state. No one thought of harm being slow, insidious, and ongoing, producing long-term damage to the environment, climate change, and the exhaustion of natural resources.[14]

"De-moralized" as a sin or vice, this complete makeover of luxury transformed the notion itself into a significant player in the new consumer society. It turned on its head the ancient concept and Greek legacy of *pleonectic*, the heart of Greek vices, meaning the grasping for more and more regardless of the consequences to friend or foe.[15] Its positive new role was to express a natural human instinct, a definition made famous by Adam Smith's *Wealth of Nations*: "the desire of bettering our condition, a desire which, though generally calm and dispassionate, comes to us from the womb, and never leaves us til we go into the grave."[16] With luxury's critics increasingly on the defensive, the idea of luxury, as it had been understood for more than twenty-five hundred years, would fade and disappear as a term of moral indictment, however inegalitarian the unintended consequences might be.[17]

At the very moment the republican experiment was launched, public confidence seemed to have reached a new low, brought about by its anxiety over the possibility of too much prosperity and abundance. Instead of progressing, things seemed to be going the other way. "To increase in numbers, in wealth, in elegance and refinements, and at the same time increase in luxury, profaneness, impiety, and a disesteem of things sacred," the New England clergyman Nathan Fiske wrote in 1776, "is to go backward and not forward."[18] Society's failure to toe the moral line of self-discipline created an apprehension of imminent ruin that would become a protean element in what we now call the Founders' debate over the evolving republican ideology.

In provincial Boston at the outset of the Revolution in 1776, luxury was all too obvious to men like John Adams and his good friend Mercy Otis Warren. Boston's economy was already showing early signs of wartime greed and corruption. The palpable existence of luxury at that critical moment had left Adams feeling unmanned, "vain, light, frivolous," not sure that he or anyone else could hold on to the essential virtues required to run a successful war and establish a principled republic along classical lines. There was more than a suspicion that England had been deliberately corrupting America for its own political ends by exporting its licentious products and manners to undermine republican simplicity. Such a possibility was made all the easier by Parliament's hated Navigation Acts, which required all imports to be sold in England or to be bought from England, regardless of competitive prices available elsewhere. British merchants were suddenly in control of what has been called an international "free-trade zone."[19]

The formidable bluestocking Mrs. Warren, poet, playwright, and historian, hardly needed the reminder. Like Adams, she had seen old New England habits threatened by "the Spirit of Commerce." In 1763, John Singleton Copley painted a portrait of a fashionable Mercy Warren wearing an elegant blue satin gown trimmed with expensive lace. But a dozen years later, she concluded that in the history of human action, "ambition and avarice" exhibited in showy finery and style were always the leading "sources of corruption" spreading "distress over the face of the earth."[20] Both Mrs. Warren and Adams held the conviction that a republican form of government required the personal commitment of every citizen and his commitment to the unquestioned virtue of "pure Religion or Austere Morals." They had little reason to believe that the uncharted American experiment combined with a radical "consumer revolution" would be, in the end, an exception to history's examples of corruption and lost liberty.[21]

The same year that Adams and Warren exchanged their growing concerns over Boston's moral decline, Adam Smith's *Wealth of Nations* was published, offering an original new perspective on economic growth and national prosperity. Smith not only saw no moral or political threats in private consumption, he believed it was "the sole end and purpose of all production; and the interest of the producer ought to be attended to, only so far as it may be necessary for promoting the consumer." He was also tolerant of private indulgence a minor vice that advanced the arts. "Noble palaces, magnificent villas, great collections of books, statues, pictures and other curiosities, are frequently both an ornament and an honour, not only to the neighbourhood, but to the whole country to which they belong. Versailles is an ornament and an honour to France. Stowe and Wilton to England." Their magnificence simply confirmed society's progress from "rudeness to refinement."[22]

The impact of Smith's revolutionary work moved far beyond the outrage triggered by Bernard Mandeville's magnum opus with its "Spacious Hive well stockt with Bees, That liv'd in Luxury and Ease."[23] While the main thrust of Smith's argument is that meddlesome government should not be allowed to disrupt the natural law of the "invisible hand" in the market place, it has been overemphasized. Like that of the French physiocrats, Smith's political economy assumed that government was naturally tied to a country's society and economy. Even though his main emphasis was on private capital accumulation, the productive use of surplus and the expenditures of the rich were not waste but served to redistribute wealth with investment for expansion and growth. But he also assumed that an enlightened government was necessary to enforce the public priorities and arbitrate the "natural law" (or jungle law) of commercial activity.

Smith was well aware that "the great mob of mankind" admired great wealth and status. But for him this unadulterated, unquestioned worship of wealth for its own sake had the possibility of destruction in a modern commercial society; it could erode the basic qualities that capitalism needed to survive and grow: "The disposition to admire, and almost to worship, the rich and the powerful, and to despise, or, at least, to neglect, persons of poor and mean condition . . . [is] the great and most universal cause of corruption of our moral sentiments."[24]

Under whatever alias "the syren luxury" traveled, many Americans still perceived it as a threat to the republican ideals of wisdom, justice, temperance, modesty, honesty, frugality, benevolence, simplicity, and sobriety. It was the elephant in the room whenever virtue was discussed. "Such were the Manners and principal Occupations of the Romans before that People had been corrupted by Riches and Luxury," an essayist on simplicity and luxury reminded his readers among the gentry in Williamsburg, Virginia that "Probity, Simplicity, and the Love of Labour were Virtues as common in Rome as they were rare in succeeding Ages."[25]

From the 1730s until the beginning of the American Revolution, a growing chorus of voices spoke out against what appeared to be a rising tide of social vices and moral declension at every level of the community. No one seemed immune. In 1741, Judge Benjamin Whitaker of South Carolina was sufficiently troubled to use his charge to a grand jury to deplore the "Luxury and Excess, which within a few Years last past, has pour'd in upon us like a Torrent" and "greatly contributed to enervate and soften our Minds, and sink us, into Indolence and Inactivity." As upright citizens, it was their civic duty "to return to our former Frugality, Temperance and moderate Enjoyments."[26]

Five years later William Stith, in a sermon preached at Bruton Parish Church in Williamsburg, Virginia, warned his congregation of the decline of "the ancient *British virtue* . . . among us" because of "the Demon, or rather Legion, of Avarice [that] has gone forth and possessed the Nation" along with "the Love of Money [that] has spread itself like a devouring Flame." Aware of the Virginia vices of elaborate entertaining, drinking, and gaming, the rector warned his audience "that national Corruption" would "certainly bring with it national Ruin."

The concerns heard in the Virginia church, whose parishioners represented the wealthy plantation establishment of the Tidewater, were repeated by the Reverend Charles Chauncey of Massachusetts, where Virginia opulence was unknown, lamenting that people were "laying out so much of the fruit of their labour" on an "extravagant . . . manner of living." The Reverend Nathaniel Potter, also of Massachusetts, spoke of "greedy Depradations . . . made upon" the moral health of the people "by the Vices of Luxury and Extravagance" to satisfy "the studied Gratifications of sensual Appetites" that had "weaken[ed], debase[d], and impair[ed] Men's Reason and Understanding." The sound of the word "luxury" was heard so often from the pulpit, one gets the feeling that the inhibited clergy got an erotic rush from the sound of its lascivious, drawn-out, syllables: "lux-ur-y."

Contrary to the critics of the advancing consumer revolution then and now, some historians have argued that ordinary colonial Americans saw themselves united as consumers, if nothing else, who could join together to withhold their material appetites for British imports. In *The Marketplace of Revolution*, T. H. Breen has argued that the colonists' invention of a consumer boycott of imported goods and, above all, luxuries, transformed colonial consumerism into a massive popular form of political protest. It was as effective as the high-flown republican rhetoric on behalf of independence and equality appearing in all the newspapers and pamphlets and heard in the political oratory of the day.[27]

The Stamp Act crisis in 1765 ignited the popular resistance to British goods, followed by the more successful struggle against the Townshend Revenue Acts of 1768 and the Tea Act of 1773. "A strategy of political resistance centered on the marketplace quickly transformed myriad private acts of consumption," according to Breen's conclusion, "into a self-conscious public declaration of resistance."[28] The ultimate goal was to secure the endless blessings of shopping, replacing the Whig republican interpretation of the blessings of liberty.

John Adams anticipated by several decades Alexis de Tocqueville's observation that the preeminent urge for material distinction was greater in a democratic society than in an Old World aristocracy. "There can be no subordination" in a democracy, Adams told Benjamin Rush, and there was no reason it would be immune to excess. At the end of the war, Adams concluded that America was "more Avaricious than any other Nation that ever existed" and that it had rushed into "a greater degree of luxury than ought to have crept in for a hundred years."[29]

Though the colonists found the reserves of personal sacrifice and patriotism required to defeat the British, the moral decay that had existed before the war did not disappear with the signing of the Peace Treaty. For some, the bottom of the problem was "the degenerate character of the people" who had been seduced "into living in a manner much more expensive and luxurious, than they have Ability to support," enthralled by "an immoderate desire of high and expensive living." Many blamed easy credit—both private and public—and a paper money system favoring debtors and speculators. No one noticed the simple economic fact that there was a shortage of hard currency to circulate. The postwar boom and the lifting of bans on international trade had produced a red-hot economy as everyone rushed to buy imported luxuries on easy credit. The Pennsylvania politician William Findley, an Irish immigrant, paraphrased Dean Swift when he observed that "we are affected in quite a different manner from all the nations upon earth, for, with others, wealth is the mother of luxury, but with us poverty has the same effect."[30]

While the postwar fears of uncertainty poured out in private letters and public protest in the 1780s, Thomas Jefferson was in Paris serving as the American minister of the Continental Congress. During those personally liberating years between 1784 and 1789, he had spent every spare moment and had over-extended his financial resources joining in the Parisian version of the consumer revolution, trolling the city's luxury shops, unequaled in the world. The new minister's elevated and decidedly unyeomanlike tastes had deeply impressed the marquis de Chastellux when he visited Jefferson at Monticello at the close of the Revolution. Having never traveled abroad, the Virginia provincial had already begun to surround himself with imported luxuries—books, wines, silver, furniture, mirrors, musical and scientific instruments—which he considered to be the essentials of the cultivated planter, and which we continue to admire at Monticello today. It seemed, the marquis wrote in his travel memoir published in Paris before Jefferson arrived, that the young patriot had "placed his mind, like his house, on a lofty height, whence he could contemplate the whole universe."[31]

What the French visitor did not mention, and his host did not acknowledge, was that the elevated domestic style that Jefferson had created for himself by "consulting the fine arts" on the edge of the frontier was made possible by the more than 150 slaves who he owned. This bondage and forced labor provided the means for his family to live so well. Like the lives of all of the Roman aristocrats whom Jefferson admired and quoted as he advanced his arguments on behalf of "life, liberty and the pursuit of happiness," his own spending on all the comforts of the complicated household at Monticello were utterly dependent on the dynamics of slavery; human chattel supported and defined his very existence. But unlike Rome's system of enslaved captives, the spoils of military victories and conquests, Virginia's "peculiar institution" was based on race and color (excluding indentured servants and a small minority of free blacks) making any route to freedom virtually impossible.

Most of the Founding Fathers accepted the institution of slavery as a part of Western civilization based on their reading of Greek and Roman literature, which gave it unquestioned status and made it an authority of acceptable morality. All agreed that without slavery there would have been no Greek state, no Greek art and science, no Roman Empire. The practice had been firmly embedded in Roman law and later adapted to European legal principles through various Germanic and English statutory codes, so the first colonists in the New World—and many regions of European conquest—had an established legal system to support the importation and use of slaves as a primary source of labor. For those who raised moral questions about the institution, ample biblical texts and Christian literature confirmed its established roots in history as a fact of life in a world that God had created. God's support was needed to justify enslaving some of His own creatures.[32] Those who acknowledged slavery corrupting both master and slave, as Jefferson did, could, as enlightened Christians, condemn its negative influence and work for its abolition while believing that Christianity's slow healing role could pave the way to its eventual end. And while Jefferson agonized over the long-term damage slavery did to the prosperity and well-being of the nation, the economics of his own life was too entangled in the institution to find any clear way out of the dilemma.

Quite aside from the familiar moralistic and legal arguments over slavery, it was Benjamin Franklin, writing in 1751 as a homegrown "economist" on contemporary trade and protectionism, who with bold originality linked slavery to the negative notion of the addiction to "luxury" as a part of the eighteenth-century debate. In the context of a pamphlet, Franklin places slavery in the middle of the debate over what made a society's population grow or decline. Slavery corrupted not only the individual but also society by spreading the habit, which led to the degradation of free, honest labor while enlarging an unacceptable gulf between the few at the top, caught up in excess, and the rest of mankind. It had a direct effect on the contemporary demographics of the untested American experiment that depended on a growing population to fill up its vast geographic space.

Franklin's eight-page pamphlet, "Observations concerning the Increase of Mankind," was circulated by hand until it was printed in Boston in 1755. It listed in Section 13 six things that "must diminish a nation." Among them was "the introduction of slaves." Here is his brief argument: "The negroes brought into the English sugar Islands have greatly diminish'd the whites there; the poor are, by this means, deprived of Employment, while a few families acquire vast estates; which they spend on foreign luxuries, and educating their children in the habit of those luxuries; the same Income is needed for the support of one that might have maintained one hundred." With their dependence on slaves to do all the work, the slave-owning families "become proud, disgusted with labour, and being educated in idleness, are rendered unfit to get a living by industry." As a foundation for an enlightened republic, slavery and its destructive effect on free people was wrong on both ethical and economic grounds in which unhealthy temptations of "luxuries" played a significant role.[33]

When Jefferson arrived in Paris, instead of renting small, furnished quarters, he first leased the Hôtel Taitbout, located in a smart district not far from the shopping galleries created by the duc d'Orleans in his family's palace. Jefferson, like most tourists, found this revolutionary introduction to popular consumption in the Palais Royal irresistible. The financially challenged duke had transformed the central courtyard arcades of the old palace into a booming commercial center, described in a tourist book as "an enchanted place . . . a small luxurious city enclosed in a large one." The magnetic attraction of its "convenient assemblage of delights" and vice was an unprecedented experiment in the burgeoning international consumer revolution. With a long and growing shopping list, the enthusiasm of this Virginia aesthete was overwhelmed by the highly charged world of the arts, fashion, and material temptations requiring endless choices of design, color, scale, and texture. This side of his character, seeming to lack self-restraint and extending himself beyond his means, is seldom commented on by biographers until he was overwhelmed by debt near the end of his life. His restive ambitions, eclectic curiosity, and high-minded tastes are reflected in his *Memorandum Book*, in which he recorded the accumulation of furnishings for his first Paris house and for the house he rented later, the Hôtel de Langeac, an elegant, aristocratic villa with an extensive garden situated on what was then the western edge of the city.

The cost of living the good life in Paris quickly strained Jefferson's financial resources, tied exclusively to the production of his slaves at Monticello. But he nevertheless extended his insatiable appetite to London where he found that "the splendor of their shops is all that is worth seeing" in that city. On one trip he couldn't resist a new English carriage and set of handmade harness with silver mounts (elegant but not "foppish"), which he ordered and had delivered to Paris in violation of the French embargo against trade with its enemy. It would take more than eighty crates to carry all of these articles of luxe and worldly accumulations when he returned to Monticello in the fall of 1789.

The Virginia patriot would insist that his passionate collecting, guided by republican "taste," represented an innate feeling and was, like moral sense, an essentially useful republican virtue untainted by Old World corruption and opulence. In a letter to John Bannister warning him against a European education, he singled out "European luxury and dissipation" to be avoided because it would breed a contempt for American "simplicity." When he returned to Virginia, he would, he told himself, set an example of enlightened, understated discrimination for his fellow Americans, "which contributes to fix us in the principles and practices of virtue." From his point of view, his aesthetic tastes expressed the necessary refinements of a cultivated country gentleman determined to follow the moral imperative, setting the tone for the newly established republic, however far removed from the life of the ideal yeoman he had venerated in his *Notes on the State of Virginia* first published in Paris in 1784. In a burst of unaccustomed piety he famously declared, "Those who labour in the earth are the chosen people of God." Although he wrote them in Paris, it was in the *Notes* that Jefferson spoke most lyrically on the virtues of the agrarian way of life, upholding moderation and avoiding the moral swamp of the city where "pestilential" luxury and excess would undermine the frugality of the virtuous farmer, who had few worldly ambitions for distracting comforts or possessions.[34]

Before he left Virginia, Jefferson was aware that despite the state's attempts to control excessive credit offered by British merchants to revive consumption of imported goods and luxuries after the war, Virginians were eager to satisfy their pent-up appetites. He was discouraged by reports from his neighbor Archibald Stuart "that Extravagance and dissipation has seized all Ranks of people" and included the importation of "Coffins from Europe."[35] He told Stuart that only firm limits on runaway credit "can restrain our disposition to luxury, and the loss of those manners which alone can preserve republican government."[36] Virginians were saddled with their prewar British debts, confirmed and reinstated in the Peace Treaty, and the accumulation of more personal debt for luxuries would only compound the problems of putting the republican experiment on a sound economic footing.[37]

For the New York patriot Alexander Hamilton, it was no longer a moral issue that the modern economics of the republic and its future were to be created by the energy of commerce and manufacturing. In *The Federalist* 12, he agreed with David Hume's theory of political economy that by freeing individual economic ambitions, the luxurious living and commercial enterprise that followed would actually strengthen a republic by raising the standard of living for everyone. The age-old tension between wealth and virtue had finally been settled. Any moral ambiguity was resolved by spreading the benefits of an essentially urban commercial society. "By multiplying the means of gratification, by promoting the introduction and circulation of the precious metals, those darlings of human avarice and enterprise, it serves to vivify all channels of industry and make them flow with greater activity and copiousness."[38]

By the spring of 1787, five months before the Philadelphia convention, James Madison wrote Jefferson, using the metaphor of disease, that America "was marked by symptoms truly alarming, which has tainted the faith of the most orthodox republicans." A writer in Philadelphia called it "galloping consumption." The unintended consequences of the Revolution had allowed government to fall into the wrong hands. As Madison would point out later in *The Federalist* 62, with "every new election in the States is found to change one half of the representatives and newer state legislatures were being filled," it was argued, with "men without reading, experience or principle."[39] There simply was not enough virtue and social character, let alone frugal tastes and manners, left in the country to resist the vice of "luxury, dissipation and extravagance" and support a virtuous republican government.[40]

A month later in April, William Hay was more explicit in his letter to the Virginian envoy in Paris. "Your Native Country exhibits at present a very gloomy Picture," Hay reported, "the most striking Traits of which are a Degeneracy of Manners, and an unequal and slow administration of Justice. The People are greatly in Debt and the Cry is, *Paper Money*. . . . The Means which, since the Peace, have fostered Luxury and extravagance are now withheld from the Bulk of the People. . . . Necessity therefore will teach us Frugality and Temperance." A month later, another Virginia friend, James Currie from Richmond, added his concerns to those already sent to Paris, telling Jefferson that the country was "on the Eve of political Damnation." "We are a Voluptuous indolent expensive people without Economy or industry. Our private and publick Virtue you can judge of it. Our public and private faith are much shaken," Currie remarked. The envoy would not read any of the letters until he had returned, in June 1787, from a leisurely, sightseeing trip through the vineyards and Roman ruins of southern France and northern Italy.[41]

To the upright old patriot-republican Samuel Adams, his dream of making Boston into a "Christian Sparta" appeared to be fading even before the war was over. By 1778, a new commercial class of rich merchants in a "Spirit of Avarice" had taken over. It was as if the town had been captured by subversives trained by the cynics of the economic school of Bernard Mandeville. Men like Adams, closely associated with the Revolution and its ideals, were increasingly depressed by the material extravagance flaunted in all directions and at every level of society. That same year, Elbridge Gerry, a signer of the Declaration of Independence, told Gen. James Warren that in time of revolution it was to be expected that "the morals of the people will be greatly injured." The general got another earful from Adams, who reported that "all manner of extravagance prevails here in dress, furniture, equipage and living, amidst the distress of the public." Three years later in 1781, Adams questioned "whether there is not more Parade among our Gentry than is consistent with republican Principles." By the mid 1780s, the signs of decline continued to spread as more and more Bostonians wallowed in consuming pleasures. Adams choked on his outrage as he repeated the litany of "the Equipage, the Furniture and expensive Living of too many, the Pride and Vanity of Dress which pervades thro every Class, confounding every Distinction between Poor and Rich."[42]

The creation of an exclusive tea club in Boston in 1785, confirmed Adams's deepest fears. As he wrote his cousin John in London, too many former colonists were "imitating the Britons in every idle amusement and expensive foppery which it is in their power to invent for the destruction of a young country." And in the words of General Warren, "Money is the only object attended to, and the only acquisition that commands respect."[43] A return to patriotic austerity was the only way to uphold old-fashioned Puritan ethics and rekindle the spirit of republican virtue.

In retrospect, the uproar created by the organization of the Tea Assembly, or Sans Souci Club, in 1785, could be dismissed as a tempest in a teapot. But to "Candidus," writing in the Boston *Independent Chronicles*, the stakes were nothing less than the future character of American society. In plain New England words, "We, my countrymen, have a character to establish,"[44] and the sudden infatuation with money, commerce, and luxury made the challenge that had preoccupied the country throughout the 1770s and 1780s all the more pressing. Now was the time to confront the crisis head-on before it was too late.

The sudden and vicious attacks in the press on the smart new club and its organizers exposed the festering tensions and turbulence brought on by the unprecedented social mobility and disarray caused by the Revolution. New people were turning up in communities all over the country. Governor James Bowdoin of Massachusetts complained that he could "scarcely see any other than new faces," which was "as remarkable as the revolution itself."[45]

But not all observers agreed that whatever passed for national virtue could or should be measured in classical republican terms underlined with useful citations of Greek and Roman writers. Just as the war was coming to a close in 1782, Gouverneur Morris made no apology when he called Americans "highly commercial, being as it were the first born children of extended Commerce in modern Times." He knew what he was speaking about, having managed to make a fortune in international business ventures during and after the Revolution. Despite the decline in manners and morals brought on by commerce, it was thought that the desire for material possessions might keep the new country's citizens from becoming, in John Adams's words, "lazy drones." It was a trade-off of vice and virtue that made practical sense. As Benjamin Franklin wrote a friend, "Is not the Hope of one day being able to purchase and enjoy Luxuries a great Spur to Labour and Industry?" Without such a spur, "people would be, as they are naturally enough inclined to be, lazy and indolent."[46] It had to be the honest labor and industry, however, of a free and independent citizenry, not the product of slaves.

The Sans Souci Club was organized as the exclusive gathering place for the new postwar gentry of Boston to dance and play cards at twenty tables. No one was allowed to bet more than a quarter of a dollar—hardly conduct that could lead to another revolution. But to Samuel Adams, Elbridge Gerry, General Warren and his kinsman Mercy Warren, the club represented a classic symptom of effeminate refinement, idle amusement, and Old World surfeit intended, "to lull and enervate these minds, already too much softened, poisoned and contaminated by idle pleasures, and foolish gratifications," an anonymous "Observer" wrote in the *Independent Chronica* (probably Samuel Adams).[47] It threatened the very foundation of the republic. "We are prostituting all our glory, as a people, for new modes of pleasure, ruinous in their expences, injurious to virtue and totally detrimental to the well being of society." "Candidus," another critic, declared that most right-thinking Bostonians considered the club to be "a very *dangerous* and *destructive institution*" that was trying to ape "the long established Courts of Europe . . . fatal to the infant republics of America."[48] To some of the most severe critics, it was the social pretensions of the club's subscribers that were so destructive to republican character "when all the individuals of a State are so nearly on an equality." As in most disputes over manners and morals in the eighteenth century, the myth of the ancient world was loudly invoked. "Did we consult the history of Athens and Rome, we should find that so long as they continued their frugality and simplicity of manner, they shone with superlative glory," a writer under the name of "Observer" declared. "But no sooner were effeminate refinements introduced amongst them, than they visibly fell from whatever was elevated and magnanimous, and became feeble and timid, dependent, slavish and false."[49]

Bored with the staid provincial life of Boston, the members of the club defended themselves as being "observant of the nicest and most scrupulous laws of delicacy," promoting the highest ideals of manners and conduct befitting a republic. One member with cheek, calling himself "Sans Souci," struck out at the would-be "Censor of the age," accusing him of introducing "the Spirit of Faction" and "fanaticism" into the community. As for Greece and Rome, "while we boast a Washington and other truly virtuous men, I cannot think the ancients were more deserving than the present age, nor can I think that you would wish us to exchange our amusements for those of Rome," such as gladiator combats and circuses. One brave defender made his argument for the club a defense of luxury itself. Without some luxury, the country would remain, "a rude imbecile people" who had abandoned commerce to live in rustic simplicity and would end up "cutting one another's throats." To "Candidus," the very idea that luxury was a republican blessing and salvation was a, "*dangerous* and *distructive institution* only appropriate in "the long established courts of Europe."[50]

To those stalwart revolutionaries who understood the warnings, holding on to virtue was not a ridiculous cause. In their provincial simplicity, bred in a world that had still managed to escape from the draining extravagance and pomp of power, they believed that with the right kind of government they could still become the new center of morality and liberty, a beacon to the world. So far they had been spared the mad waste and squandering that would become the hallmark of late consumer society in the following centuries, the fourth stage of social progression "from the lowest and rudest state" to the final achievements of civilized "polish and refinement." Their very isolation without the evils of great wealth or imperial ambitions of domination might spare them. The debate in Boston pitted those who held on to moral reform of republicanism and regeneration as the only remedy for men's foolish inner passions against those who looked to utilitarian, legal methods, or to something subjective and mysterious, like Adam Smith's "invisible hand" of the marketplace, to somehow curb luxury and vicious corruption, "diseases most incident," in the words of James Madison "to republican government."

It is easy enough to see how, in the eyes of American republicans, the notion of "luxury" and all it implied automatically carried the taint of decadence, and tyranny, luxury's ancient legacy of immorality. While simple manufacturing to serve basic needs was acceptable, Americans were not to be transformed into factory slaves. Large-scale manufacturing in France and England was considered "the remains of that feudal system, which are yet to be traced in the policy of European governments, [that] enables the rich individuals to immerse in the deadly shades of their manufacturing houses, many thousands of miserable slaves."[51]

As the historian Drew McCoy has argued in *The Illusive Republic*, by the time the Constitution was debated and the government formed, "the ideological environment" over the relevance of luxury to republican virtue in a commercial society was increasingly perplexing. The former meaning and moral implications of luxury seemed wobbly, to some irrelevant. For most Americans there was simply no easy formula to resolve the questions and problems about the nature of American society and its future. The journal *The American Museum* offered a prize for "the best answer to the influence of luxury and morals" and how "to restrain the pomp and extravagance of ambitious or vain individuals . . . that was consistent with republican freedom."[52]

The question raised by the essay competition was at the core of Madison's deep concern for individual freedom and the economic basis of that independence. As a fatalist, Madison could only urge that the new constitution be drawn in a way to accommodate future unforeseen changes. Recognizing that the presence of excessive wealth concentrated in the hands of the few who supported and controlled an impenetrably complex financial system to maintain their power would destroy the equilibrium of a true republic, Hamilton argued in Number 36 of *The Federalist Papers* that it should be "a fixed point of policy in the national administration to go as far as may be practicable in making the luxury of the rich tributary to the public treasury, in order to diminish the necessity of those impositions which might create dissatisfaction in the poorer and most numerous classes of the society." The policy was to find a balance between the "proper distribution of the public burthens" and the protection "of the least wealthy from oppression."[53] Hamilton's support of progressive taxation on excessive wealth in a capitalist society can be traced to Adam Smith's position on economic inequalities in *The Wealth of Nations*, published a decade before *The Federalist Papers*:

> The necessities of life occasion the great expense of the poor. . . . The luxuries and vanities of life occasion the principal expense of the rich; and a

magnificent house embellishes and sets off to the best advantage all the other luxuries and vanities which they possess. . . . It is not very unreasonable that the rich contribute to the public expense, not only in proportion to their revenue, but something more than in that proportion.[54]

In defense of the new constitution, Madison understood the American paradox of a republican system of government; the task was to create a social order that would not only encourage a virtuous citizenry but also an arrangement of political power that would guarantee the security of the government without destroying the ideals of individual liberty. The Virginian was without illusions: such a government could only survive if the people had the "virtue and intelligence to select men of virtue and wisdom. Is there no virtue among us?—If there be not, we are in a wretched situation. No theoretical checks— no form of Government can render us secure."[55]

Hamilton, Madison's partner (along with John Jay) in drafting the arguments in support of the Constitution, was also without illusions. So that the country could reach the highest stage of social development, he promoted a republic of manufacturing and commerce that would define a different quality of the country's characteristic habits, policies, and institutions. For Hamilton the future was clear: there would and should be absolutely nothing to limit the exploitation of an unexplored continent with untold natural resources. To do otherwise was to attempt to reverse both natural laws and economic common sense.

It was a vision ideologically at odds with Madison's ideal society of independent farmers and small shopkeepers expressing "a greater simplicity of manners, consequently a less consumption of manufactured superfluities and a less proportion of idle proprietors and domestic."[56] The New Yorker's primary emphasis was on mercantile production as the main source of capital rather than Smith's liberated consumer. Hamilton made clear that his economic policy unleashing individual ambition and ingenuity would transform the dowdy, outdated image of Protestant ethic and frugality into the latest secular fashion plate of what Madison called "caprices of fancy."

"As riches increase and accumulate in a few hands; as luxury prevails in society," Hamilton told the New York Ratifying Convention in 1788, "virtue will be in a greater degree considered as only a graceful appendage of wealth and the tendency of things will be to depart from the republican standard. This is the real disposition of human nature."[57] Republican virtue would be replaced by Madison's system of checks and balances to somehow implement Smith's "invisible hand." The "advantage of character," Hamilton declared without apology, "belongs to the wealthy." The litmus test and sign of worldly grace was to be wealth and the things it could buy. This was a stunning break with the ideals of republican virtues of simplicity and moderation promoted by Madison and Jefferson. For them, an alternative political economy of controlled growth of commerce and manufacture—small, local, humane, idealist—would have to be worked out within a mixed economic society that could "grow prosperous and civilized but not avaricious."[58]

Both Madison and Jefferson understood that in the end, their republican revolution would only be an experiment defined and tested by time.

POSTLOG
Enough Is Enough

—◦◦—

*The earliest customs of peoples seem to send us a warning that
in accepting what we receive so abundantly from nature we
should guard against a gesture of avarice. For we are able to
make Mother Nature no gift of our own.*
—WALTER BENJAMIN

The age-old anxiety over the effects of luxury and excess did not end in the eighteenth century. Many of these venerable preoccupations with limits or lack of them have reappeared in our growing reaction to the present global crisis over the destruction of the environment that has been fueled with abandon by generations of consumption without limits and fanned by "the emotional addiction to materialism."[1] The moral crisis created by the illusion of endless growth has been compounded by the promises of global market economies. Consumers are driven by the worship of individual gain or at least the search for an ever-greater variety of things, not according to individual needs but to achieve an artificial standard of living created by marketing strategies that includes designed obsolescence.[2] This consumption-based economic system leads to increased inequality, widening the gulf between the rich and the poor while exhausting the earth's natural resources and undermining the psychic well-being and happiness of the individual. Experts and leaders around the world recognize that the planet has already passed its capacity to support this growth-obsessed system. The passing of these limits is not a philosophical, moral, or theological issue using the euphemism of "luxury"; it is one of scientific, quantifiable fact. And it turns out that capitalism's gravediggers are not Marx's revolutionary proletariats but "its own delusional Cardinals" as the Indian novelist and critic Arundgati Roy has written, who "have difficulty comprehending reality or grasping the science change, which say quite simply that capitalism (including the Chinese variety) is destroying the planet."[3]

In his essay on the alarming increase of robbers in London in 1751, Henry Fielding identified the root of the problem in "the vast Torrent of Luxury, which late Years hath poured itself on the Nation," making eighteenth-century England sound very much like the run-up to the near destruction of world economies in first decade of the twenty-first century and the scandals of the contemporary "robbers" hiding in full sight among their surfeit of bling.[4] Newspapers and commentators rush to catalogue the causes of the spreading public disquiet caused by deepening unemployment, political slogans of hope that turn out to be hopeless, the failure of the education system and its dwindling failure to produce workers or citizens, a generation of youth to which no political representation corresponds.

It would be easy enough to translate and use similar examples of the long cautionary history of excess to target the contemporary dangers of overindulgence and greed to force ourselves to ask the right, fundamental questions of public policy: Is it right, fair, just? Does it help to create a better society? One that is less materialistic and self-centered? It would appear that the system has no real interest in, or cultural authority to, address these fundamental moral issues.

The threat of the collapse of our ecosystem on a global scale and the mounting instability caused by plunging public confidence in the financial markets present an unprecedented epic moment for the transformation of public opinion and policy. It offers a chance to return to a model of restraint and moderation with all of its accumulated moral lessons, even if the restraints are not totally voluntary and would be met with all the usual skepticism of the cynics preaching the Gospel of Wealth and growth, the doomed mantra of denial. Instituting such policies would create a world far more livable and secure than our single-minded consumer society of "private privilege and public indifference" that has now lost its way.

The rich and the poor have always been with us, but the concentrated wealth of the very few at the expense of the common good is greater now than at any time in living memory. This extreme, unprecedented materialism and selfishness of contemporary life, however, as late and heroic Tony Judt has pointed out, is not inherent in the human condition. In a short time "we have made a virtue out of the pursuit of material self-interest: indeed this very pursuit now constitutes whatever remains of our sense of our collective purpose."[5] Much of what seems "natural" in our pathological mania for the excesses of wealth for wealth's sake and our uncritical belief in an infallibly rational market economy deluded by the illusion of endless growth actually dates no further back than the early 1980s.

The now undeniable and precipitous depletion of the earth's natural resources should open the way for world leaders to innovatively address these seismic warnings, creating new moral sanctions to firmly establish social priorities for mankind's essential, life-sustaining needs. There are few alternatives. Dwindling, irreplaceable natural resources are no longer adequate to fulfill the material desires of the industrialized nations, let alone the dreams of the rest of the world's populations. This stark reality ought to promote rational debate over the line between ordinary, achievable things we need and the lust for the redundant, ephemeral accumulations bought in the shopping mall and online, created mostly by an invented demand through relentless consumer advertising. It is all paid for with unsupportable personal debt promoted by an increasingly weakened financial system dependent on the state to bail it out.

For decades, leading world scientists have warned that unfettered consumption by the advanced industrial countries, followed by those third world developing countries that aspire to its standards, is not only unsustainable, it has put us on a collision course with the natural environment and its shrinking, nonrenewable resources. When we consider that it took one million years for nature to create the fossil fuel consumed in just one year, public discussion of human limits with references to the apocalyptic visions of the decline of Greece and Rome are beside the point.

According to the distinguished biologist and environmentalist E. O. Wilson, our ravenous human appetites lead us to consume annually between 20 and 40 percent of the solar energy captured in organic material by land plants.

His studies show "there is no way that we can draw upon the resources of the planet to such a degree without drastically reducing the state of most other species."[6] Our level of excessive consumption beyond our means has run up not only a staggering economic debt but an even larger debt on the planet and nature. Wilson estimates that with existing technology it would take the resources of four additional planets for every person in the world to reach the present level of per capita consumption in the United States. Or put in terms of the inevitable exhaustion of global physical and biological limits, according to Wilson consumption now equals 1.3 to 1.5 times the earth's ability to maintain sustainability. It is another version of the old metaphors for irredeemable excess, the luxuria and avarita understood by the ancients, inevitably leading to ruin.

But debts, like the sins of yore, have a due date and are eventually collected. It has occurred to some that we will have to give up many of our "luxuries" if we are going to stop overheating the earth's atmosphere to the point that it cannot support intelligent life.

It will be interesting to see how the industrialized countries will react to the mandatory limitations increasingly imposed on "market freedom" by economic and even more devastating environmental forces as we move into an accelerating downward spiral of scarcity and ecological devastation. As it seeks to catch up, China will consume more coal; in thirty years its coal consumption is predicted to throw more megatons of carbon dioxide into the atmosphere annually than the rest of the industrialized world combined.

Accompanying the mounting abuse of the environment has been the spectacular collapse of corporate and boardroom ethics within the largely unregulated capitalist system, a culture exhibiting a virulent greed that defies all ethical or moral reason. In fact, the phenomena are clearly intertwined. When the wealthiest elites in any society usurp a disproportionate chunk of that society's resources and power to support their exclusive lifestyle and supremacy, they then persuade everyone else that they too might some day reach such meaningless heights of limitless extravagance, however absurd the delusion. As a result, the charade takes the entire society hostage to the hubris of the benighted few. Here we are getting closer to luxury's mythic reputation as a universal vice in contemporary terms, disdained and feared throughout history, no matter what name it has been called.[7]

The most calamitous global crisis of the financial system since the Great Depression, erupting in 2007–2009, exposed a widening inequality brought about by systemic corporate avarice used to advance personal status and power of top executives and financial professionals exceeding anything in recent memory. The spectacular number of boardroom and management abuses at the highest levels of the financial system confirms the worst suspicions about what happens to money in an "invisible hand" and the deadly arrogance of power it can breed. The ongoing crisis has already stirred up a healthy and salutary reaction of protest and alarm, however. The very legitimacy of capitalism has been called into question with growing protests in the streets. In 2009, the financier Warren Buffett compared the financial crisis to a global epidemic of venereal disease. The novelist Tom Wolfe, whose *Bonfire of the Vanities* famously told a cautionary tale of earlier Wall Street excess, recently remarked to the *New York Times*, "The whole order of things has changed."[8]

The twisted values of the boom years have also reached far beyond the corporate and financial world. The ivory towers of nonprofit, public institutions—foundations, universities, libraries, museums, health organizations, even mega-churches—have also been corrupted by corporate rhetoric, values, ambition, and avarice: think of the "million-dollar galas" that could, until recently, raise a million dollars any night of the week in New York City; or consider the cozy university boards who saw to it that their presidents' salaries matched those of the highest-paid CEOs of major corporations. Before he was forced to resign, a recent secretary of the Smithsonian Institution was paid $200,000 a year just to use his house for entertainment—in addition to his nearly million-a-year salary.[9] The salary of the president of the New York Public Library was recently upped to a figure twice the annual pay of the president of the United States. And no one seemed shocked that Lawrence Summers, while president of Harvard, was at the same time on the payroll of a lucrative hedge fund without a single eyebrow being raised among the university's board of overseers.

This infectiously close relation linking our institutions representing educational and cultural dignity to the prevailing economic and moral standards of the business community was wryly anticipated by Thorstein Veblen in the final chapter of his 1899 classic on the leisure classes. Already he had seen the dubious shift in leadership: a "tendency lately to substitute the captain of industry in place of the priest, as heads of seminaries of the higher learning." It was not a good sign. These new heads recruited from finance and industry combined, in his mordant conclusion, "pecuniary with sacerdotal efficiency . . . a commitment of the modern transition from conspicuous leisure," represented by the positive qualities of educated, independent scholarship, to modern "conspicuous consumption," where "administration ability and skill in advertising the enterprise" of the university, library, or museum, was far more important and valuable than teaching and research.[10]

Forty years ago, the social critic Christopher Lasch also reflected on a moral compass that he presciently saw spinning out of control: "Older conceptions of success presupposed a world in accelerated motion, in which fortunes were rapidly won and lost and new opportunities unfolded every day. Yet they also presupposed a certain stability, a future that bore some recognizable resemblance to the present and the past." But the widespread loss of a "sense of historical continuity" (and community) has transformed the worn-out Protestant ethic, carrying the "underlying principles of a capitalist society to its logical conclusion."[11] Where individual self-realization is reduced to mere calculation and projections of consumption, it cannot impose any limits on human satisfactions or, in the words of Lasch, "on the immediate gratification of every desire no matter how perverse, insane, criminal or merely immoral." Echoing Alexis de Tocqueville's earlier observation, Lasch concluded that the ultimate product of bourgeois individualism "is psychological man who lives utterly for the present, demands instant gratification and yet exists in a state of restless, unsatisfied yearning."[12]

All the recent images of tabloid profligacy that any reader can conjure from our overloaded databank of information will not, in themselves, be sufficiently shocking to restore luxury's ancient potency to the level of a taboo and a moral signal to accept restraint. And for many people, the litany of glut and the pointless, exhausting pursuit of the spoils of materialism in the first decade of the twenty-first century would be a tedious and redundant closing chapter of shared indignation.

Human nature being what it is and what it has always been, the vice of excess (or vice versa) will always be with us. And there will always be disputes about where to draw the line—what does or doesn't violate the normal rules of rational public values and responsibilities. In defense of a winner-take-all economy where "luxury," from the piquant to the grotesque, has always thrived, the writings of Adam Smith are, like the Bible, most often invoked in support of pure market forces versus the so-called welfare state. But, Smith was far more nuanced and less doctrinaire than many of his followers would have us believe. In his *Wealth of Nations*, Smith actually spoke of another deeper concern for things the market has ignored, with regard to the broader, humane Western values essential to the "ease of body and peace of mind" of the individual and the community. Call it enlightened self-interest, it nevertheless throws a different light on the simplistic interpretation of Smith's philosophy as merely a guide for the pursuit of power and lucre, the devil take the hindmost.

He did not hesitate to approve of luxury taxes on fancy carriages, alcohol, sugar, and tobacco. He worried, as the economist Alan Krueger has pointed out, that corporations pursuing their own interests in the bottom line and led by the market's "invisible- and unaccountable-hand," could easily manipulate government at the expense of the common good.[13] In discussing laws against usury, Smith argued for state regulation to protect people from what he called over-enthusiastic "prodigals and projectors," speculators taking wild, excessive financial risks of boom and bust to maximize their profit, ignoring its cost to public welfare.

In his less well-known first book, *The Theory of Moral Sentiments*, Smith advances the strong need for public policies expressing moral values that go beyond the singular profit motive of the market, arguing that "humanity, justice, generosity and public spirit are the qualities most useful to others" in a truly civilized world. In the chapter "Of Utility," Smith observes that when Providence divided the earth between the powerful few with their "own vain and insatiable desires" and everyone else, "it neither forgot nor abandoned those who seemed to have been left out of the partition." In whatever makes up real happiness of human life, everyone deserves the same opportunities. With that conviction, the sole end of "the great system of government" is to serve that goal and support "those institutions which tend to promote the public welfare," his eloquence rising with these famous lines:

Nothing tends so much to promote public spirit as the study of politics, of
the several systems of civil government, their advantages and disadvan-

tages, of the constitution of our own country, its situation and interest in regard to foreign nations, its commerce, its defense, the disadvantages it labours under, the dangers to which it may be exposed, how to remove the one, and guard against the other.[14]

As we saw, both Plato and Aristotle agreed that restraint and moderation were required to produce a stable, self-sufficient, balanced individual and society and that limitless appetites should be controlled to introduce health, safety, and harmony into every sphere of human activity. It was perennial instability that Solon is asked to address in the economic and moral decline of Athens. Nor were these concerns confined to philosophical and political debate. Greek myths expressed with even more instructive power a similar worry over infinite desires that could alienate the individual from the gods, from nature and the rest of humanity, defying even the instinct of self-preservation.

As our all-consuming culture of a limitless freedom of exchange extracts its revenge on the environment and future generations, it recalls the myth of Erysikhthon, the king of Thessaly, first recorded two and a half millennia ago. To build a banqueting hall for entertaining, the king ruthlessly cut down the sacred grove of Demeter, the goddess of the harvest. Outraged "beyond telling" when she heard her trees falling, the goddess took her diabolical revenge by making the king's hunger insatiable.

> "Yea, yea, build thy house, dog, dog, that thou art, wherein thou shalt hold festival; for frequent banquets shall be thine hereafter." So much she said and devised evil things for Erysikhthon. Straightway she sent on him a cruel and evil hunger—a burning hunger and a strong—and he was tormented by a grievous disease. Wretched man, as much as he ate, so much did he desire again.[15]

When nothing else would satisfy the curse of his unquenchable cravings, Erysikhthon finally devoured his own flesh.

Notes

CHAPTER 1. A WORD OF WARNING

1. David E. Shi, *The Simple Life: Plain Living and High Thinking in American Culture* (New York: Oxford University Press, 1985), 22.
2. Ibid.
3. J. H. Plumb, *In the Light of History* (London: Allen Lane, 1972), 190.
4. Joseph Epstein, *Envy: The Seven Deadly Sins* (New York: New York Public Library and Oxford University Press, 2003), 85; Mae West, "If a little is great, and a lot is better, then way too much is just about right!"
5. F. Scott Fitzgerald, *The Great Gatsby* (1925; repr., New York: Scribner Classics, 1996), 152. Fitzgerald's original title of the novel was *Trimalchio*, taken from the name of the flamboyant Neronian party-giver described in the *Satyricon* by Petronius, so the myth of the excesses of Rome were on his mind and he had underlined them in his copy of the book. The trophy document in the Gates library is Leonardo da Vinci's notebook "Codex Leister," which Gates bought for $30.8 million.
6. In 2010 Anthony Hayward, CEO of British Petroleum at the time of the Gulf disaster, refused to miss watching his yacht compete for the J. P. Morgan trophy at the international yacht race at Cowes while the catastrophic oil spill in the Gulf continued out of control.
7. Alina Tugend, "Envy, Anxiety, Secrecy, Taboos: The Subject Must Be Money," *New York Times*, February 3, 2007.
8. Alexis de Tocqueville, *Democracy in America*, Reeves text rev. Francis Bowen, (New York: Alfred A. Knopf, 1976), 2:51.
9. Frank Rich, "The Rabbit Ragu Democrats," *New York Times*, October 3, 2009.
10. Kisari Mohan Ganguli, trans., *The Mahabharata* (1883–1896; Internet Sacred Text Archive, 2006), bk. 12, sec. 157, 346–47, http://www.sacred-texts.com/hin/maha/index.htm.

11. Sallust, *The Jugurthine War [and] The Conspiracy of Catiline*, trans. S. A. Handford (Baltimore: Penguin Books, 1963), 182.

12. Daniel Horowitz, *The Morality of Spending: Attitudes toward the Consumer Society in America, 1875–1940* (Baltimore: Johns Hopkins University Press, 1985), xxiv–xxv.

13. Gustave Flaubert, *Madame Bovary*, trans. Lydia Davis (New York: Viking, 2010), 126.

14. Thorstein Veblen, *The Theory of the Leisure Class*, ed. John Kenneth Galbraith (Boston: Houghton Mifflin, 1973), xiv. Galbraith's own "cool and penetrating" reading of Veblen's classic thesis remains unmatched.

15. Ibid., 42.

16. Alan Hunt, *Governance of the Consuming Passions: A History of Sumptuary Laws* (New York: St. Martin's, 1996), 93.

17. Polybius, *The Rise of the Roman Empire*, trans. Ian Scott-Kilvert (London: Penguin Books, 1979), 341.

18. Dio Chrysostom, *Discourses*, trans. J. W. Cohoon and H. Lamar Crosby, vol. 3, Discourse 31–36 (Cambridge, MA: Harvard University Press, Loeb Classical Library, 1940), Discourse 33:26, 299.

19. Werner Sombart, *Luxury and Capitalism*, trans. W. R. Dittmar (Ann Arbor: University of Michigan Press, 1967), 60–61. Although Sombart's work was first published in 1913, it is still stimulating and controversial. Even if he does not prove that there are clear links between luxury, sex, consumption, and capitalism, it is nonetheless a richly rewarding book. For all the unanswered questions raised and unsolved problems posed in his thesis, consider his closing line as a synoptic climax: "Luxury, then, itself a legitimate child of illicit love—as we have seen—gave birth to capitalism."

20. Ibid., xxii.

21. In *The Marketplace of Revolution: How Consumer Politics Shaped American Independence* (New York: Oxford University Press, 2004), author T. H. Breen has made the alternative argument that the Revolution was in fact fueled by the politicized consumer market: the rebels mobilized on a large scale when they joined in the embargo against British consumer goods in favor of American products.

22. Adam Ferguson, *An Essay on the History of Civil Society* (Edinburgh, 1767), 375.

23. Epstein, *Envy*, xxiv.

24. Gouverneur Morris to George Washington, October 13, 1789, in Jared Sparks, *The Life of Gouverneur Morris, with selections from his correspondence and miscellaneous papers. . . .* (Boston: Gray & Bowen, 1832), 2:1–5.

25. Andrew Jackson to Commodore Jesse D. Elliott, March 27, 1845; Mary Beard, unpublished Mellon lectures, National Gallery of Art, Washington, DC, 2011. Lecture 6.

26. Brad Gregory, *The Unintended Reformation: How a Religious Revolution Secularized Society* (Cambridge, MA: Belknap Press of Harvard University Press, 2012), 289.

27. Christopher Lasch, *The Culture of Narcissism: American Life in an Age of Diminishing Expectations* (New York: Norton, 1978), 11.

28. Shi, *Simple Life*, 270–77.

29. Phyllis A. Tickle, *Greed: The Seven Deadly Sins* (New York: Oxford University Press, 2004), 45.

CHAPTER 2. THE GREEKS: LESS IS MORE

1. John Sellars, *Stoicism* (Berkeley: University of California Press, 2006), 122–34. In his useful introduction to *Stoicism*, Sellars points out that it is above all an attitude and way of life rather than a fixed, articulated philosophy.

2. Edward Gibbon, *The History of the Decline and Fall of the Roman Empire* (London: Penguin Books, 1995), 1:35–36.

3. *Hesiod*, trans. Richmond Lattimore (Ann Arbor: University of Michigan Press, 1973), 29.

4. *Grief Lessons: Four Plays by Euripides*, trans. Anne Carson (New York: New York Review Books, 2006), 51.

5. *The Complete Greek Tragedies*, ed. Richard Lattimore, vol. 2, *Sophocles* (Chicago: University of Chicago Press, 1959), 169.

6. Richard Seaford, *Money and the Early Greek Mind: Homer, Philosophy, Tragedy* (Cambridge: Cambridge University Press, 2004), 1, 164, 196–97, 294–95; Sophocles, *Antigone*, trans. Elizabeth Wyckoff (Chicago: University of Chicago Press, 1959), 2:169. Seaford's stimulating study can only be briefly referenced here but chapter 14, "Individualism," on the invisible, destabilizing power of money and its ability to "dehumanize" the individual and isolate him from the realities of the community, is particularly valuable.

7. E. R. Dodds, *The Greeks and the Irrational* (Berkeley: University of California Press, 1951), 139–40. While I take Professor Dodds's warning "against treating the book as if it were a history of Greek religion" seriously, his dense, illuminating text provides a persuasive understanding of puritanism and its rejection of the dangers inherent in the notion of luxury and excess.

8. Patrick Leigh Fermor, "Gluttony," in *The Seven Deadly Sins*, Angus Wilson et al. (New York: Quill, 1992), 54.

9. Teresa M. Shaw, *The Burden and the Flesh: Fasting and Sexuality in Early Christianity* (Minneapolis, MN: Fortress Press, 1998), 31.

10. Dodds, "The Greek Shaman and the Origin of Puritanism," chap. 5 in *The Greeks*.

11. Donald Friedman, *Marvell's Pastoral Art* (Berkeley: University of California Press, 1970), 75, 210. See also 1 Pet. 2:2 (Revised King James Version).

12. Robert Renehan, "On the Greek Origins of Concepts Incorporeality and Immateriality," *Greek, Roman, and Byzantine Studies* 21 (1980): 109. See also Shaw, *Burden and Flesh*, 27–52.

13. Quoted in Charles Freeman, *The Closing of the Western Mind: The Rise of Faith and the Fall of Reason* (New York: Alfred Knopf, 2003), 234.

14. Ibid., 29–30.

15. Ibid., 155–56.

16. André Lacks, "Soul, Sensation and Thought," in *The Cambridge Companion to Early Greek Philosophy*, ed. A. A. Long (Cambridge: Cambridge University Press, 1999), 253. Lacks points out that whether the author of the quotation is actually Democritus or Plutarch, it is close to Plato's, Socrates's, and Aristotle's concepts of the soul in the fifth century.

17. *The Republic / Plato*, trans. Benjamin Jowett (New York: Heritage Press, 1944), bk. 2, 105.

18. Aristotle, *The Nicomachean Ethics*, trans. J. A. K. Thomson; (New York: Penguin, 1976), 76.

19. Ibid., 81.

20. Ibid., 91.

21. Ibid., 92.

22. Ibid., 93n1.

23. Quoted in William D. Desmond, *The Greek Praise of Poverty: Origins of Ancient Cynicism* (Notre Dame, IN: University of Notre Dame Press, 2006), 53.

24. James Davidson, *Courtesans and Fishcakes: The Consuming Passions of Classical Athens* (New York: St Martin's, 1998), 194–95.

25. Xenophon, *Memorabilia and Oeconomicus*, trans. E. C. Marchant (Cambridge, MA: Harvard University Press, 1968), 3:xiii, 1–5, 249–51.

26. Paul Cartledge, *Ancient Greece: A History of Eleven Cities* (Oxford: Oxford University Press, 2009), 3.

27. Desmond, *Greek Praise of Poverty*, 154–57.

28. Ibid., 27.

29. Ibid., 2.

30. Davidson, *Courtesans and Fishcakes*, 283–84.

31. Desmond, *Greek Praise of Poverty*, 17.

32. Frederick Raphael, *Some Talk of Alexander* (New York: Thames & Hudson, 2006), 265. The author does not identify the translation from Plutarch's *Lives of the Greeks*. But it is superior to any others I have read. Plutarch closed his narrative by remarking that when Solon was dismissed, he left the king with "some pain but no instruction."

33. By the 390s BC, Alcibiades had already provoked widespread interest and biographies. See Jasper Griffin, *Latin Poets and Roman Life* (Chapel Hill: University of North Carolina Press, 1986), 36, 37n20.

34. *The Complete Essays of Montaigne*, trans. Donald M. Frame (Stanford: Stanford University Press, 1965), 124. Montaigne sketched out an unfinished essay on the frugality of the Romans; David Gribble, *Alcibiades and Athens: A Study in Literary Presentation* (Oxford: Oxford University Press, 1999), 61–69. I am indebted to Gribble's account and interpretation throughout this section, particularly his survey of the early histories in "The Alcibiades Traditions," 32–43. See also Davidson, *Courtesans and Fishcakes*, 298–99.

35. Davidson, *Courtesans and Fishcakes*, 299.

36. Plutarch, *The Rise and Fall of Athens: Nine Greek Lives. . . .*, trans. Ian Scott-Kilvert (London: Penguin Books, 1960), 258; *The Greek Historians: The Complete and Unabridged Historical Works. . . .*, ed. Francis R. B. Godolphin (New York: Random House, 1942), 1:859, "Thucydides," 16.

37. *Isocrates*, trans. George Norlin (Cambridge, MA: Harvard University Press, 1968), 2:107.

38. Quoted in Andrew Wallace-Hadrill, *Rome's Cultural Revolution*, (Cambridge: Cambridge University Press, 2008), 321. In his chapter on luxury, Wallace-Hadrill attempts to "bridge the gap between two discourses," one as a "moralizing discourse" showing "luxury as a threat to the fabric of Roman social order" and the other, "a contemporary anthropological discourse to see in material culture a language or semiotic system out of which social meaning and order can be constructed," 318.

39. Plutarch, *Rise and Fall of Athens*, 177–78, 206.

40. *Isocrates*, 2:7, 21.

41. Plutarch, *Lives of the Noble Greeks*, ed. Edmund Fuller (New York: Dell Publishing Company, 1971), 50.

42. Ibid., 50–51.

43. Ibid., 61–62.

44. In the second century AD, the Christian convert Tertullian issued his own warning on architectural excess: "If you have renounced temples, make not your own gate a temple. If you have renounced stews, clothe not your own house with the appearance of a new brothel."

45. Davidson, *Courtesans and Fishcakes*, 230–31. The growing concern for environmental issues and climate change may give a new moral edge to architectural criticism.

46. Demosthenes, *Olynthiac* 3, 26, 29; Demosthenes, III, "Against Meidias, Androntion, Aristocrates, Timocrates, Aristogeiton," trans. J. H. Vince (Cambridge, MA: Harvard University Press, 1964), 158–59, 109–10.

47. Thomas M. Kavanagh, *Enlightened Pleasures: Eighteenth-Century France and the New Epicureanism* (New Haven, CT: Yale University Press, 2010), 4.

48. Jonathan Barnes, "Hellenistic Philosophy and Science," in *The Oxford History of the Classical World*, eds. John Boardman, Jasper Griffen, and Oswyn Murray (Oxford: Oxford University Press, 1986), 372. Barnes's section on ethics provides useful background beyond the specific focus of this exercise.

49. *The Essential Epicurus: Letters, Principal Doctrines, Vatican Sayings, and Fragments,* trans. Eugene O'Connor (Buffalo, NY: Prometheus Books, 1993), 66.

50. Ibid.

51. Dirk Baltzly, "Stoicism," in *The Stanford Encyclopedia of Philosophy*, ed. Edward N. Zalta, (Palo Alto, CA: Metaphysics Research Lab, Center for the Study of Language and Information, Stanford University, 2008). Virtue is "an expertise (*techne*) concerned with the whole of life," so a trained "soul" would reject luxury.

52. Epictetus believed that while external events were controlled by fate, individuals were responsible for their own actions, which they could control through rigorous inner examination and self-discipline. Writers in the twentieth century from James Joyce to J. D. Salinger to Tom Wolfe refer to him in their novels. See A. A. Long, *Epictetus: A Stoic and Socratic Guide to Life* (Oxford: Clarendon Press, 2002).

53. "On Tranquility," in *The Stoic Philosophy of Seneca: Essays and Letters*, trans. Moses Hadas (New York: W. W. Norton, 1958), 77–106.

54. Ibid., 76.

55. Ibid., 91.

CHAPTER 3. ROME: THE ROAD TO RUIN

1. Gibbon, *Decline and Fall*, 6:135. The title of this chapter is inspired by Gibbon, who more than two hundred years ago expressed the belief "that Rome had declined and fallen." Most subsequent historians agreed with Gibbon that it was mainly the fault of the Christians and barbarians. But in 1971, Peter Brown's *The World of Late Antiquity*, offered new interpretation and "transformed the end of Rome," in the words of G. W. Bowersock, "into the rise of late antiquity. Transformation replaced decline and fall." *From Gibbon to Auden: Essays on the Classical Tradition* (New York: Oxford University Press, 2009), 198.

2. As Donald Earl makes clear in his study *The Moral and Political Tradition of Rome* (Ithaca, NY: Cornell University Press, 1967), when we speak of "Rome" and "the Romans" throughout the Republic and later, we mean the "small, literate upper class" who produced the only written record of the period that is available to us.

3. Polybius, *Roman Empire*, 308–11.

4. Albert O. Hirschman, *The Passions and the Interests: Political Arguments for Capitalism before Its Triumph* (Princeton, NJ: Princeton University Press, 1977), 9–10; See also A. W. Lintott, "Imperial Expansion and Moral Decline in the Late Republic," *Historia* 21 (1972): 626–38. Lintott's argument is a fair example of the prevailing rejection of the role of luxury and moral decline in the fall of the Republic, but he agrees nevertheless that many believed it at the time.

5. Juvenal, "Satire IX" in *The Sixteen Satires*, trans. Peter Green, (London: Penguin Books, 1998), 105.

6. Ibid., "Satire I," 6.

7. Ovid, *The Art of Love and Other Poems*, ed. G. P. Goold, trans. J. H. Mozley (Cambridge, MA: Harvard University Press, 1979), 127.

8. Seneca, *Ad Lucilium Epistulae Morales*, trans. R. M. Gummere (Cambridge, MA: Harvard University Press, 1971), 3:307.

9. Pliny, *Natural History*, 37, 13–14 , quoted in Mary Beard, *The Roman Triumph* (Cambridge, MA: Belknap Press of Harvard University Press, 2007), 9–10. With her usual vibrant style, Beard's analysis of the Roman triumph is a model of a focused study of ancient history. As she says at the outset, "it is as much about *how* we know as *what* we know." Her advice is particularly relevant to the subject of this chapter and to the entire study of luxury.

10. Karl Galinsky, *Augustan Culture: An Interpretive Introduction* (Princeton, NJ: Princeton University Press, 1996), 187.

11. Sallust, *Jugurthine War*, 181; In *The Roman Revolution* (Oxford: Oxford University Press, 1939), 452–53, author Ronald Syme argues that "the whole conception of the Roman past on which [Augustus] sought to erect the moral and spiritual basis of the New States was in large measure imaginary or spurious."

12. Gordon S. Wood, *The Creation of the American Republic, 1776–1787* (Chapel Hill: University of North Carolina Press, 1998), 53.

13. See Hugh Trevor-Roper, "Gibbon and the Publication of Decline" in *History and the Enlightenment* (New Haven, CT: Yale University Press, 2010), 151–57.

14. Wallace-Hadrill, *Rome's Cultural Revolution*, 331.

15. Quoted by Peter Green from D. Konstan's essay "Sexuality and power in Juvenal's second satire," in notes on the same satire. Green, 128–29.

16. Cicero, *De Finibus*, trans. H. Rackham (New York: Loeb Classical Library, 1931), 3:64.

17. Plutarch, *Fall of the Roman Republic. . . .*, trans. Rex Warner (London: Penguin Classics, 1972), 248, 296.

18. Ibid., 341.

19. Gibbon, *Decline and Fall*, 4:192.

20. Livy, *The Rise of Rome: Books 1–5*, trans. and ed. T. J. Luce (Oxford: Oxford University Press, 1998), preface, 4.

21. Livy, *The Dawn of the Roman Empire, Books 31–40*, trans. J. C. Yardley (Oxford: Oxford University Press, 2000), 427–28.

22. Ibid., 429.

23. Ibid., 428; Keith Hopkins and Mary Beard, *The Colosseum* (Cambridge, MA: Harvard University Press, 2005), 68.

24. Alan E. Astin, *Cato the Censor* (Oxford: Oxford University Press, 1978), 91. Author's paraphrase of quote.

25. Hopkins and Beard, *The Colosseum*, 147–48.

26. *The Letters of Cicero*, trans. E. Shuckburgh (London: George Bell, 1899), 1:7.3.1.7.

27. Jasper Griffin, "Augustan Poetry and the Life of Luxury," *Journal of Roman Studies* 66 (1976): 91.

28. Diane Favo, "Making Rome a World City," in *Cambridge Companion to the Age of Augustus*, ed. Karl Galinsky (Cambridge: Cambridge University Press, 2005), 214–63.

29. Sallust, *Jugurthine War*, 181.

30. Ibid., 182.

31. Emily Gowers, *The Loaded Table: Representations of Food in Roman Literature* (Oxford: Oxford University Press, 1993), 19.

32. Ibid., 12–13. Roman moralists regularly pointed out physical (or imagined) traces of their past such as the alleged hut of Romulus, the founder of Rome— "nothing more distinguished," in the patriotic words of Seneca.

33. Ibid., 18; Seneca, *Letters from a Stoic. Epistulae morales ad Lucilium*, trans. Robin Campbell (London: Penguin, 1969), xviii, 67.

34. Petronius Arbiter, *The Satyricon*, trans. William Arrowsmith (Ann Arbor: University of Michigan Press, 1959), xvi. Arrowsmith speaks of hubris, like *luxuria*, transforming a man for the worse "so that he eventually loses his sense of his specific function of virtue . . . . He surpasses himself luxuriating into other things and forms."

35. Plutarch, *Makers of Rome: Nine Lives. . . .*, trans. Ian Scott-Kilvert (Baltimore: Penguin Books, 1965), 124–25.

36. *The Epistles of Horace*, trans. David Ferry (New York: Farrar, Straus, and Giroux, 2001), 119.

37. Horace, Ode 3:29, trans. Charles Tomlinson, in *The Odes: New Translations by Contemporary Poets*, ed. J. D. McClatchy (Princeton, NJ: Princeton University Press, 2002), 239.

38. Mary Beard and Michael Crawford, *Rome in the Late Republic*, 2nd ed. (London: Duckworth, 1999), 12–15.

39. Wallace-Hadrill, *Rome's Cultural Revolution*, 329–35. The author's fresh analy-

sis of the social discourse on Roman luxury within the context of sumptuary laws is particularly useful.

40. Sallust, *Jugurthine War*, 178.
41. Ibid., 181.
42. When the ambitious Mark Antony invited Cleopatra to meet him in Greece, according to Plutarch, she set out to seduce the Roman using all the Eastern guile at her disposal, and her genius for luxurious showmanship inspired Shakespeare's imagined description of the event in *Antony and Cleopatra*.
43. Peter Green, *The Hellenistic Age: A Short History* (New York: The Modern Library, 2007), 80–81.
44. Forster called Augustus "one of the most odious of the world's successful men." E. M. Forster, *Alexandria: A History and a Guide and Pharos and Pharillon* (London: André Deutsch, 2004), 33.
45. Suetonius, *Lives of the Caesars*, trans. Catharine Edwards, (Oxford: Oxford University Press, 2000), 81.
46. I am particularly indebted to M. I. Finley for his chapter "The Emergence of a Slave Society" in *Ancient Slavery and Modern Ideology*, ed. Brent D. Shaw (Princeton, NJ: Marcus Wiener Publishers, 1998), 135–60.
47. Finley, *Ancient Slavery*, 133. In his essay "Generalizations in Ancient History," Finley addresses the difficulty of applying the sweeping label of "slave" and "slavery" in antiquity without some mischaracterization. He admits that "at present, on this particular topic, the use of classificatory labels and concepts is in an unsatisfactory state." *The Use and Abuse of History* (New York: Viking Press, 1975), 64.
48. Green, *The Hellenistic Age*, 77.
49. Finley, *Ancient Slavery*, 90.
50. Keith Hopkins, *Conquerors and Slaves* (Cambridge: Cambridge University Press, 1978). I have relied extensively on Hopkins throughout this discussion of Roman slavery and the issue of luxury.
51. Benjamin Franklin, *Essays on General Politics, Commerce, and Political Economy*, ed. Jared Sparks, (1836; repr., New York: A. M. Kelley, 1971), 316.
52. Griffin, *Latin Poets*, 29–31.
53. For the most comprehensive study of the Roman water system, see A. Trevor Hodge, *Roman Aqueducts and Water Supply*, 2nd ed., (London: Gerald Duckworth & Co., 2002), 191. Hodge suggests military conscripts constructed the aqueduct system and does not mention the use of slave labor, but given the sheer scale of the project, slave labor for the heavy lifting seems to be the only plausible conclusion.
54. Polybius, *Roman Empire*, 529.

55. Dio Chrysostom, Discourse 49, 43:2–4, quoted in Galinsky, *Augustan Culture*, 98.

56. Anyone interested in Roman spectacles should begin with *The Roman Triumph* by Mary Beard. I have used it as a stimulating source for the summary treatment of the luxury of slavery and the Roman spectacle.

57. Hopkins and Beard, *The Colosseum*. This study represents the latest and most thorough guide and account of the complex. See also Sallust, *Jugurthine War*, 181.

58. R. H. Barrow, *Slavery in the Roman Empire* (1928; repr., New York: Barnes & Noble, 1986), 25; Keith Bradley, *Slavery and Society at Rome* (New York: Cambridge University Press, 1994), 62–67.

59. Petronius, *Satyricon*, xi.

CHAPTER 4: FEAR AND LOATHING: LUXURY AND CHRISTIAN SALVATION

1. Gregory, *Unintended Reformation*, 246.

2. Shaw, *Burden and Flesh*, 32–31.

3. Mark 10:23–24 (Revised King James Version).

4. Matt. 6:19–20 (Revised King James Version).

5. Luke 6:21, 24–25 (Revised King James Version). I owe many details and much else to Elaine Pagels's *Adam, Eve, and the Serpent* (New York: Vintage Books, 1988), particularly chap. 1, "The Kingdom of God is at Hand." See also L. William Countryman, *The Rich Christian in the Church of the Early Empire: Contradictions and Accommodations* (New York: E. Mellen Press, 1980), 83–86. It has been argued that Matthew's version, "Blessed are the poor *in spirit*," watered down the troubling literal reading of Jesus's words in order to appeal to a wider audience.

6. Although the word is now an archaic cliché drained of much of its original stigma of moral compromise, surprisingly its meaning still survives more or less intact but ignored in many modern languages. As late as the nineteenth century, Thomas Carlyle lamented that the growing power of materialism and the consumer society, seduced by "the Gospel of Mammonism," personified the age's selfish greed.

7. 1 Corinthians 7:29 (Revised King James Version).

8. Ibid., 7:30–31. Tertullian, the second century Christian convert in Carthage, invoked this passage in his sermon condemning women's excesses in dress and ornaments.

9. Matt. 19:21; Mark 8:36 (Revised King James Version).

10. Gibbon, *Decline and Fall*, 3:149, 1:504–6.

11. Ramsay MacMullen, *Paganism in the Roman Empire* (New Haven, CT: Yale University Press, 1981), 40; Robert L. Wilken, *The Christians as the Romans Saw Them* (New Haven, CT: Yale University Press, 1984), 66.

12. Dodds, *The Greeks*, 212.

13. Tacitus, *The Annals and The Histories*, ed. Moses Hadas, trans. A. J. Church and W. J. Brodribb (New York: Modern Library, 2003), 351.

14. 1 Tim. 6:9 (Revised King James Version).

15. 1 Tim. 6:10 (Revised King James Version).

16. Matt. 19:21 (Revised King James Version).

17. Dodds, *The Greeks*, 138–39, 212.

18. Gal. 3:27–28 (Revised King James Version); see esp. Peter Brown, *The Body and Society: Men, Women and Sexual Renunciation in Early Christianity* (New York: Columbia University Press, 1988), 45–50.

19. 1 Tim. 2:9–10 (Revised King James Version).

20. Heb. 13:14 (Revised King James Version).

21. Quoted in Pagels, *Adam, Eve, and Serpent*, 32.

22. Ibid., 58–59.

23. For all the vicious cruelty of Greek and Roman slavery, neither the high-minded Stoics nor the later Christians offered any arguments for its abolition. In their emphasis on heavenly rewards for earthly suffering, the early Christians accepted slavery with "entire obedience." It may also have been for the practical reason that the economic structure of contemporary society was built on slavery, and the ostentatious use of slaves by the rich to reinforce their status was too embedded in Roman society to be challenged by a struggling new, upstart cult. Paul, Col. 3:22–24 (Revised King James Version). Slavery as a means of displaying wealth lasted much longer than as a method of producing wealth. See generally Hopkins, *Conquerors and Slaves*.

24. E. M. Forster, *Alexandria: A History and Guide: And Pharos and Pharillon* (London: Andre Deutsch, 2004), 19.

25. Green, *The Hellenistic Age*, 49. Green's list of Alexandrian pleasures is paraphrased from Herodas's *Mimes*.

26. *Clement of Alexandria*, trans., G. W. Butterworth (Cambridge, MA: Harvard University Press, 1979), 271–367.

27. Ibid., 282–83.

28. Forster, "Clement of Alexandria," in *Alexandria: History and Guide*, from the first edition published in 1922, 210–13; Brown, 125. Brown's chapter, "A Faint Image of Divine Providence" is a rich study of sex and the pre-Constantinian church.

29. Forster, *Alexandria: History and Guide*, 47. Hadrian's exasperation was primarily because the Christians refused to worship the emperors. Forster notes that Hadrian's letter is only attributed to him and the date is a speculation.

30. L. Michael White, "Scholars and Patrons: Christianity and High Society in Alexandria," in *Christian Teaching: Studies in Honor of LeMoine G. Lewis*, ed. Everett Ferguson (Abilene, TX: Abilene Christian University Book Store, 1981), 330.

Scholars have counted the names of more than three hundred pagan writers scattered through his works who have now disappeared from history.

31. Clement, "Exhortation to the Greeks," in Clement of Alexandria; 55–83; Pagels, *Adam, Eve, and Serpent*, 45.

32. Clement, "Exhortation," 271–73.

33. Ibid., 277; Countryman, *The Rich Christian*, 60.

34. Christopher J. Berry, *The Idea of Luxury: A Conceptual and Historical Investigation* (New York: Cambridge University Press, 1994), 90.

35. Countryman, *The Rich Christian*, 70.

36. Tertullian, "On the Apparel of Women," *Ante-Nicene Fathers*, eds. Alexander Roberts and James Donaldson (Edinburgh: T&T Clark, 1867–1873, 10 vols; repr. Grand Rapids: Eerdman, 1962), vol. 3 accessed: http://earlychristian writings.com/text/tertullian27.html. All of the following quotations are from this text.

37. Peter Brown, "The Tale of Two Bishops and a Brillant Saint," *New York Review of Books* 54, no. 4 (March 8, 2012): 32.

38. J. G. Davies, *Daily Life of Early Christians* (New York: Duell, Sloan, and Pearce, 1953), 157–58.

39. Saint Augustine, *The City of God*, trans. Marcus Dods (New York: Modern Library, 2000), 135–36.

40. In my discussion here and following, I have leaned on John Sekora's opening essay in *Luxury: The Concept in Western Thought, Eden to Smollett* (Baltimore: The Johns Hopkins University Press, 1977), 39–47, and Pagels, "The Politics of Paradise," Chap. 5 in *Adam, Eve and Serpent*.

41. Mark 12:17 (Revised King James Version).

42. Herbert A. Deane, *The Political and Social Ideas of St. Augustine* (New York: Columbia University Press, 1963), 37.

43. Ibid, 38.

44. Ludwig von Pastor, quoted in Anthony Majanlahti, *The Families Who Made Rome: A History and a Guide* (London: Chatto & Windus, 2005), 76.

45. Stephen Bailey, "Metamorphoses of the Grimani 'Vitellius,'" *J. Paul Getty Museum Journal* 5 (1977): 105–22. See also Mary Beard, "Warts and All? Emperors Come Down to Earth," (third A. W. Mellon Lecture, National Gallery of Art, Washington, D.C., 2011). To be published. Titian used the same piece of sculpture as a model of Pilate in his *Christ Mocked*, and Rubens used it for his head of Bacchus in the Hermitage.

CHAPTER 5. UNINTENDED CONSEQUENCES: INDULGENCE AND THE REFORMATION

1. Quoted in Charles E. Mee, *White Robe, Black Robe: A Duel Biography of Pope Leo X and Martin Luther* (London: Harrap, 1973), 120.

2. John Addington Symonds, *The Renaissance in Italy* (New York: The Modern Library, 1935), 1:219.

3. Silvio A. Bedini, *The Pope's Elephant: An Elephant's Journey from Deep in India to the Heart of Rome* (London: Penguin Books, 2000), 84.

4. The "Throne of Saint Peter" is used here metaphorically. According to Vatican historians, until the fourteenth century the newly elected pope was regularly seated in the historic relic believed to be Saint Peter's chair until the papacy was moved to Avignon. It would later be brilliantly encased in bronze to designs by Bernini in the 17th century and installed in the bascilica as a center piece of papal ceremony.

5. Euan Cameron, ed. "The Power of the Word: Renaissance and Reformation," in *Early Modern Europe* (Oxford: Oxford University Press, 1999), 86–87.

6. Evelyn Welch, *Shopping in the Renaissance: Consumer Cultures in Italy: 1400–1600* (New Haven, CT: Yale University Press, 2005), 300.

7. George Monbiot, "Selling Indulgences," *The Guardian*, October 18, 2006, posted at Monbiot.com, October 19, 2006.

8. Mee, *White Robe, Black Robe*, 46.

9. Symonds, *Renaissance in Italy*, 1:219.

10. Mee, *White Robe, Black Robe*, 196.

11. Sombart, *Luxury and Capitalism*, 2, 64. See also the section on "The Courts," 63–112, and the role of court life in the spread of luxury.

12. Ibid., 64–65.

13. Lauro Martines, *Fire in the City: Savonarola and the Struggle for Renaissance Florence* (Oxford: Oxford University Press, 2006), 286.

14. Ibid., 113.

15. Catherine Kovesi Killerby, *Sumptuary Law in Italy, 1200–1500* (New York: Oxford University Press, 2002), 44.

16. Sombart, *Luxury and Capitalism*, 61–62.

17. Ibid., 61. Chap. 4, "The Development of Luxury" provides a useful summary of the growth of luxury in European courts from the sixteenth to the eighteenth centuries.

18. Sekora, *Luxury*, 40–41. My direction here is taken from Sekora's introduction.

19. Jasper Griffin, "Virgil Lives!" review of *The Virgilian Tradition: The First Fifteen Hundred Years*, eds., Jan M. Ziolkowski and Michael C. J. Putnam (New Haven, CT: Yale University Press, 2008), *New York Review of Books*, June 26, 2008, 24.

20. The critique of "luxury" has often been used to confront general signs of national degeneration and moral decline calling for radical reform of popular conduct, particularly if there are hints of sexual or sensual elements involved. The action of the chairman of the FCC against CBS television for not blocking the public exposure of Janet Jackson's breast for nine-sixteenths of a second

when her costume "malfunctioned" during a halftime sequence of the Super Bowl in 2004 takes the most extreme attempt of fleshly regulation into the constitutional realm of the First Amendment.

21. Hunt, *Consuming Passions*, 231.

22. Commentary on Isa. 2:12–16 (Revised King James Version).

23. *The Miracle of the Dutch Republic as Seen in the Seventeenth Century: An Inaugural Lecture Delivered at University College London 6 November 1967 by K. W. Swart* (London: H. K. Lewis, 1969), 3.

24. Ibid., 10–11.

25. Jonathan Israel, *The Dutch Republic: Its Rise, Greatness, and Fall 1477–1806* (Oxford: Clarendon Press, 1995), 106. For a comprehensive analysis of early modern Dutch society see chap. 6, "Society before Revolt."

26. Kasper von Greyerz, *Religion and Culture in Early Modern Europe: 1500–1800* (New York: Oxford University Press, 2008), 80–82. I am particularly indebted to Greyerz's introductory chapter on the Reformation and his discussion of the Dutch Reformed Church's distinctive history in the context of the Reformation.

27. Max Weber, *The Protestant Ethic and the "Spirit" of Capitalism and Other Writings* (New York: Penguin Books, 2002), 86.

28. Simon Schama, *The Embarrassment of Riches: An Interpretation of Dutch Culture in the Golden Age* (Berkeley: University of California Press, 1988), 124.

29. Ibid., 191.

30. Ibid., 155.

31. Bernard Mandeville, *The Fable of the Bees: or Private Vices, Publick Benefits*, ed. F. B. Kaye (Oxford: Oxford University Press, 1924), 148–49.

32. Timothy Brook, *Vermeer's Hat: The Seventeenth Century and the Dawn of the Global World* (London: Bloomsbury Press, 2008), 74.

CHAPTER 6. PLAIN LIVING AND HIGH THINKING: PIETY AND PROSPERITY IN THE AMERICAN COLONIES

1. Weber's critics have questioned his linking of Calvinism and the Protestant work ethic to the origin of capitalism. He argues that removing a sense of guilt from material pursuits encouraged the systematic accumulation of wealth as a sign of God's blessing. But Calvin and other Puritan theorists never equated worldly gain with salvation and were thoroughly suspicious of the "inebriation of prosperity." See Shi, "The Puritan Way," chap. 1 in *The Simple Life*.

2. William A. Dyrness, *Reformed Theology and Visual Culture: The Protestant Imagination from Calvin to Edwards* (New York: Cambridge University Press, 2004), 68.

3. Richard Baxter, *The Saints' Everlasting Rest* (New York: Fleming H. Nevell Company, 1962), 130. Before Baxter died in 1691, the book had reached twelve editions.

4. Dyrness, *Reformed Theology*, 304. There are as many varieties of ascetic Protestantism as there are scholars of the subject, but the basic, austere tenets are common to radical Calvinists, Puritans, Baptists, Mennonites, Methodists, and Quakers.

5. Over time, and particularly in the American South, sexual sins have continued to overshadow all other sins, particularly too much money unwisely spent.

6. Patrick Collinson, *The Elizabethan Puritan Movement* (Oxford: Clarendon Press, 1990).

7. Andrew Delbanco, *The Puritan Ideal* (Cambridge, MA: Harvard University Press, 1989), 26.

8. Peter Stanlis, "Acceptable in Heaven's Sight: Robert Frost at Bread Loaf 1939–1941," in *Frost: Centennial Essays*, vol. 3, ed. Jac Tharpe (Jackson: University Press of Mississippi, 1978).

9. Godfrey Hodgson, *The Myth of American Exceptionalism* (New Haven, CT: Yale University Press, 2009), 8–9.

10. Shi, *The Simple Life*, 11.

11. George Santayana, *The Genteel Tradition: Nine Essays*, ed. Douglas L. Wilson (Lincoln: University of Nebraska Press, 1998), 17.

12. Cynthia Griffin Wolff, "Literary Reflections of the Puritan Character," *Journal of the History of Ideas* 29, no. 1 (January–March 1968): 18–20.

13. Frederick B. Tolles, "Of the Best Sort But Plain: The Quaker Esthetic," *The American Quarterly* 11, no. 4 (Winter 1959): 496.

14. Shi, *The Simple Life*, 18–19.

15. *The John Winthrop Papers* (Boston: Massachusetts Historical Society, 1929–47), 2:136.

16. Shi, *The Simple Life*, 16.

17. Weber, *The Protestant Ethic*, 81.

18. Edmund S. Morgan, *The Puritan Dilemma: The Story of John Winthrop*, ed. Oscar Handlin (Boston: Little, Brown, 1958), 8.

19. Ibid., 11.

20. Shi, *The Simple Life*, 11–12.

21. Dyrness, *Reformed Theology*, 213.

22. Ibid., 8–9.

23. John Bunyan, *The Pilgrim's Progress*, ed. Roger Sharrock (New York: Penguin, 1987), 79.

24. James Hosmer, ed., *Winthrop's Journal, "History of New England, 1630–1649"* (New York: C. Scribner's Sons, 1908), 1:77.

25. Frederick B. Tolles, *Quakers and the Atlantic Culture* (New York: Macmillan, 1960), 485.

26. Jean R. Soderlund, ed., *William Penn and the Founding of Pennsylvania 1680–1684: A Documentary History* (Philadelphia: University of Pennsylvania Press, 1983), 4.

27. Tolles, *Quakers*, 491.

28. Ibid., quoted on page 491.

29. Ibid., 82.

30. Ibid., 73.

31. William Penn, preface to *No Cross, No Crown* (London, 1669).

32. Shi, *The Simple Life*, 32.

33. Soderlund, *Founding of Pennsylvania*, 58–66.

34. Ibid., 58–59. Italics in the original.

35. Robert Barclay, *An Apology for the True Christian Divinity* (London, 1687; Philadelphia: Friends' Bookstore, 1908), 503. Citations refer to the Friends' edition.

36. Samuel Fawconer, *An Essay on Modern Luxury* (London: 1765), 50.

37. Linda Levy Peck, *Consuming Splendor: Society and Culture in Seventeenth-Century England* (Cambridge: Cambridge University Press, 2005), 8.

38. Breen, *Marketplace of Revolution*, 184–85. Italics in the original.

CHAPTER 7. THE AGE OF ANXIETY: LUXURY AND THE EIGHTEENTH CENTURY

1. G. W. Bowersock, "The Vanishing Paradigm of the Fall of Rome," *Bulletin of the American Academy of Arts and Sciences* 49, no. 6 (May 1996): 29–43, 31. In a thoughtful piece in The New York Review of Books Blog (March 10, 2011), the poet Charles Simic wrote on the growing feeling of pessimism in America that he believes has its roots in the excesses of political, economic, and cultural power it has unwisely wielded over the past thirty years: "The reason pessimists are multiplying is that we dishonor the intellect and the knowledge of history in this country by refusing to admit that corruption is the source of our ills."

2. Catherine Ingrassia, *Authorship, Commerce and Gender in Early Eighteenth Century: A Culture of Paper Credit* (New York: Cambridge University Press, 1998), 4.

3. See Sophie Gee, *Making Waste: Leftovers and the Eighteenth-Century Imagination* (Princeton, NJ: Princeton University Press, 2010), 44. Gee focuses on the growing signs of waste as a byproduct of affluence and its impact on value, viewed by some Enlightenment writers as having new significance. While the issue of luxury as the central phenomenon of my study is only implied, her succinct background on the relationship between waste and depreciation is stimulating.

4. Mandeville, *Fable of the Bees*, 2:108.

5. Shi, *The Simple Life*, 85.

6. Mandeville, *Fable of the Bees*, 1: preface, 11.

7. Ibid.

8. J. G. A. Pocock, *Virtue, Commerce and History: Essays on Political Thought and History, Chiefly in the Eighteenth Century* (Cambridge: Cambridge University Press, 1985), 121; Wood, "The Vices of the System," chap. 5 in Wood's *Creation*, 423, for an important discussion of the issues republican virtue versus consumer capitalism.

9. Istvan Hont, "The Early Enlightenment Debate on Commerce and Luxury," in *The Cambridge History of Eighteenth-Century Political Thought*, eds. Mark Goldie and Robert Wokler (Cambridge: Cambridge University Press, 2006), 379–80. This essay is a useful introduction into the intellectual debate of the period.

10. The apt expression "the new empire of things" comes from Emma Rothschild's *The Inner Life of Empires: An Eighteenth-Century History* (Princeton, NJ: Princeton University Press, 2011).

11. Breen, *Marketplace of Revolution*, 90.

12. Hannah Arendt, *On Revolution* (New York: Viking Press, 1963), 134–35. Arendt's chapter "The Pursuit of Happiness" has been deeply stimulating for the author in this closing chapter beyond this brief hint in the text.

13. Shi, *The Simple Life*, 84.

14. See Melissa Lane, *Eco-Republic: What the Ancients Can Teach Us About Ethics, Virtue, and Sustainable Living* (Princeton, NJ: Princeton University Press, 2012), 66–67. Lane's stimulating argument that classical virtues are still relevant in addressing contemporary issues add to my own analysis.

15. Ibid., 32–33.

16. Adam Smith, *An Inquiry into the Nature and Causes of the Wealth of Nations*, eds. R. H. Campbell, A. S. Skinner, and W. B. Todd (Indianapolis, IN: Liberty Classics, 1981), 2:ii, 28.

17. Berry, *The Idea of Luxury*, 101. I have used and benefited extensively from Berry's chapter 5 "The demoralization of luxury," where he probes into philosophical issues surrounding luxury in the eighteenth century.

18. Wood, *Creation*, 108.

19. Breen, *Marketplace of Revolution*, 88.

20. Historians have discovered that, in the best tradition of Bostonian frugality, Mrs. Warren passed the dress along to several friends to wear in their portraits.

21. January 8, 1776, *Warren-Adams Letters, Collections of The Massachusetts Historical Society Collections* (Boston: AMD Press, 1972), 1:201–202; Mercy Otis Warren, *History of the Rise, Progress and Termination of the American Revolution*, ed. Lester H. Cohen (Indianapolis, IN: Liberty Fund, 1989), 3.

22. Smith, 2:iii, 39.

23. Mandeville, *Fable of the Bees*, 1:17.

24. Adam Smith, *The Theory of Moral Sentiments* (1759; repr., Mineola, N.Y.: Dover Publication Classics, 2006), 59.

25. "An essay on simplicity and luxury," *The Virginia Gazette*, Williamsburg, VA, September 5, 1771.

26. Jack P. Greene, *Imperatives, Behaviors, and Identities: Essays in Early American Cultural History* (Charlottesville: University Press of Virginia, 1992). The quotes here and in the three following paragraphs were taken from Greene's perceptive discussion on "The Concept of Virtue," chap. 9, where luxury figures prominently.

27. Breen, *Marketplace of Revolution*, introduction, xi–xviii, and particularly chap. 6, "Strength Out of Dependence: Strategies of Consumer Resistance in an Empire of Goods," 195–234.

28. Ibid., xvi.

29. Wood, *Creation*, 575.

30. Ibid., 416.

31. François Jean, marquis de Chastellux, *Travels in North America in the Years 1780, 1781, and 1782*, ed. Howard C. Rice (Chapel Hill: University of North Carolina Press, 1963), 2:389–96.

32. Finley, *Ancient Slavery and Modern Ideology*, 18. Finley's first chapter is a good summary of the ideological conflicts for and against slavery in the eighteenth and nineteenth centuries.

33. Franklin, *Essays*, 316.

34. William Howard Adams, *The Paris Years of Thomas Jefferson* (New Haven, CT: Yale University Press, 1997), 78–83.

35. Archibald Stuart to Thomas Jefferson, October 17, 1785, *The Jefferson Papers*, ed. Julian P. Boyd (Princeton, NJ: Princeton University Press, 1955), 9:645.

36. Ibid., 9:218.

37. Herbert E. Sloan, *Principle and Interest: Thomas Jefferson and the Problem of Debt* (New York: Oxford University Press, 1995), 32–33. Sloan's opening chapter "The Thralldom of Debt" puts economic and philosophical dilemma in historical perspective.

38. Jacob E. Cooke, ed., *The Federalist* (Middletown, CT: Wesleyan University Press, 1961), 73–74.

39. Wood, *Creation*, 477.

40. Ibid., 479.

41. James Madison to Jefferson, March 19, 1787; William Hay to Jefferson, April 26, 1787; James Currie to Jefferson, May 2, 1787; *Jefferson Papers*, 10:219, 318–19, 328–29.

42. Quoted in Wood, *Creation*, 421–23.

43. Charles Warren, "Samuel Adams and the Sans Souci Club of 1785," *Proceedings of the Massachusetts Historical Society* 60 (May 1927): 3:320; Wood, *Creation*, 422.

44. Wood, *Creation*, 476.

45. James Bowdoin to Thomas Pownall, Nov. 20, 1285, quoted in ibid., 126.

46. Ibid., 476; Drew R. McCoy, *The Elusive Republic: Political Economy in Jeffersonian America*, (Chapel Hill: University of North Carolina, 1980), 96–97.

47. Wood, *Creation*, 422.

48. Ibid.

49. Warren, "Samuel Adams," 323; Wood, *Creation*, 422.

50. Warren, "Samuel Adams," 325.

51. McCoy, *Elusive Republic*, 111. The third and fourth chapters of McCoy's study of the political economy of Jeffersonian republicanism is relevant throughout this discussion.

52. Ibid., 135. See also *American Museum*, VI (July 1789).

53. Cooke, *The Federalist*, 228–29.

54. Smith, *Wealth of Nations*, 1065.

55. Bernard Bailyn, *To Begin the World Anew: The Genius and Ambiguities of the American Founders* (New York: Vintage Books, 2003), 34.

56. James Madison to Jefferson, June 18, 1786, *Jefferson Papers*, 9:660.

57. *The Papers of Alexander Hamilton*, ed. Harold C. Syrett (New York: Columbia University Press, 1962), 5:42.

58. McCoy, *Elusive Republic*, 237.

POSTLOG: ENOUGH IS ENOUGH

1. Paul Gilding, *The Great Disruption: Why the Climate Crisis Will Bring on the End of Shopping and the Birth of a New World* (New York: Bloomsbury Press, 2011), 185. His chap. 16, "Yes, There is Life After Shopping," is incendiary.

2. Arendt, *On Revolution*, 136.

3. Arundhati Roy, "Capitalism in Crisis," *Financial Times*, January 14/15, 2012.

4. *Henry Fielding: Enquiry into the Cause of the Late Increase of Robbers and Other Related Writings*, ed. Malvin R. Zirker, (1751; repr., Oxford: Clarendon Press, 1988).

5. Tony Judt, "Ill Fares the Land," *New York Review of Books*, 57 no. 7 (April 29, 2009): 17. I am indebted to Judt throughout this brief Postlog and to his book, an expanded version of the essay, *Ill Fares the Land* (New York: The Penguin Press, 2010).

6. Edward O. Wilson, *The Diversity of Life* (Cambridge, MA: Belknap Press of the Harvard University Press, 1992), 272. See also his even bleaker study *The Future of Life* (New York: Alfred A. Knopf, 2002).

7. Paul Ehrlich and Anne Ehrlich, *One with Nineveh: Politics, Consumption, and the Human Future* (Washington: Island Press, 2004), 12.

8. Andrew Ross Sorkin, "The Titans Take It on the Chin," *New York Times*, January 26, 2009. http://www.nytimes.com/2009/01/27/business/27sorkin.html?_r=0.

9. Jacqueline Trescott and James V. Grimaldi, "Smithsonian's Small Quits in Wake of Inquiry," *Washington Post*, March 27, 2007, http://www.washingtonpost.com/wp-dyn/content/article/2007/03/26/AR2007032600643.html.

10. Veblen, *Theory of the Leisure Classes*, 241–42. Veblen's determination to pursue his own academic career undaunted by criticism of both his scholarship and private life—women found him irresistible—helped to shape the sardonic, deadpan insights of the chapter on the corruption of American higher education.

11. Lasch, 68. After fifty years, *The Culture of Narcissism* is still a controversial critique and "hellfire sermon" against the excesses of the consumer society.

12. Ibid., 69.

13. Alan B. Krueger, introduction to *Wealth of Nations*, by Adam Smith (New York: Bantam Classic, 2003), xviii.

14. Smith, *Moral Sentiments*, 184–86, 189–90. See also Amartya Sen, "Capitalism Beyond the Crisis," *New York Review of Books*, March 26, 2009, 56:5, 27–30. Sen has persuasively argued for "a new approach to organization of economic activity" including "consensus building policies" and regulations that would not depart from either the spirit or letter of Smith's philosophy. When we run out of words to condemn those who brought on the recent financial crisis, Sen suggests appropriating Smith's nouns "prodigals and projectors."

15. Callimachus, *Hymns and Epigrams*, trans. A. W. Mair (Cambridge, MA: The Loeb Classical Library, Harvard University Press, 1969), 129–31; Ovid, *Metamorphosis*, bk. 4, "Gorg'd his own tattered flesh, and gulph'd his gore. Wounds were his feast, his life to life a prey, Supporting nature by its own decay." See also Richard Seaford, "World without Limits," *Times Literary Supplement*, June 19, 2009, 14–15.

Selected Bibliography

Adams, William Howard. *The Paris Years of Thomas Jefferson*. New Haven, CT: Yale University Press, 1997.

"An Essay on Simplicity and Luxury." *The Virginia Gazette* (Williamsburg, VA), September 5, 1771.

Arendt, Hannah. *On Revolution*. New York: The Viking Press, 1963.

Aristotle. *Eudemian Ethics*. Translated by Harris Rackham. London: Loeb Library, 1952.

———. *The Nicomachean Ethics*. Translated by J. A. K. Thomson. London: Penguin Books, 1953. Reprinted with revised notes and appendices by Hugh Tredennick. New York: Penguin, 1976. Page references are to the 1976 edition.

———. *The Politics*. Translated by T. A. Sinclair. London: Penguin Books, 1981.

Astin, Alan E. *Cato the Censor*. Oxford: Oxford University Press, 1978.

Augustine. *The City of God*. Translated by John Healey. London: J. M. Dent, 1945.

Bagnani, Gilbert. *Arbiter of Elegance: A Study of the Life and Works of C. Petronius*. Toronto: University of Toronto Press, 1954.

Bailyn, Bernard. *To Begin the World Anew: The Genius and Ambiguities of the American Founders*. New York: Vintage Books, 2003.

Baltzly, Dirk. "Stoicism." In *The Stanford Encyclopedia of Philosophy*. Edited by Edward N. Zalta. Palo Alto, CA: Metaphysics Research Lab, Center for the Study of Language and Information, Stanford University, 2008. http://www.science.uva.nl/~seop/archives/fall2008/entries/stoicism/.

Barnes, Jonathan, ed. *The Cambridge Companion to Aristotle*. Cambridge: Cambridge University Press, 1995.

Barnes, Jonathan. "Hellenistic Philosophy and Science." In *The Oxford History of the Classical World*. Edited by John Boardman, Jasper Griffin, and Oswyn Murray. Oxford: Oxford University Press, 1986.

Barrow, R. H. *Slavery in the Roman Empire*. 1928. Reprint, New York: Barnes & Noble, 1968.

Baudrillart, Henri Joseph Léon. *Histoire du luxe privé et public depuis l'aniquité jusqu'à nos jours.* 4 vols. Paris: Hachette, 1880.

Baxter, Richard. *The Saints' Everlasting Rest.* New York: Fléming H. Nevell Company, 1962.

Beard, Mary. *A Don's Life,* a blog in *The Times Literary Supplement,* March 8, 2008. http://timesonline.typepad.com/dons_life/2008/03/index.html.

———. *The Roman Triumph.* Cambridge, MA: Belknap Press of Harvard University Press, 2007.

Beard, Mary, and Michael Crawford. *Rome in the Late Republic.* 2nd ed. London: Duckworth, 1999.

Bedini, Silvio A. *The Pope's Elephant: An Elephant's Journey from Deep in India to the Heart of Rome.* London: Penguin Books, 2000.

Benjamin, Walter. *Reflections.* New York and London: Harcourt Brace Jovanovich, 1978.

———. *The Writer of Modern Life: Essays on Charles Baudelaire.* Edited by Michael W. Jennings. Cambridge, MA: The Belknap Press of Harvard University Press, 2006.

Berry, Christopher J. *The Idea of Luxury: A Conceptual and Historical Investigation.* New York: Cambridge University Press, 1994.

Botton, Alain de. *Status Anxiety.* New York: Pantheon, 2004.

Bowersock, Glen. "The Vanishing Paradigm of the Fall of Rome." *Bulletin of the American Academy of Arts and Sciences* 49, no.6 (May 1996): 29–43.

Boyd, Julian P., ed. *The Jefferson Papers.* Princeton, NJ: Princeton University Press, 1955.

Bradley, Keith. *Slavery and Society at Rome.* New York: Cambridge University Press, 1994.

Braund, D. "The Luxuries of Athenian Democracy." *Greece and Rome* 41 (1994): 41–48.

Breen, T. H. *The Marketplace of Revolution: How Consumer Politics Shaped American Independence.* New York: Oxford University Press, 2004.

Brook, Timothy. *Vermeer's Hat: The Seventeenth Century and the Dawn of the Global World.* New York: Bloomsbury Press, 2008.

Brown, Peter. *The Body and Society: Men, Women and Sexual Renunciation in Early Christianity.* New York: Columbia University Press, 1988.

———. *The Making of Late Antiquity.* Cambridge, MA: Harvard University Press, 1978.

Bunyan, John. *The Pilgrim's Progress.* Edited by Roger Sharrock. New York: Penguin, 1987.

Callimachus. *Hymns and Epigrams.* Translated by A. W. Mair. Cambridge, MA: The Loeb Classical Library, Harvard University Press, 1969.

Cameron, Euan. "The Power of the Word: Renaissance and Reformation." In *Early Modern Europe: An Oxford History*, 86–87. Oxford: Oxford University Press, 1999.

Cartledge, Paul. *Ancient Greece: A History of Eleven Cities*. Oxford: Oxford University Press, 2009.

Chadwick, Henry. *Early Christian Thought and the Classical Tradition: Studies in Justin, Clement, and Origen*. New York: Oxford University Press, 1966.

Chadwick, Henry, and John E. L. Oulton, eds. *Alexandrian Christianity: Selected Translations of Clement and Origen*. Philadelphia: Westminster Press, 1954.

Chastellux, François Jean, marquis de. *Travels in North America, in the Years 1780, 1781, and 1782*. Edited by Howard C. Rice. 2 vols. Chapel Hill: University of North Carolina Press, 1963.

Cicero. *De Finibus*. Translated by H. Rackham. New York: Loeb Classical Library, 1931.

———. *The Letters of Cicero*. Translated by E. Shuckburgh. London: George Bell, 1899.

Clarke, John R. "Augustan Domestic Interiors: Propaganda or Fashion?" In *The Cambridge Companion to the Age of Augustus*, edited by Karl Galinsky. Cambridge: Cambridge University Press, 2005.

Clement of Alexandria. *Clement of Alexandria*. Translated by G. W. Butterworth. Cambridge, MA: Harvard University Press, 1979.

———. *The Writings of Clement of Alexandria*. Translated by W. Wilson. Edinburgh: T. & T. Clark, 1857.

Cocceianus, Cassius Dio. *Dio's Rome: an historical narrative originally composed in Greek during the reigns of Septimus Severus, Geta and Caracalla, Macrinus, Elagabalus and Alexander Severus: and now presented in English form*. Edited by Herbert Baldwin Foster. 6 vols. Troy, NY: Pafraets Book Co., 1905–6.

Connolly, Peter, and Hazel Dodge. *The Ancient City: Life in Classical Athens and Rome*. Oxford: Oxford University Press, 1998.

Cooke, Jacob E., ed. *The Federalist*. Middletown, CT: Wesleyan University Press, 1961.

Countryman, L. William. *The Rich Christian in the Church of the Early Empire: Contradictions and Accommodations*. New York: E. Mellen Press, 1980.

Crevecoeur, J. Hector St. John de. *Letters from an American Farmer and Sketches of Eighteenth-Century America*. Reprint, New York: Penguin Books, 1986.

Davidson, James. *Courtesans and Fishcakes: The Consuming Passions of Classical Athens*. New York: St Martin's, 1998.

Davies, J. G. *Daily Life of Early Christians*. New York: Duell, Sloan, and Pearce, 1953.

Davis, John H. *Venice: Art and Life in the Lagoon City*. New York: Newsweek Books, 1973.

Deane, Herbert A. *The Political and Social Ideas of St. Augustine*. New York: Columbia University Press, 1963.

De Graaf, John, David Wann, and Thomas Naylor, eds. *Affluenza: The All Consuming Epidemic*. San Francisco: Berrett-Koeher Publishers, 2001.

Delbanco, Andrew. *The Puritan Ideal*. Cambridge, MA: Harvard University Press, 1989.

Demosthenes. *Olynthiac*. Translated by J. H. Vance. Cambridge, MA: Harvard University Press, 1964.

Desmond, William D. *The Greek Praise of Poverty: Origins of Ancient Cynicism*. Notre Dame, IN: University of Notre Dame Press, 2006.

Dio Chrysostom. *Discourses*. Translated by J. W. Cohoon and H. Lamar Crosby. Cambridge, MA: Harvard University Press, Loeb Classical Library, 1940.

Diogenes Laertius. "Life of Zeno." In *Essential Works of Stoicism*, edited by Moses Hadas. New York: Bantam Books, 1961.

Dodds, E. R. *The Greeks and the Irrational*. Berkeley: University of California Press, 1951.

Dorcey, Peter F. *The Cult of Silvanus: a Study in Roman Folk Religion*. New York: E. J. Brill, 1992.

Dyrness, William A. *Reformed Theology and Visual Culture: The Protestant Imagination from Calvin to Edwards*. New York: Cambridge University Press, 2004.

Earl, Donald. *The Moral and Political Tradition of Rome*. Ithaca, NY: Cornell University Press, 1967.

Ehrlich, Paul, and Anne Ehrlich. *One with Nineveh: Politics, Consumption, and the Human Future*. Washington: Island Press, 2004.

Epicurus. *The Essential Epicurus: Letters, Principal Doctrines, Vatican Sayings, and Fragments*. Translated by Eugene O'Connor. Buffalo, NY: Prometheus Books, 1993.

Epstein, Joseph. "Envy." In *The Seven Deadly Sins*. New York: New York Public Library and Oxford University Press, 2003.

Euripides. *Grief Lessons: Four Plays by Euripides*. Translated by Anne Carson. New York: New York Review Books, 2006.

Fielding, Henry. *Henry Fielding: An Enquiry into the Causes of the Late Increase of Robbers and Related Writings*. Edited by Malvin R. Zirker. 1751. Reprint, Oxford: Clarendon Press, 1988.

Finley, M. I. *The Ancient Economy*. Updated. Berkeley: University of California Press, 1999.

———. *Economy and Society in Ancient Greece*. New York: Penguin Books, 1983.

———. "The Emergence of a Slave Society." In *Ancient Slavery and Modern Ideology*, edited by Brent D. Shaw. Princeton, NJ: Marcus Wiener Publishers, 1998.

———. *The Use and Abuse of History*. New York: Viking Press, 1975.

Fitzgerald, F. Scott. *The Great Gatsby*. New York: Scribner Classics, 1996. First published 1925 by Scribner.

Flaubert, Gustave. *Madame Bovary*. Translated by Lydia Davis. New York: Viking, 2010.

Forde, Nels W. *Cato the Censor*. New York: Twayne, 1975.

Forster, E. M. *Alexandria: A History and a Guide and Pharos and Pharillon*. London: André Deutsch, 2004.

Franklin, Benjamin. *Essays on General Politics, Commerce and Political Economy*. Edited by Jared Sparks. 1836. Reprint, New York: A. M. Kelley, 1971.

Freeman, Charles. *The Closing of the Western Mind: The Rise of Faith and the Fall of Reason*. New York: Alfred Knopf, 2003.

Friedman, Donald. *Marvell's Pastoral Art*. Berkeley: University of California Press, 1970.

Galbraith, John Kenneth. *The Affluent Society*. Boston: Houghton Mifflin, 1958.

Galinsky, Karl. *Augustan Culture: An Interpretive Introduction*. Princeton, NJ: Princeton University Press, 1996.

———. *Cambridge Companion to the Age of Augustus*. Cambridge: Cambridge University Press, 2005.

Ganguli, Kisari Mohan, trans. *Mahabharata*. Reprint of 1883–1896 edition, Internet Sacred Text Archive, 2006. Available at, http://www.sacred-texts.com/hin/maha/index.htm.

Gee, Sophie. *Making Waste: Leftovers and the Eighteenth-Century Imagination*. Princeton, NJ: Princeton University Press, 2010.

Gibbon, Edward. *The History of the Decline and Fall of the Roman Empire*. 6 vols. London: Penguin Books, 1995.

Godolphin, Francis R. B., ed. *The Greek Historians: The Complete and Unabridged Historical Works of Herodotus, Thucydides, Xenophon, and Arrian*. 2 vols. Translated by George Rawlinson, Benjamin Jowett, Henry G. Dakyns, and Edward J. Chinnock. New York: Random House, 1942.

Goldsmith, Maurice M. *Private Vices, Public Benefits: Bernard Mandeville's Social and Political Thought*. Cambridge: Cambridge University Press, 1985.

Goldsmith, Oliver. *The Works of Oliver Goldsmith*. 5 vols. London: G. Bell and Sons, 1885.

Gowers, Emily. *The Loaded Table: Representations of Food in Roman Literature*. Oxford: Oxford University Press, 1993.

Green, Peter. *The Hellenistic Age: A Short History*. New York: The Modern Library, 2007.

Greene, Jack P. *Imperatives, Behaviors, and Identities: Essays in Early American Cultural History*. Charlottesville: University Press of Virginia, 1992.

Greyerz, Kasper von. *Religion and Culture in Early Modern Europe: 1500–1800.* New York: Oxford University Press, 2008.

Gribble, David. *Alcibiades and Athens: A Study in Literary Presentation.* Oxford: Oxford University Press, 1999.

Griffin, Jasper. "Augustan Poetry and the Life of Luxury." *Journal of Roman Studies* 66 (1976): 87–105.

———. *Latin Poets and Roman Life.* Chapel Hill: University of North Carolina Press, 1986.

———. "Virgil Lives!" Review of *The Virgilian Tradition: The First Fifteen Hundred Years*, Jan M. Ziolkowski and Michael C. J. Putnam, eds. (New Haven, CT: Yale University Press, 2008), *New York Review of Books*, June 26, 2008, 24.

Herodotus. *The Histories.* Translated by Aubrey de Sélincourt. London: Penguin Books, 1996.

Hesiod. *Hesiod.* Translated by Richmond Lattimore. Ann Arbor: University of Michigan Press, 1973.

Hirschman, Albert O. *The Passions and the Interests: Political Arguments for Capitalism before Its Triumph.* Princeton, NJ: Princeton University Press, 1977.

Hodge, A. Trevor. *Roman Aqueducts and Water Supply*, 2nd ed. London: Gerald Duckworth & Co., 2002.

Hodgson, Godfrey. *The Myth of American Exceptionalism.* New Haven, CT: Yale University Press, 2009.

Hollander, Anne. *Seeing Through Clothes.* New York: Penguin Books, 1988.

Hont, Istvan. "The Early Enlightenment Debate on Commerce and Luxury." In *The Cambridge History of Eighteenth-Century Political Thought*, edited by Mark Goldie and Robert Wokler. Cambridge: Cambridge University Press, 2006.

Hopkins, Keith. *Conquerors and Slaves.* Cambridge: Cambridge University Press, 1978.

Hopkins, Keith, and Mary Beard. *The Colosseum.* Cambridge, MA: Harvard University Press, 2005.

Horace. *The Epistles of Horace.* Translated by David Ferry. New York: Farrar, Straus, and Giroux, 2001.

———. *The Odes: New Translations by Contemporary Poets.* Edited by J. D. McClatchy. Princeton, NJ: Princeton University Press, 2002.

Horne, Thomas A. *The Social Thought of Bernard Mandeville: Virtue and Commerce in Early Eighteenth-Century England.* London: Macmillan, 1978.

Horowitz, Daniel. *The Morality of Spending: Attitudes toward the Consumer Society in America, 1875–1940.* Baltimore: The Johns Hopkins University Press, 1985.

Hosmer, James, ed. *Winthrop's Journal, "History of New England," 1630–1649.* 2 vols. New York: C. Scribner's Sons, 1908.

Hume, David. *An Inquiry Concerning the Principles of Morals*. New York: Liberal Arts Press, 1957.

Hunt, Alan. *Governance of the Consuming Passions: A History of Sumptuary Laws*. New York: St. Martin's, 1996.

Ingrassia, Catherine. *Authorship, Commerce and Gender in Early Eighteenth Century: A Culture of Paper Credit*. New York: Cambridge University Press, 1998.

Isocrates. *Isocrates*. Translated by George Norlin. 3 vols. Cambridge, Mass.: Loeb Classical Library, Harvard University Press, 1968.

Israel, Jonathan. *The Dutch Republic: Its Rise, Greatness, and Fall 1477–1806*. Oxford: Clarendon Press, 1995.

Judt, Tony. *Ill Fares the Land*. New York: Penguin Press, 2010.

Juvenal. *The Sixteen Satires*. Translated by Peter Green. London: Penguin Books, 1998.

Kammen, Michael. *People of Paradox: An Inquiry Concerning the Origins of American Civilization*. New York: Knopf, 1972.

Killerby, Catherine Kovesi. *Sumptuary Law in Italy, 1200–1500*. New York: Oxford University Press, 2002.

Lacks, André. "Soul, Sensation and Thought." In *The Cambridge Companion to Early Greek Philosophy*, edited by A. A. Long, 253. Cambridge: Cambridge University Press, 1999.

Lasch, Christopher. *The Culture of Narcissism: American Life in an Age of Diminishing Expectations*. New York: Norton, 1978.

Leigh Fermor, Patrick. "Gluttony," In *The Seven Deadly Sins*, 54. New York: Quill, 1992.

Levy, Michael. *Giambattista Tiepolo: His Life and Art*. New Haven: Yale University Press, 2004.

Lintott, A. W. "Imperial Expansion and Moral Decline in the Roman Republic." *Historia* 21 (1972): 626–38.

Livy. *The Dawn of the Roman Empire, Books 31–40*. Translated by J. C. Yardley. Oxford: Oxford University Press, 2000.

Long, A. A. *Epictetus: A Stoic and Socratic Guide to Life*. Oxford: Clarendon Press, 2002.

MacMullen, Ramsay. *Paganism in the Roman Empire*. New Haven, CT: Yale University Press, 1981.

Majanlahti, Anthony. *The Families Who Made Rome: A History and a Guide*. London: Chatto & Windus, 2005.

Mandeville, Bernard. *The Fable of the Bees: or Private Vices, Publick Benefits*. Edited by F. B. Kaye. Oxford: Oxford University Press, 1924.

Martines, Lauro. *Fire in the City: Savonarola and the Struggle for Renaissance Florence*. Oxford: Oxford University Press, 2006.

McCoy, Drew R. *The Elusive Republic: Political Economy in Jeffersonian America.* Chapel Hill: Published for the Institute of Early American History and Culture by the University of North Carolina, 1980.

McKendrick, Neil, John Brewer, and A. H. Plumb. *The Birth of a Consumer Society: The Commercialization of Eighteenth Century England.* London: Hutchinson, 1983.

Mee, Charles L. *White Robe, Black Robe: A Dual Biography of Pope Leo X and Martin Luther.* London: Harrap, 1973.

Mitchell, H. *The Economics of Ancient Greece.* Cambridge: Cambridge University Press, 1940.

Monbiot, George. "Selling Indulgences." *The Guardian,* October 18, 2006.

Monro, David H. *The Ambivalence of Bernard Mandeville.* Oxford: Clarendon Press, 1975.

Montaigne, Michael de. *The Complete Essays of Montaigne.* Translated by Donald M. Frame. Stanford: Stanford University Press, 1965.

Morgan, Edmund S. *The Puritan Dilemma: The Story of John Winthrop.* Edited by Oscar Handlin. Boston: Little, Brown, 1958.

Ovid. *The Art of Love and Other Poems.* Edited by G. P. Goold. Translated by J. H. Mozley. Cambridge, MA: Harvard University Press, 1979.

Pagels, Elaine. *Adam, Eve, and the Serpent.* New York: Vintage Books, 1988.

Peck, Linda Levy. *Consuming Splendor: Society and Culture in Seventeenth-Century England.* Cambridge: Cambridge University Press, 2005.

Penn, William. *No Cross, No Crown.* London, 1669.

Petronius Arbiter. *The Satyricon.* Translated by William Arrowsmith. Ann Arbor: University of Michigan Press, 1959.

Plato. *The Republic.* Translated by Benjamin Jowett. New York: Heritage Press, 1944.

Plumb, J. H. *In the Light of History.* London: Allen Lane, 1972.

Plutarch. *Fall of the Roman Republic: Marius, Sulla, Crassus, Pompey, Caesar, Cicero: Six Lives.* Translated by Rex Warner. London: Penguin Classics, 1972.

———. *Lives of the Noble Greeks.* Edited by Edmund Fuller. New York: Dell Publishing Company, 1971.

———. *Makers of Rome: Nine Lives Coriolanus, Fabius Maximus, Macellus, Cato the Elder, Tiberius Gracchus, Gaius Gracchus, Sertorius, Brutus, Mark Antony.* Translated by Ian Scott-Kilvert. Baltimore: Penguin Books, 1965.

———. *The Rise and Fall of Athens: Nine Greek Lives: Theseus, Solon, Themistocles, Aristides, Cimon, Pericles, Nicias, Alcibiades, Lysander.* Translated by Ian Scott-Kilvert. London: Penguin Books, 1960.

Pocock, J. G. A. *The Machiavellian Moment: Florentine Political Thought and the Atlantic Republican Tradition.* Princeton, NJ: Princeton University Press, 2003.

———. *Virtue, Commerce, and History: Essays on Political Thought and History, Chiefly in the Eighteenth Century*. Cambridge: Cambridge University Press, 1985.

Polybius. *The Rise of the Roman Empire*. Translated by Ian Scott-Kilvert. London: Penguin Books, 1979.

Prose, Francine. "Gluttony." In *The Seven Deadly Sins*. Oxford: Oxford University Press, 2003.

Raphael, Frederick. *Some Talk of Alexander*. New York: Thames & Hudson, 2006.

Rawson, Elizabeth. *The Spartan Tradition in European Thought*. Oxford: Clarendon Press, 1969.

Renehan, Robert. "On the Greek Origins of Concepts Incorporeality and Immateriality." *Greek, Roman, and Byzantine Studies* 21 (1980): 109.

Rich, Frank. "The Rabbit Ragu Democrats." *New York Times*, October 3, 2009, Op-Ed.

Sallust. *The Jugurthine War [and] The Conspiracy of Catiline*. Translated by S. A. Handford. Baltimore: Penguin Books, 1963.

Scheidel, Walter. "The Roman Slave Supply." In *The Cambridge World History of Slavery*, edited by Keith Bradley and Paul Cartledge, 1: 287–311. New York: Cambridge University Press, 2011.

Schimmel, Solomon. *The Seven Deadly Sins: Jewish, Christian, and Classical Reflections on Human Psychology*. New York: Oxford University Press, 1997.

Seaford, Richard. *Money and the Early Greek Mind: Homer, Philosophy, Tragedy*. Cambridge: Cambridge University Press, 2004.

———. "World Without Limits." *Times Literary Supplement*, June 19, 2009, 14–15.

Sekora, John. *Luxury: The Concept in Western Thought, Eden to Smollett*. Baltimore: The Johns Hopkins University Press, 1977.

Sellars, John. *Stoicism*. Berkeley: University of California Press, 2006.

Sen, Amartya. "Capitalism Beyond the Crisis." *New York Review of Books*, March 26, 2009, 56:5, 27–30.

Seneca. *Ad Lucilium Epistulae Morales*. Translated by R. M. Gummere. Cambridge, MA: Harvard University Press, 1971.

———. *Letters from a Stoic. Epistulae morales ad Lucilium*. Translated by Robin Campbell. London: Penguin, 1969.

———. *The Stoic Philosophy of Seneca: Essays and Letters*. Translated by Moses Hadas, New York: W. W. Norton, 1958.

Shaw, Teresa M. *The Burden of the Flesh: Fasting and Sexuality in Early Christianity*. Minneapolis, MN: Fortress Press, 1998.

Shi, David E. *The Simple Life: Plain Living and High Thinking in American Culture*. New York: Oxford University Press, 1985.

Sidgwick, Henry. "Luxury." *International Journal of Ethics* 5 (1894): 1–16.

Slater, William J., ed. *Dining in a Classical Context*. Ann Arbor: University of Michigan Press, 1991.

Sloan, Herbert E. *Principle and Interest: Thomas Jefferson and the Problem of Debt*. New York: Oxford University Press, 1995.

Smith, Adam. *An Inquiry into the Nature and Causes of the Wealth of Nations*. Edited by R. H. Campbell, A. S. Skinner, and W. B. Todd. 2 vols. Indianapolis, IN: Liberty Classics, 1981.

———. *The Theory of Moral Sentiments*. Edited by D. D. Raphael and A. L. Macfie. 1759. Reprint, Mineola, NY: Dover Publication Classics, 2006.

Soderlund, Jean R., ed. *William Penn and the Founding of Pennsylvania, 1680–1684: A Documentary History*. Philadelphia: University of Pennsylvania Press, 1983.

Sombart, Werner. *Luxury and Capitalism*. Translated by W. R. Dittmar. Ann Arbor: University of Michigan Press, 1967.

Sophocles. *Antigone*. Translated by Elizabeth Wyckoff. 4 vols. Chicago: University of Chicago Press, 1959.

Sparks, Jared. *The Life of Gouverneur Morris, with selections from his correspondence and miscellaneous papers; detailing events in the American Revolution, the French Revolution, and in the political history of the United States*. 3 vols. Boston: Gray & Bowen, 1832.

Stanlis, Peter. "Acceptable in Heaven's Sight: Robert Frost at Bread Loaf 1939–1941." In *Frost: Centennial Essays*, edited by Jac Tharpe, vol 3. Jackson: University Press of Mississippi, 1978.

Swart, K. W. *The Miracle of the Dutch Republic as seen in the Seventeenth Century: an inaugural lecture delivered at University College London 6 November 1967, by K. W. Swart*. London: H. K. Lewis, 1969.

Syme, Ronald. *The Roman Revolution*. Oxford: Oxford University Press, 1939.

Symonds, John Addington. *The Renaissance in Italy*. 2 vols. New York: The Modern Library, 1935.

Syrett, Harold C., ed. *The Papers of Alexander Hamilton*. New York: Columbia University Press, 1962.

Tacitus. *The Annals and The Histories*. Edited by Moses Hadas. Translated by A. J. Church and W. J. Brodribb. New York: Modern Library, 2003.

Tertullian. "On the Apparel of Women." In *The Ante-Nicene Fathers*, edited by Alexander Roberts and James Donaldson, 4: Edinburgh: T&T Clark, 1867–1873. Reprint Grand Rapids: Wm. B. Eerdmans, 1962. Available online, http://early christianwritings.com/text/tertullian27.html.

Thornton, Peter. *Seventeenth Century Interior Decoration in England, France, and Holland*. New Haven, CT: Yale University Press, 1978.

Tickle, Phyllis A. "Greed." In *The Seven Deadly Sins*. New York: Oxford University Press and The New York Public Library, 2004.

Tocqueville, Alexis de. *Democracy in America*, Reeves text rev. Francis Bowen, vol. 2. New York: Alfred A. Knopf, 1976.

Tolles, Frederick B. "Of the Best Sort But Plain: The Quaker Esthetic." *The American Quarterly* 11, no. 4 (Winter 1959): 496.

———. *Quakers and the Atlantic Culture*. New York: Macmillan, 1960.

Tugend, Alina. "Envy, Anxiety, Secrecy, Taboos: The Subject Must Be Money." *New York Times*, February 3, 2007.

Veblen, Thorstein. *The Theory of the Leisure Classes*. Edited by John Kenneth Galbraith. Boston: Houghton Mifflin, 1973.

Veyne, Paul, ed. *From Pagan Rome to Byzantium*. Translated by Arthur Goldhammer. Vol. 1 of *A History of Private Life*, edited by Philippe Ariès and Georges Duby. Cambridge, MA: Belknap Press, 1992.

Veyne, Paul. *Le pain et le cirque: Sociologie historique d'un pluralisme politique*. Paris: Seuil, 1976.

Wallace-Hadrill, Andrew. *Rome's Cultural Revolution*. Cambridge: Cambridge University Press, 2008.

Warren-Adams Letters, Collections of The Massachusetts Historical Society. Boston: AMD Press, 1972.

Warren, Charles. "Samuel Adams and the Sans Souci Club of 1785." *Proceedings of the Massachusetts Historical Society* 60 (May 1927): 3.

Warren, Mercy Otis. *History of the Rise, Progress and Termination of the American Revolution*. Edited by Lester H. Cohen. 2 vols. Indianapolis, IN: Liberty Fund, 1989.

Waszek, Norbert. "Two Concepts of Morality: A Distinction of A. Smith's Ethics and its Stoic Origin." *Journal of the History of Ideas* 45 (October 1984): 591–606.

Weber, Max. *The Protestant Ethic and the "Spirit" of Capitalism and Other Writings*. New York: Penguin Books, 2002.

Welch, Evelyn. *Art and Society in Italy 1350–1500*. New York: Oxford University Press, 1997.

White, L. Michael. "Scholars and Patrons: Christianity and High Society in Alexandria." In *Christian Teaching: Studies in Honor of LeMoine G. Lewis*, edited by Everett Ferguson. Abilene, TX: Abilene Christian University Book Store, 1981.

Wilken, Robert L. *The Christians as the Romans Saw Them*. New Haven, CT: Yale University Press, 1984.

Williams, G. "Poetry in the Moral Climate of Augustan Rome." *Journal of Roman Studies* 52 (1962): 28–46.

Wilson, Edward O. *The Diversity of Life*. Cambridge, MA: Belknap Press of the Harvard University Press, 1992.

————. *The Future of Life*. New York: Alfred A. Knopf, 2002.

Winthrop, John. *The John Winthrop Papers*. Boston: Massachusetts Historical Society, 1929–1947.

Wolff, Cynthia Griffin. "Literary Reflections of the Puritan Character." *Journal of the History of Ideas* 29, no. 1 (January–March 1968): 18–20.

Wood, Gordon S. *The Creation of the American Republic, 1776–1787*. Chapel Hill: University of North Carolina Press, 1998.

Xenophon. *Memorabilia and Oeconomicus*. Translated by E. C. Marchant. Cambridge, MA: Harvard University Press, 1968.

Index

211

About the Author

William Howard Adams is an independent scholar and lecturer working on books about Thomas Jefferson and also the history of the garden. He is a fellow of the International Research Center for Jefferson Studies in Charlottesville, Virginia, and served for sixteen years as a trustee of the Thomas Jefferson Memorial Foundation. Mr. Adams has also served as a Senior Fellow of the Garden History Library at Dumbarton Oaks, Harvard University.

Mr. Adams has been a member of the faculty of the school of Architecture and Regional Planning at Columbia University, the Cooper Union, and Distinguished Lecturer, the School of Architecture, the University of Houston. In 1993 Mr. Adams was named to the President's Advisory Committee on the Arts at the University of Virginia.

His study, *The French Garden: 1500–1800*, and his monograph, *Jefferson's Monticello*, published in 1984 by Abbeville Press, have been widely acclaimed. *Jefferson's Monticello* received the English Speaking Union award for outstanding nonfiction. As director of national programs at the National Gallery of Art, he was curator in 1976 of the Bicentennial Exhibition, "The Eye of Thomas Jefferson," and editor of the catalog of the same name. The catalog, *The Eye of Thomas Jefferson*, has been continuously in print since its first publication and was most recently reprinted in 1993 by the University of Missouri Press as part of Jefferson's 250th anniversary celebration.

For several years, Mr. Adams worked on a major international study of the history of the garden titled *Nature Perfected*. The book was published in

November 1991 by John Murray in London and by Abbeville Press in the United States, and was translated into French. Two of Adams's other titles have also been translated into French. British television in London sponsored the production of a twelve-part documentary television series, also called "Nature Perfected," based on the book. The programs were written and narrated by Mr. Adams.

In 1991 Mr. Adams was invited by the Museum of Modern Art to curate the museum's first exhibition devoted to the work of a landscape architect. The exhibition focused on the twentieth-century Brazilian artist Roberto Burle Marx.

Mr. Adams attended the University of Missouri and received his law degree from Washington and Lee University. He was admitted to the Missouri Bar in 1951. In 1958 Mr. Adams took an active role in the reorganization of the Jackson County Historical Society, now one of the leading historical societies in the country. In 1961 Governor John M. Dalton named him Chairman of the Governor's Committee on the Arts, and after successfully securing the passage of the legislation for the Missouri Council of the Arts, he was named the first Chairman of the Council for the first state arts council in the nation. In 1964 he joined Nancy Hanks at the Rockefeller Brothers Fund to organize the American Council of the Arts. He was the founder of the National Assembly of State Arts Agencies. In 1969 he became a senior officer of the National Gallery of Art in Washington, D.C.

Mr. Adams lives at Hazelfield in Jefferson County, West Virginia.